MICK WALKER'S
GERMAN
RACING
MOTORCYCLES

REDLINE
BOOKS

This very special book is dedicated to the memory of my son
Gary Walker, whose life and developing skills on the track were cruelly
cut short by the sport he loved so much.

British Library Cataloguing in Publication Data

A catalogue record for this book is available
from the British Library

ISBN: 0 9531311 2 2

Designed and published in 1999 by
Redline Books
2 Carlton Terrace, Low Fell, Tyne & Wear, NE9 6DE.

Contents

Introduction

MZ's Walter Kaaden is generally accepted today as the father of the modern two-stroke. New Zealander John Hempleman is seen here on one of his 125 singles during the 1960 Isle of Man TT.

In this, the third of the Racing Motorcycles series, it is Germany's turn to come under the spotlight. For a considerable period covered by this book, there were two distinct Germanys; West and East. Although run under very different political doctrines, they both produced some highly innovative and competitive racing machinery.

Not only were German motorcycles often in the very vanguard of technical progress, but they were also good enough to win world titles. In this respect, the top names in the solo categories were NSU and Kreidler, while BMW, Fath, Munch and König did the business on three wheels.

Like the Japanese, the Germans were faced with rebuilding a shattered country following their defeat at the hands of the Allies at the end of World War 2. And like the Japanese, they overcame all the problems not only to create an economic miracle, but also to construct world-beating motorcycles. Much of this success was thanks to Germany's pool of skilled engineers, both at factory and private level.

There were lone geniuses such as Roland Schnell, Helmut Fath, Gustav Baumm, Dieter König, Friedl Munch and Daniel Zimmermann. At factory level, engineers were actively encouraged to display their skills in their employers' race departments. Among them were Kurt Grasmann and Jan Friedrich Drkosch (Adler), Alex von Falkenhausen (BMW), Erich Wolf and Helmut Gorg (DKW), Johannes Hilber (Kreidler), Gunther Schier (Maico), Walter Kaaden (MZ), and Albert Roder and Walter Froede (NSU).

Start of the 1961 250cc West German GP at Hockenheim.

These men did not confine their expertise to certain-capacity classes, but created racing bikes of all types from 50cc upwards, together with sidecar machines. In addition, Germany was particularly strong in the record-breaking field, a tradition it had held since the very dawn of motorcycle sporting activities.

Although not so prolific as the British or Italians, German riding talent was also quite effective, particularly in the sidecar field. A short list of German solo stars includes Ernst Henne, Georg Meier, August Hobl, Werner Haas, Hans Georg Anscheidt, Walter Zeller, Ernst Degner and Dieter Braun. While the names of Wilhelm Noll, Willi Faust, Fritz Hillebrand, Walter Schneider, Helmut Fath, Max Deubel, Klaus Enders, Horst Oswesle and Rolf Steinhausen may not sound as familiar, all had the distinction of winning the world sidecar title at least once - and on German machinery.

Built by an Amsterdam BMW dealer the Ro Scuderia 4-valve R1100RS-based racer proved a race winner in Dutch BOTT (Battle of the Twins) racing during 1996.

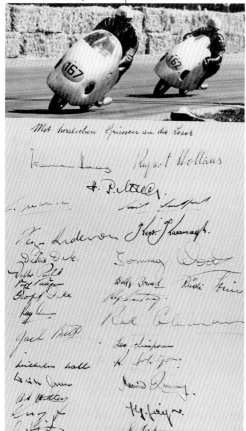

Post-war, the Grand Prix has been held at five circuits within the German borders. The most famous of these was the Nürburgring, initially the original 14 mile ultra-demanding course, followed later by the shorter South Loop section. Solitude was an extremely picturesque location just outside Stuttgart, now no longer used for racing. The same could be said of the 10 mile Schotten circuit. Used for the national Grand Prix only once, it was viewed by many riders as being positively dangerous.

Sachsenring in the East had been the home of the German GP in pre-war days, and was reintroduced with the advent of a separate East German classic in the early 1960s. Finally, there was the Hockenheim Ring. Still used today, it is essentially a pair of straights connected by loops at each end, making the speed of the machines the dominant factor.

Thus, Germany could be said to have contributed to the development of the sport in a wide variety of ways - engineers, machines, riders, circuits, and even record-breakers. The Germanic motorcycle racing story has them all, which made this particular title so interesting to compile.

Many good people helped in some way in the completion of German Racing Motorcycles. As I have discovered in the past, the vast majority were only too pleased to provide whatever assistance they could, and I will always be in their debt.

Unfortunately, the list is almost endless, so I must apologise to those whose names I have not been able to mention, but I shall be eternally grateful to them for the help given.

So I offer acknowledgement to the following, in no particular order of merit: the late Brian Woolley, Doug Jackson, Barry Hickmott, Don Mitchell, John Fernley, the late Fred Secker, Phil Higston, Emlyn Evans and Dominique Tellier.

I should also like to make special mention of the help received from fellow author Alan Cathcart, who kindly provided additional information on the SMZ (Maico) twin, raced by Dieter Braun in the early 1970s.

The photographs came from a number of sources, including Doug Jackson's World Motorcycle News Agency, Vic Bates, Colin Perkins, Neil Emmott, Mick Woollett, John and Joan Milligan, Nick Nicholls, George Nutall, Robin Saker, BMW archives and my own collection. I have used as many previously unpublished photographs as I could, but occasionally it has been necessary to use a 'familiar' picture due to its historic importance. I would also record the patience shown by my dear wife Susan.

Mick Walker's German Racing Motorcycles spans the decades to bring its reader the widest possible coverage of an intriguing subject. It is the third of a series of titles looking at both major and minor players throughout the world who have produced racing machines of significant interest. All that is left is to hope that you gain as much enjoyment reading the finished product as I have had in compiling it.

Mick Walker
Wisbech, Cambridgeshire,
July 1999.

Helmut Fath is still the only man to have won a motorcycling road racing world championship using an engine designed and built by himself; a feat he achieved in 1968 with the URS four- cylinder sidecar outfit.

Double 250cc world champion Werner Haas with one of the Rennmax twins, summer 1953. Haas was arguably Germany's finest post-war racer. He was killed in an air crash in 1955.

Max Deubel with Emil Horner in the chair at Quarter Bridge during the 1963 Isle of Man TT. The pair were world champions for BMW in 1961, 1962, 1963 and 1964.

Adler

One of Germany's most respected industrial brand names, Adler (Eagle), was not only a pioneer in the manufacture of both cars and motorcycles, but also lives on to this day in the office equipment manufacturing field.

Adler's founder was Heinrich Kleyer, who was born in 1853. His father was a factory owner, and the young Kleyer attended the Darmstadt Technical University. His first job was with an ironware and machinery company in Frankfurt. This was followed by four years in Hamburg with a firm that imported machinery, which led him to work in America with the Sturevant Mill Company of Boston.

Heinrich Kleyer returned to Germany in 1886 and founded Adler Fahradwerke AG in Frankfurt am Main. At first, Adler imported American-made pedal cycles, but within a year was manufacturing its own range of bicycles. The period in America had convinced Kleyer of the great potential for future transport requirements, and the business possibilities these offered. His production facilities were housed in a six-storey building (at the time, the highest in Frankfurt), where customers could test the machines on the top floor.

Within a decade, Kleyer's organization had produced its 100,000th bicycle, and in 1898, it came up with the first German-made typewriter. In that year, the company gained the services of Dip. Ing. Franz Starkloph as chief designer and works manager of the Adler bicycle works. Other business ventures at the time included owning the German distribution rights for Dunlop tyres.

The M250 launched in 1952 was destined to be the company's biggest selling post-war model. At its heart was a 247cc (54 x 54mm) piston port two-stroke twin which owed much to the earlier M200 of 1951.

"Adler"

Adler (Eagle) pioneered the modern twin-cylinder two-stroke, featuring a turbine-smooth 247.3cc engine with equal bore and stroke dimensions of 54 x 54mm, during the early 1950s.

In 1898, a licence was also taken out to build French De Dion-Bouton tricyles, but little use was made of this. Instead, Kleyer instructed Starkloph to design a light car powered by a De Dion-Bouton engine. This entered production in 1900. Of more significance to this chapter, however, is the fact that Adler also employed a De Dion engine, a single-cylinder four-stroke, to power its first motorcycle two years later in 1902.

Early race-kitted MB250 twin with air-cooled cylinders and plunger rear suspension.

From 1903 onwards, Adler also manufactured its own engines, both single- and twin-cylinder and, again, four-stroke. These early Adler machines were of excellent quality and were also raced in some of the pioneer events, with considerable success, by Kleyer's two sons, Erwin and Otto.

However, Adler, together with many other German motorcycle marques of the era, ceased production at the end of 1907 to concentrate on other (more profitable!) engineering enterprises - in Adler's case, cars, bicycles and typewriters. Furthermore, except for a brief return to powered two-wheelers in 1931, during the worst part of the depression, when it introduced an engine-assisted bicycle of 74cc, the Frankfurt company stayed away from motorcycles for some four decades.

The front-wheel-drive Adler Trumpf Junior was one of the most popular German cars of the 1930s, while the company's range of typewriters were market leaders.

However, all had not been as easy as it appeared on the surface. During World War 1, Adler built trucks, transmissions for tanks and aero engines under licence from Daimler-Benz. In 1916, Heinrich Kleyer had taken an interest-free war loan of 4,000,000 reichmarks from the government, but the loan was never repaid fully, the result being that control of the company passed to the Deutsche Bank in 1920. This was because the repayment of the loan was rendered almost worthless by the high inflation which took place within Germany following the end of hostilities.

The engine which started it all, the Adler twin-cylinder M200 195cc (48 x 54mm) of 1951.

Factory-supported Adler 250 water-cooled twin at Assen, Dutch TT July 1955. It was ridden into 8th place by Gunter Beer.

Fortunately for the Kleyer family, the bankers allowed them to retain managerial control, so the Frankfurt company was able to continue and prosper, avoiding this potential disaster. Shortly after the Trumpf car was introduced in 1932, Heinrich Kleyer died at the age of 79. He was succeeded by his son Erwin, whose interest in streamlining led to some very advanced four wheel designs during the mid and late 1930s.

With the arrival of World War 2, Adler's production facilities were turned to military requirements once again, in particular staff cars, ambulances and even half-tracked vehicles with Maybach engines.

At the war's end in the spring of 1945, very little remained of the Adler factories, which were centrally located in Frankfurt where destruction was around 80 percent! Somehow, the existing Adler corporate boss, Ernst Hagemeyer, succeeded in setting the wheels in motion to ensure recovery of his shattered empire. It was decided that first typewriter manufacturing and then automobile assembly were to be restarted as soon as it was possible to do so.

At first, Hagemeyer envisaged making cars and returning to motorcycle production, for which he engaged the services of the talented engineer, Karl Jentschke. Jentschke was charged with creating a new motorcycle and modernising the Trumpf Junior car with a 995cc engine. However, although prototypes appeared, the latter project was soon abandoned. Instead, it was decided to concentrate on the two wheel venture.

First, a new factory was built, its managing director and chief engineer being Herman Friedrich. Initially, it was intended to produce a 60cc two-stroke commuter machine, as this was the capacity limit imposed on the German manufacturers by the Allied Commission in 1946.

However, by the time production of the new Adler got under way in 1949, these rules had been relaxed. The result was a 98cc (50 x50 mm) machine, coded M100.

This first post-war Adler motorcycle was hardly the commercial success that the management team hoped it would be. Even so, it led Friedrich and his engineers to consider other designs, and when the giant Frankfurt Show took place in October 1951, Adlerwerke had three different models to display. These comprised the M100 and its larger brother, the M125, plus a brand-new design, the trend-setting M200 twin. The last machine was to point the way to future Adler developments over the next few years.

This was a much bolder move than may at first be appreciated, because at the time, designing small capacity two-stroke twins produced a major problem - how to achieve effective crankcase sealing. Friedrich and his engine specialist, Felix Dozekal, came up with a solution that was ingenious, but complicated.

The two separate crankshafts needed to be located side by side in a common crankcase assembly, the serrated joints of which were held together by a long through-bolt. A roller bearing and a pair of seal rings were housed in the central web of the crankcase. To tighten the through-bolt, a specially-designed tool was inserted through a hole in the offside to locate on a radial serration on the bolt head. The complete crank assembly was supported at both ends in bearing housings which, in turn, were located in the crankcase walls. The cranks were placed at 180 degrees.

ADLER

With a capacity of 195cc (48 x 54mm), the M200 employed cast-iron cylinder barrels and alloy heads. These were inclined forward from the vertical by 45 degrees.

The primary drive to the four-speed gearbox was by helical gears. Of particular note was the wet, multi-plate clutch, which was mounted in an outrigger location on the nearside end of the crankshaft.

To cope with the increase in both power and weight, Adler built a more robust version of the M125 frame. This had plunger rear suspension, while the front forks still retained the 'clockspring' suspension pioneered on the original M100; 16in wheels were specified to provide a low riding position capable of 65mph. The M200 was well received by both press and customers alike. The influential journal *Das Motoradd* commented: 'a super quality motorcycle in a class by itself; a genuine jewel of German motorcycle production.'

However, the real headline maker was launched in 1953 as the M250. Essentially a larger and improved M200, the new quarter-litre challenger was truly a trend-setting machine, its turbine-smooth engine having equal bore and stroke measurements of 54 x 54mm and a capacity of 247.3cc.

The year before, Adler had proved the quality of the twin-cylinder concept when all four of their machines entered in the 27th ISDT in Austria had completed the gruelling rigour of six days in the world's toughest motorcycle test. At the end, they had three golds and a bronze medal to show for their efforts.

This success was instrumental in triggering more competition activity, and soon the first Adler riders began to appear in road races on home-tuned models. Among them were Walter Vogel, Willi Bilger, Hubert Luttenberger and the Kramer brothers, Klaus and Ulrich.

However, it was the Nurnburg rider Hans Hallmeier who could claim to have been the first to use a race-kitted M250 twin, which had been tuned by his father. This was in September 1953 in the 20th Eilenriede Rennen held at Hanover. Although the event was won by NSU star and World Champion Werner Haas, it was the Adler twin that commanded the attention of the press boys, not only for its speed, but also its vivid acceleration.

Englishman Richard Williats rode an Adler with considerable success on British short circuits in the early 1960s. He is pictured here at Castle Coombe in April 1963.

Hallmeier's performance prompted the factory into building a batch of over-the-counter racing models for sale to private customers. These were based on the standard production M250 roadster.

The prototype of the new machine, the RS (Renn Sport), made its debut at the Dieburg circuit in the spring of 1954. Its rider was Hubert Luttenberger, who finished this first round of the German national championships in a mid-field position. However, he clearly showed the potential of the newcomer.

Besides its specially-tuned engine, which pumped out a claimed 24bhp, the most interesting features were the entirely new frame and suspension. These were the responsibility of Jan Friedrich Drkosch. The frame was neatly crafted from lightweight, aircraft-quality steel tubing, while the suspension featured a swinging arm with pivoted fork at the rear and a pair of hydraulically-damped, leading-link forks up front.

RS250 Adler with water-cooling and Italian Dell'Orto carbs; this was the usual format from 1955 onwards.

The engine of the RS was largely the work of former aero-engine expert Kurt Grasmann. The same man had developed the M250 power unit for long distance trials, such as the ISDT, where Adler also enjoyed considerable success.

Grasmann spent a considerable time on the gasflow characteristics of the Adler twin-cylinder engine, including experimenting with varying inlet and exhaust tract lengths and different expansion chambers. In fact, Adler was carrying out very similar work to that which was being undertaken at the same time by two-stroke rival DKW at Ingolstadt. Both companies were to have a profound influence on the development of the modern two-stroke engine.

The main areas of development undertaken by Grasmann were in the exhaust system, cylinders and carburettors. The last were 24mm Amal TT instruments specially imported from Britain. Although Adler never officially had a works team, private riders were to achieve some quite outstanding successes over the next few years, both inside Germany and in other countries.

During their first season, the RS Adlers lined up against the all-conquering NSU Rennmax works double-knocker twins. Even so, Hallmeier and Vogel finished third and sixth respectively in the 1954 German GP at Solitude. Moreover, in the Swiss GP at Berne, Vogel repeated the performance with another sixth - excellent results indeed. The maximum speed of the 1954 RS250 was almost 120mph, a truly stunning performance for what was, after all, a production-based 250.

By 1955, a handful of the leading Adler tuners had begun to water-cool their engines. This was to maintain the optimum power output for a longer period. With the standard air-cooled cylinders, the

Adler 250 water-cooled twin, circa 1955.

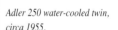

performance would drop as the engine became hotter after a few laps. However, with a water-cooling jacket, the power would remain constant throughout the race. This was particularly important in Grand Prix events which, in some cases, could be up to three hours in duration.

Water-cooling also allowed further tuning to take place. This enabled privately-entered RS250s to give race-winning performances throughout the remainder of the 1950s and well into the 1960s. In fact, some of the best performances by Adlers in road racing came after the factory ceased production! This was because, from early 1956, the Frankfurt company had found the going ever more difficult, until eventually the giant Gründig electrical empire took over Adler (and also the German Triumph concern) in the winter of 1957-8. However, Gründig had no interest in continuing with the motorcycle side, having taken over the ailing company for its typewriter expertise alone.

Adler RS250 engined special, using a mixture of parts, including forks and front wheel from a Ducati, circa 1962.

Kestermann-developed 500 four-cylinder engine, using Adler components and raced by sidecar star Fritz Scheidegger in 1963.

Adler had become caught up in the drastic decline in two-wheeler sales which hit Germany in the mid 1950s and led to severe financial crises amongst the vast majority of manufacturers. Adler's fall from grace, however, was not the end of the marque's track successes because, in 1958, Dieter Falk on a home-tuned RS twin, finished fifth overall in the 250cc World Championship series. This included a couple of third places at Assen and the Nürburgring and, perhaps most sensational of all, a magnificent fifth in the Isle of Man TT. Falk was also German champion that year. Gunther Beer, on another Adler, also gained some leaderboard placings in the classics during this period.

Tuned by men such as Willi Klee, the final 250 Adlers in water-cooled form, were pumping out 38-40 bhp and could reach almost 140mph. All this was most impressive, and the potential of the Frankfurt two-strokes was not only realised in Germany itself, but overseas.

In Japan, both Suzuki's and Yamaha's experimental departments imported examples of the M250, and designs such as the Colleda (Suzuki) and the YD 1 (Yamaha) owed much to the German machine. In Britain, the Val Page-designed Ariel Leader/Arrow was another machine that borrowed Adler technology.

Another water-cooled Adler special at a Dutch exhibition during the early 1970s.

Even though the German eagle had fallen from grace, its descendants were destined to soar to glories anew. The Adler was the first really modern two-stroke twin, a type that was to dominate on road and track in the quarter-litre class many years later under the Honda and Yamaha marques. This, above all else, is the most fitting tribute to the Adler concept, and is something of which its German creators can be truly proud.

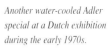

BMW Solos

2

BMW Kompressor 1949.

The Bayerische Motoren Werke (Bavarian Motor Works) came into existence following a merger, in 1913, between two aero engine manufacturers: the Karl Rapp Motorwerke and the Gustav Otto Flugmotorenfabrik. The new company became the Bayerische Flugzeugwerke in 1916, and BMW the following year.

Both BFW and then BMW were major suppliers of engine units to the German Air Force, and the vital men in the formation of BMW were an Italian-born Austrian banker, Camillo Castiglione, and a young Austrian naval engineer, Franz Josef Popp. The two first came into contact at the Austro-Daimler aircraft engine company. When BMW came into existence on 29th July 1917, Popp was appointed its managing director - a post he was to hold until 1942.

During late 1917 and into 1918, the new company's growth was incredible. It became one of the largest engineering-based companies in Germany which, at its wartime peak, employed over 3,500 people. However, when the war finally came to an end in November 1918, its fall was equally spectacular.

After the Armistice, BMW was forbidden to manufacture aero engines, and subsequently branched out into other fields, including motorcycles.

In 1923, BMW produced its first complete machine, the R32. This had two notable features: shaft drive and a flat-twin engine. Conceived by Max Friz, the 493cc (68 x 68mm) machine was the star of the Paris show that year and was to influence BMW motorcycle design over the next 75 years.

FICM Diploma awarded to Ernst Henne and BMW for setting a new world record on 19th September 1929...

...Henne preparing for the run.

Henne's original record breaker, Paris Show 1930.

*1939 supercharged BMW
(Meier TT winner).*

It was the R37 which first put BMW's sporting efforts on the map in 1924, when Fritz Bieber aboard a tuned version of the company's new sports roadster won the German national road racing championship. From then on until comparatively recently, race breeding played a vital part in the future of the BMW motorcycle, and added greatly to the company's prestige within the motorcycle world.

The R37's designer, Rudolf Scheicher, was not only responsible for the preparation of Bieber's championship winning racer, but rode a BMW successfully in the 1926 ISDT held in Britain. His gold medal-winning performance gave the company additional publicity in one of the export markets in which BMW were just starting to take an increasing interest.

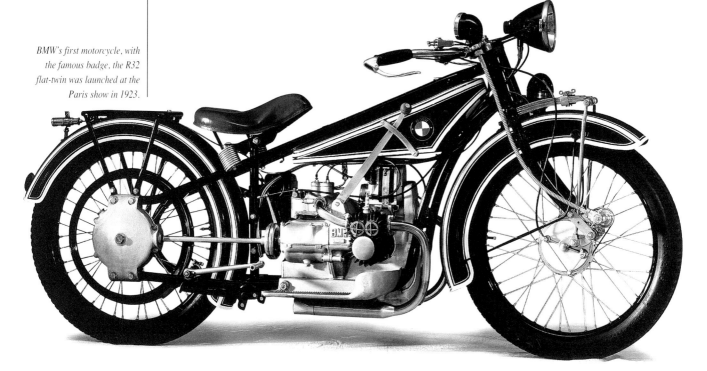

In all, BMW built some ten special racing versions of the R37, using them to experiment not only with tuned engines, but also an improved frame and for the first time, novel alloy cylinder heads. Its last major success was a victory in the 1926 German Grand Prix by Paul Koppen.

In the late 1920s, prior to the onset of financial austerities brought on by the Great Depression, Ernst Henne waved the BMW flag by breaking a number of world speed records on his 736cc speedster. Henne raced against the stopwatch at the heavily banked Avus circuit in Berlin and on Germany's first autobahn at Ingoldstadt near Munich. Among these records, he achieved the world's fastest for a motorcycle, at 137.58mph. This set a pattern for another run of outstanding performances by BMW, demonstrated by Henne again in 1932 when he retook the record which had been lost to Joe Wright's Zenith-JAP, with a speed of 151.77mph at Tat, Hungary in the summer of 1932.

*BMW's first motorcycle, with
the famous badge, the R32
flat-twin was launched at the
Paris show in 1923.*

The next year Adolf Hitler came to power, and for BMW a year of competition success at the ISDT in Wales. The works trials team, mounted on R4 machines, took ISDT golds at Garmisch Partenkirchen in its native Bavaria in 1934.

There were more speed records too, when Ernst Henne raised his own record to 152.81mph at Gyon - again in Hungary. On a different front, a 12-cylinder BMW aero engine was used to power an experimental propellor driven train to a world record speed of 143mph.

Henne broke his own new record again in 1935, this time on a new section of autobahn just outside Frankfurt, with an average speed of 159.01mph. The following year he was back at the same venue, but this time with a new, supercharged 500cc engine, as competitions manager Schleicher acknowledged that the 750 had finally been superseded. Also new was an all-enclosing body shell for machine and rider, which featured a prominent tail fin. This took the speed up to 168.92mph.

Some six months later, lone Englishman Eric Fernihough shattered BMW's record on his home-built and tuned 996cc supercharged JAP. But it was only his for a short time before it fell again to Piero Taruffi's supercharged, water-cooled Gilera four. Within some five weeks of the Italian team's triumph, on 28th November 1937, Henne had his BMW back in the record books again - pushing the world record to 173.681mph where it was destined to stay for fourteen years until 1951.

The supercharging technology that helped to make this possible for Henne and BMW, had been under development since 1929 when a production R63 had a positive displacement blower mounted on the top of the gearbox and driven by the magneto shaft. Lessons learnt from this were applied not only to record breaking, but also to the BMW Kompressor 500 works road racers which bore a close resemblance to Henne's machine under the skin. Both were fitted with a Zoller blower built onto the front of the crankcase assembly and coupled to the rearward facing inlets by

Ernst Henne preparing to enter his streamlined, supercharged 500cc BMW twin on 28th November 1937, before setting a new world record of 173.681mph (279.5kph). This speed stood until 1951 when it was beaten by NSU.

Pre-war German racing stars, left to right: Wiggerl Kraus (BMW), Walfreid Winkler (DKW) and Georg Meier. Mechanic Sepp Hopl is holding one of BMW's supercharged 500 twins.

Ernst Henne's record breaker

During the interwar period, the ultimate prize for many of the world's motorcycle manufacturers was not winning on the track, but setting the world land-speed record. At first American and British marques dominated the proceedings, but in September 1929, a new contender appeared on the scene in the shape of BMW, and its star rider, Ernst Henne. Together, they set a new record speed of 137.58mph on Germany's inaugural autobahn at Ingoldstad, establishing a pattern of achievement that would last for almost a decade.

At first BMW employed a specially prepared 736cc ohv version of its famous flat-twin design, with a bore and stroke of 83 x 68mm. Then, in 1936, BMW engineers decided to decrease the engine's capacity from 736 to 493cc. This might have appeared a backward move, but there was a sound basis for this technical change. Although previous machines that Henne had piloted looked crude and were reminiscent of 1920s creations, the BMW newcomer was entirely different. Whilst the

motorcycle still retained the flat-twin engine and shaft final drive, everything else was at the very edge of technical advance. The 493cc (66 x 72mm) engine sported double overhead cams, whilst a Zoller supercharger was mounted on the front of the

long pipes passing over the cylinders. The capacity was 492.6cc (66 x 72mm) and the dohc twin generated in excess of 80bhp at 8,000rpm, offering a maximum speed of around 140mph - subject to circuit conditions.

The first of these 500-class racers appeared in 1935 and used telescopic front forks at a time when no other racing teams used them. But it was not until the end of 1936 that BMW began using plunger rear suspension as well - and when it came, the plunger type did not automatically give the Munich factory a competitive edge or even equal other machines, notably the British Norton singles.

By 1937, the 500s were in contention throughout Europe. And that included Germany, where BMW veteran Karl Gall became the National Champion. On the Isle of Man, after finishing sixth in the Senior TT, Jock

West went on to win the Ulster Grand Prix in Northern Ireland aboard one of the rapid BMW supercharged twins. There were high hopes for the following year, 1938, but Karl Gall was injured during practice for the Isle of Man, while Georg Meier (destined to become European Champion that year) was forced to retire on the starting line. This left West, who rode his BMW to the limit and succeeded in taking the flat-twin into fifth spot.

Schorsch Meier crosses the finishing line to win the Senior TT, June 1939.

Just in time for its diamond jubilee a high honour was conferred upon the flat-twin: The Deutsche Bundespost issued a stamp in 1983 showing the BMW motorcycle on which Ernst Henne set a new world speed record with 279.5km/h in 1937.

Georg Meier was also involved in long distance trials, gaining several medals on BMW machines. Then in 1939 Meier became the first foreign rider to take the Isle of Man Senior TT, then the most important motorcycle race in the world. Meier's team-mate, Jock West, came home second but this resounding 1-2 was tinged with sadness owing to the death in practice of the third member of the team, Karl Gall, a great BMW rider throughout his long career. Following the TT, Kraus joined the works team in his place, with additional riders usually being recruited from the host country as the Grand Prix circus moved around. For a short time, the 4-cylinder Gilera offered BMW a real challenge, but all too soon such contests would be shelved by the outbreak of war.

One of the bright spots for BMW in the immediate post-war period was the restart of racing activities, albeit in a very limited way. BMW was forced to use pre-war machines including the BMW Kompressor 500 twin, on which Georg Meier, now 36, was once again in winning form. Several of the works machines had survived the conflict either to race on German soil again, or to end their days as war booty. Both John Surtees in Britain and Walter Zeller in Germany were later to claim ownership of Meier's actual TT winning machine - a controversy which will probably never be resolved.

Georg (Schorsch) Meier's 1939 Senior TT winning machine.

crankshaft, and there were rearward-facing inlets of long pipes passing over the cylinders. With a power output of between 105 and 108bhp at 8,000rpm, the running gear was suitably uprated. The Henne speed record machine featured a tubular duplex frame with telescopic front forks and a plunger rear suspension. The entire machine and its rider were clad in an aluminium body shell with detachable top section that allowed Henne to get in and out. This supercharging technology had been under development since 1929, when a production R63 model had been equipped with a positive displacement blower which was mounted atop the gearbox and driven by the magneto shaft.

After Henne broke his own record in 1936 with a speed of 168.92mph, two teams surpassed his new mark. But within a few weeks, Henne and BMW were back on top for the seventh and final time in eight years. On 28th November 1937, the German pair clocked an amazing 173.681mph, a record that was to remain unbroken until 1951.

Georg (Schorch) Meier's
1939 TT winning machine.

Georg (Schorch) Meier, 1948.

In 1946, Meier formed the Veritas team and chose a BMW for his campaign to win the German road racing championship. And in 1949, Georg Meier was voted Sportsman of the Year in Germany - the first time a motorcyclist had received the honour.

All this was in local competitions only, for German factories and German riders were still banned from FIM-organised international events. But competition still began as eagerly as ever for the 1950 season, and there were some notable battles between supercharged BMW and NSU twins ridden by such luminaries as Meier for BMW and Fleischmann for NSU. All this was due to come to an end as Germany was re-admitted to the FIM, though it had banned the use of supercharging.

Even so, BMW was ready for the world stage again as it demonstrated by the debut of a new flat-twin on 29th April 1951, at the Eilenreide Rennen meeting near Hanover. Unlike the also-new NSU four (described in chapter 12), the BMW not only lasted the distance, but took the victor's spoils. There was a new rider too, and new star for the company, 23 year old Walter Zeller who took the flag from veteran Meier, also BMW mounted. In the wider field of international competition, there was still some way to go. After eight rounds of the Grand Prix circuit, there were still no placings in the top six.

In 1951, even though Germany was now officially admitted to international competition, the Grand Prix results did not alter significantly from the performances previously turned in by the privateers. Top six placings still eluded BMW in any of the enlarged, eight-round 500cc solo series.

As the 1952 season opened, BMW received a considerable amount of publicity regarding their projected racing plans - solo and sidecar - and much was expected. The official team, announced early in April, comprised Georg Meier and Walter Zeller on solos, and Kraus/Hauser as a sidecar team - plus two reserve riders. One of these was Hans Baltisberger (formerly rider of a 1950 dohc Norton single) and the other was Ernst Riedlbauch, who already had a number of wins as a privateer aboard BMWs.

However, when the first classic opened at Berne in Switzerland, no BMWs had entered for the Swiss GP, and it was only later in June that an official reason was given. This was the factory's preoccupation with the ISDT. It was widely rumoured that the German Trophy team were to use 500 and 600 BMWs and that the race team was being entered in all possible long distance trials since the final ISDT team selection was to be based on those results. The team was said to include Hans Meier, Georg's 20 year old brother.

By mid-July, almost on the eve of the German GP at Solitude which was to be held on 20th July, the new BMW racing bikes were still very much in the development stage. Four different types of 500 were in evidence. All four had short-stoke engines with dohc valve operation - a design which was eventually to emerge as the Rennsport model. They also sported a new, more shapely tank and a pair of long, narrow-tapering megaphone exhausts. Otherwise, there were notable variations from machine to machine. Two of them had new frames with widely-splayed front downtubes, additional bracing in the region of the rear bevel drive, and horizontal tubes below the fuel tank acting as additional engine supports. Georg Meier's mount had the cardan shaft housed inside the right-hand leg of the rear swinging arm - the first time this drive/suspension layout had been used. However, Meier was none too happy about the steering of his machine in the early testing sessions, but after attention to the suspension system, improvement was noticeable. It had much the same telescopic forks as before, but now a pair of bridge pieces were used. Meanwhile, Hans Baltisberger's bike was fitted with newly modified brakes.

A pre-war supercharged 500 twin of the type used by Georg Meier to win the 1939 Senior TT.

Rumours were rife in Germany and abroad at the end of 1952, that Georg Meier would be retiring from racing. However, the pundits were proved wrong when early in January 1953 an official statement from BMW listed the team men for the new season. Meiers name appeared along with Baltisberger and Zeller.

*Walter Zeller on the works
BMW Rennsport with which
he set a new 500cc lap record
of 112.1mph at the Avus
circuit in Berlin , on the
16th August 1953.*

On a cold windy day, with the snow-capped tops of the nearby Black Forest emphasising that winter had only just past, 120,000 enthusiasts gathered at the 4.75 mile Hockenheim Ring near Heidelberg for DMV's annual international Rhein Pokal Rennen, held on Sunday 10th May 1953. A trio of works BMW solos were entered, sporting Earles forks for the first time and using auxiliary dampers to give increased control.

The race was a tour de force for the brand-new four-cylinder in-line Moto Guzzis. Fergus Anderson recorded the fastest lap before retiring, and Enrico Lorenzetti raced to victory. But it was to be the new model's only major win, and following another retirement by Les Graham's MV Agusta, the second and third places went to Meier and privateer Mette's BMWs.

BMW's lone entry for the solo class in the Isle of Man TT was Walter Zeller, who *Motor Cycling* described as 'very good indeed' during the practice session. It was his first visit to Mona's Isle. After trying both conventional carburettors and fuel injection, he opted to use the latter system. However, no opportunity was available to study performance in the race, owing to Zeller's early retirement following a spill at Signpost Corner on lap two after lying ninth at the end of lap one.

*Rennsport with partial
enclosure, of the 'bird beak'
type, used by several factory
teams including Moto Guzzi and
NSU during the early 1950s.*

After the TT, Zeller with the rest of the solo riders, concentrated his efforts within the German borders. Typical of the results gained was Zeller's victory at the Avus circuit in East Germany, near Berlin on 16th August. Despite tropical heat, Zeller established a new class record by averaging 112.1mph for the entire race.

The 1954 season started for the BMW team with an entry in the international Rhein Pokal road races at Hockenheim in South West Germany on Sunday 9th May. This was an important meeting, with not only members of BMW's team in attendance, but also representatives of Guzzi, NSU and MV Agusta.

*Front end details of
Hans Bartl's machine. Note
2LS front brake, Earles forks
and alloy fairing.*

In the 500 race, after retirement by Fergus Anderson on the in-line four Guzzi, victory finally went to Ken Kavanagh on the new Guzzi single. Walter Zeller made it a well-deserved second ahead of Nello Pagani's MV four, followed by BMW new boy Hans Bartl.

Following quickly after the Hockenheim success came an even bigger one for the BMW, when four days later on 12th May the factory gained their first post-war international speed records. Using a streamlined version of the 494cc Rennsport racing model, this put them on top of the world in the 8 and 9 hour bracket for the 500, 750 and 1000cc solo classes. The venue was Montlhéry, outside Paris, where riders Georg and Hans Meier and Walter Zeller set up speeds of 103.55mph (166.64kph) and 102.70mph (165.28kph) for the 8 and 9 hours respectively.

Next came the 17th International Eifelrennen over the famous 14.16 mile Nürburgring. The event took place under dull, clouded skies on a bitterly cold day - but was still attended by large crowds. A notable experiment was carried out at the meeting by BMW, with a hydraulically-operated front brake system on one of their solos.

A non-starter in the 500 race was Walter Zeller, who had come off in practice. Up to the time of his accident, he had been the fastest rider in his class. But his injury, a broken ankle, was unfortunately serious enough

BMW works riders, Georg Meier (1) and Walter Zeller (21), during a German championship meeting in May 1951.

to make him a non-runner not only in this race, but also for the Isle of Man TT. Without Zeller, the race was won by Norton works rider Ray Amm. But the real surprise was the second place taken by Georg Braun on a single-cylinder Horex. He proved faster than all the remaining BMWs, including Hans Meier, who came third.

Then came the TT. Without Zeller, BMW's only solo entry was Bartl, riding a production Rennsport, rather than an official works bike. And as things turned out, he too was a non-starter.

Although the company found a success on the three-wheel racing front (see chapter 3), achieving the same fortunes in the solo classes was something altogether more difficult. While Noll and BMW were taking their first classic victory in the sidecar race at the German Grand Prix, held at the Solitude circuit on Sunday 25th July before record crowds, things were going decidedly differently for Zeller and co in the 500 race. Zeller, now recovered from his accident at the Nürburgring in May, retired with little more than a lap completed when his engine suddenly ceased firing. The first BMW home was privateer Knijnenburg in eleventh spot.

Another form of full-enclosure being tested during the 1950s by BMW's competition department.

At Solitude, a modified fuel injection system (first tried on the sidecars of Noll and Hillebrand) was seen on Zeller's solo, with Bosch injector pumps replacing the BMW units previously fitted. Mounted on the front of the timing covers and driven from the timing gear, the new pumps each contained two plungers operated by a swash plate on the pump spindle. Fuel was injected directly into the combustion chambers on the side remote from the spark plug. Injection was regulated by induction pressure - the control pipe being taken from a point between the guillotine throttle slide and the inlet valve.

One of the official BMW works racers used in 1951, very much a normally aspirated version of the old pre-war model.

Zeller's machine also featured duplex single-leading shoe front brakes in place of the former single, twin-leading shoe design. And for the first time on a solo BMW racer streamlining was used. However, unlike the fully-enclosed shells of contemporaries like NSU and Guzzi, this was a modest affair in hand-beaten alloy, around the steering head and handlebar.

Lone factory entry Walter Zeller with one of the Earles-fork Rennsports he used during the mid 1950s.

Despite difficulties during the season, on 8th August Zeller became the new German 500 Champion because of his win in the last but one of the German Championship series. It was staged over the 10 mile Schotten circuit, the scene a year earlier of the sensational riders' strike at the 1953 German Grand Prix.

In front of around 170,000 spectators, Zeller got away to a good start, but with the roads still very wet after a heavy shower, Ray Amm (Norton) collided with Carlo Bandirola (MV). The Norton star was delayed until the rest of the field had departed, but nonetheless fought back to second place, although he was unable to catch the flying Zeller. In the sidecar race, BMWs dominated, with Fraust taking victory from Schneider and Noll.

On the same day at Tubbergen in Holland, Knijnenburg took his production Rennsport to victory in the 500 race ahead of Norton-mounted Frank Perris (later to become a Suzuki star in the 1960s).

On the 3rd and 4th October 1954, Australia saw the inauguration of a 24-hour race for production motorcycles. It was to be the first of its kind. Staged at the Mount Druitt circuit near Sydney, the rules specified teams of three riders for each machine. From the start Jack Forrest took the lead on a 600cc R68, a lead which he and team mates Don Flynn and Les Roberts succeeded in maintaining throughout. They put in 648 laps of the 2.25 mile circuit at an average speed of nearly 60mph and covered 1,433 miles in the allotted time. In the combined 250 solo and sidecar class, an R25 came home first.

BMW's only solo entry in the 1955 TT was the Australian Jack Forrest, but he was a non-starter. However, at the German Grand Prix, Walter Zeller was to give a hint of what might have been had he been allowed to compete. Both he and John Surtees - on his one and only BMW

Privateer Hans Bartl in action on his Rennsport during 1955. He achieved some excellent placings that year in German national events.

Australian Jack Forrest setting a new national speed record of 149.06mph at Coonarabran, New South Wales, in early 1957.

ride - were entered on BMWs with an interesting modification in the form of a hydraulic steering damper between a bracket on the frame and the top of the left fork stanchion.

The event was held at the legendary and demanding Nürburgring circuit for the first time since 1931. However, this appeared to pose no problem for the BMW team leader. He proceeded to emerge as the chief threat to the World Champion Geoff Duke on his mighty four-cylinder Gilera 'fire engine'. For Zeller was an experienced rider on the twists and turns of the tortuous 14.16 mile circuit, having lapped only 2.6 seconds slower than the champion. Duke had not previously raced on the circuit, and in his determination to off-set the handicap, had covered 55 laps by car before practice commenced. On his second practice lap on the Gilera, he broke the lap record.

In the race itself, Duke made a super-slick start, and powered into the lead as the flag dropped. Building up a 15 second lead over Zeller in the early laps, he maintained this position virtually constantly for the next five laps. Then, piling on the coals, he swept his Gilera on to gain another three seconds from Zeller. For the first two and a half laps, Bandirola on an MV four held third spot, but was then passed by Armstrong on another Gilera four, though the Irishman was soon fated to retire.

1954 RS54 Rennsport
(production racer)

Engine: Bevel-driven, double overhead camshaft flat-twin
Capacity: 492cc
Bore & Stroke: 66 x 72mm
Maximum power: 45bhp @ 8,000rpm
Carburation: Twin Fischer-Amals 30mm, with remote float chambers
Ignition: Bosch magneto
Lubrication: Wet sump
Gearbox: Four-speeds
Clutch: Single plate, dry
Frame: Duplex, all-steel construction
Front forks: Earles type or telescopic type
Rear suspension: Swinging arm, twin shock absorbers
Brakes: Front: 200mm twin leading shoe, drum.
Rear: 200mm single leading shoe, drum

Tyres: Front 3.25 x 19. Rear 3.50 x 19
Dry weight: 132kg (291lb)
Maximum speed: 126mph (203kph)
Note: Factory racing model (as used by Walter Zeller) had oversquare 70 x 64mm bore and stoke dimensions and more power. Also choice of carbs or fuel injection.

The 1954 Rennsport engine

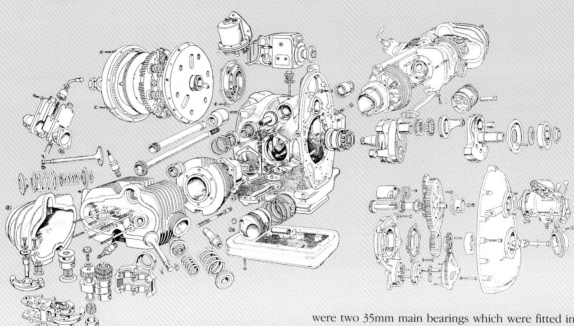

The definitive Rennsport appeared in 1954, and all subsequent factory and 'private' machines were developments of this basic layout.

Originally, the Rennsport engine was a long-stroke unit with 66 x 72mm bore and stroke measurements, giving a capacity of 492cc. In this form, maximum power was produced at 8,000rpm. Later, however, with the need for more power, the bore and stroke measurements were altered to be square at 68 x 68mm (493.9cc), resulting in the engine revolutions rising to 9,500rpm.

The crankshaft, with its 180-degree throws, was of built-up construction. Mainshafts were hollow and integral with their flywheels, which embodied balance weights. Each crankpin hole in the elliptical medial web of the shaft had a shallow counterbore on the side of the web, adjacent to the respective big-end. The radius of the counterbore was greater than that of the end of the web and of the big-end eye so that the shaft's overall length could be kept to the bare minimum.

Like the mainshafts, the hollow crankpins were of 35mm diameter; one end of each was pressed into the medial web and locked in position by a solid, forced-in expander plug. After the big-end bearings and connecting rods had been assembled on the pins, the cheeks were pressed on and further expander plugs driven in. The plugs at the outer ends of the pins differed from the inner type by having a small longitudinal hole for big-end lubrication.

There were three crankshaft main bearings. The one at the rear was of the self-aligning variety, embodying a special type of roller, while the one at the front was a conventional ball-race type. Another conventional ball-race bearing was housed in the front cover as an outboard support for the timing pinion.

The crankcase was a one-piece Electron casting. There were two 35mm main bearings which were fitted in separate housings. These housings were manufactured from different materials - cast-iron at the front, steel at the rear.

Integral with the forward main bearing housing was the rear wall of the oil pump; the aluminium-alloy pump body carrying the gears was fitted into a recess in the housing to which it was bolted.

The pump itself was of the duplex-gear type, one part feeding the main big-end, while the other supplied the cam gear. Wet-sump lubrication was employed, a 2.8-litre-capacity sump (again in Electron) being bolted to the base of the crankcase.

Oil for the cam gear flowed from the pump, through a series of oilways in the crankcase, to external pipes which lay between the cylinders. These pipes were flanked by a larger-diameter pipe through which the oil returned to the sump.

Lubricant from the other pump circulated from each main bearing housing into a trap secured by screws to the adjacent face of each crankshaft cheek. The trap was essentially a disc which had its periphery turned inwards through 180 degrees to form an annular channel. Oil from the bearing housing was directed by centrifugal force into the channel; it reached the big-end through a small hole in the trap wall that aligned with the aforementioned hole in the crankpin plug. Each of the crankpins had two radial holes and, since they diverged outwards, the oil flow had the maximum centrifugal assistance.

This type of layout minimized internal oilways which otherwise could have weakened the whole crankshaft assembly. In addition, it simplified building up the shaft because no holes had to be aligned.

Finally, the traps acted as very efficient centrifugal filters for collecting sludge and the like, which is why only a gauze suction oil filter system was needed. Each big-end bearing comprised fourteen rollers measuring 10 x 7mm. Housed in a duralumin cage, these ran directly on the crankpin and the con-rod eye, both pin and eye featuring specially hardened surfaces.

The connecting rods themselves were of particular interest, as they employed a very unusual flat section, rather than an I-section between the big and small-ends. Each rod was quite short, about 180 per cent of the stroke. BMW engineers tried the far more conventional I-section type, but discovered that these were far more prone to breakages, fatigue cracks developing at the radius between the flange and web.

The gear case at the front of the engine contained three pairs of spur gears. A steel gear on the crank drove an alloy half-speed gear immediately above it; the gears were lubricated by jet from the front main bearing housing. Also on the crankshaft was a steel gear that meshed with the alloy oil pump driving gear. It was found necessary to embody a cush-drive in the steel gear to prevent the teeth of the alloy gear from breaking under the load produced by full throttle acceleration or deceleration of the crankshaft.

A steel gear on the half-speed shaft meshed with the alloy magneto gear which featured slotted holes for timing adjustment. In front of the half-speed gear, and driven from it by a pair of pegs, was a ported sleeve which ran in the Electron front cover and served as a timed engine breather.

The breather sleeve contained the coupling for the fuel-injection pump drive. This coupling had holes that engaged with three pegs projecting from the end of the half-speed shaft, and it was splined internally at its forward end to receive male splines on the pump-unit shaft.

At the rear end of the half-speed shaft, which was carried in a pair of ball bearings in a duralumin housing, was a bevel gear. This meshed with two more bevel gears embodying short, hollow shafts which transmitted the drive, via solid shafts, to the camshafts.

Engaging with the splines of the hollow shafts were male splines at the inboard end of the solid drive shafts. Each of these shafts had an integral bevel gear at its outer end and ran in a ball-bearing pressed into the inboard half of a cast-iron housing. Split longitudinally in the vertical plane, the housing

was held to the cylinder head by three pairs of studs; the two outer pairs also served to retain the Electron cambox covers.

BMW engineers employed a most unconventional arrangement for the double-overhead-camshaft system. In each cylinder head, the two camshafts lay close together within a split housing, and each operated its respective valve through a short, straight rocker. The design was a compromise between the usual sohc and the conventional 'double-knocker' layouts because, although the reciprocating weight with the rockers was higher than with directly-operated valves, there was less power loss since two spur gears replaced the normal five. No doubt, this helped the Rennsport engine to run safely at over 9,500rpm.

Camshafts and rockers ran on needle rollers, while the rocker spindles were carried in the cam housings and had eccentric ends for valve-clearance adjustment.

Typical of the engineering skills shown in its design, the method of locking the rocker spindles was both simple and ingenious. On one end of each spindle was a serrated washer which was located on the spindle by flats. The serrations engaged similar serrations on a short arm, the other end of which was bolted to the housing. If the bolt was slackened and the serrations were disengaged, the spindle could be turned by one serration, or more, and then the serrations re-engaged. For valve timing, there was a vernier coupling between each camshaft and its driving gear.

Each cylinder head contained a part-spherical combustion chamber that provided quite a wide valve included angle of 82 degrees. Inlet and exhaust valve seats were in different materials: manganese steel for the inlet, bronze for the exhaust. Both valve guides were also of bronze.

Valve diameters were 40mm inlet, and 36mm exhaust, the latter being sodium-cooled. Duplex coil valve springs and a stepped form of split collet were employed to keep cylinder head width to a minimum.

The downdraught angle of the inlet ports was 15 degrees, and their bore at the flange 32mm. On the 1954 works-type Rennsport engine, as used by BMW team members that year, the third type of fuel-injection system (already described) was employed. Like the fuel pump, magneto and spark plugs, the injector nozzles were of Bosch manufacture and had a minimum delivery pressure of 570 psi.

Fuel was gravity-fed from the 25-litre tank to a paper cartridge filter mounted on the offside of the crankcase, above the cylinder. From the filter, petrol passed to the pump, which was of the plunger type (similar to pumps used on diesel engines). There was no direct rider control of pump delivery.

A 1954 fuel injected Rennsport engine showing inlet manifolds, fuel injection delivery pipe and throttle slide.

In the pump body was a diaphragm, which was subjected on one side to induction-pipe depression by means of a balance-pipe system connected to the two throttle boxes. Attached to the diaphragm was a rack-rod, which engaged with a gear on each of the two plungers. Movement of the diaphragm, activated by opening or closing the throttle, rotated the plungers; such rotation varied the internal porting and, with it, the amount of fuel delivered by the plungers. Surplus fuel was pumped back into the tank. An adjusting screw permitted basic setting of the mixture strength. Lubrication of the pump was taken care of by engine oil from a separate container.

Apart from providing a useful gain in performance, BMW also claimed, at the time, that its fuel-injection system produced a 15-per-cent improvement in fuel consumption.

Another aspect of the Rennsport engine, which was of considerable technical interest, was the piston design. Almost fully-skirted, the 10.2:1 pistons had an oil scraper ring below the bosses of the gudgeon pin. Three compression rings were also fitted in the conventional position, the lowest of these having a tapered face and drainage holes to assist oil control.

The piston crown was of nearly pent-roof shape and fitted closely into the head space at each side to promote squish. To accommodate the contour of the valve head, the valve cutaways under the inlet and exhaust valves were convex and concave respectively.

The cylinder barrels normally featured shrunk-in cast-iron liners, but BMW also tried chromium-plated bores - the finish being applied directly to the aluminium - with complete success.

A taper at the rear of the crankshaft accommodated a flywheel car-type clutch. The clutch body was in two halves, which were held together by a ring of eight bolts; the inner face of the rear half formed one of the driving surfaces. Sandwiched between that face and the pressure plate was a single, faced driven plate. This had a splined centre which transmitted the drive to the gearbox mainshaft.

The rear half of the clutch body had internal peripheral teeth which engaged with similar external teeth on the pressure plate. Actuating force for the pressure plate was supplied by six non-adjustable springs that were seated in the front half of the clutch body. Clutch withdrawal was by means of a thrust rod passing through the hollow gearbox mainshaft; a hemispherical pad, jointed to the end of the rod, sat on a cup in the centre of the pressure plate.

The forward half of the clutch body had a spigot that fitted into a bore in the back of the rear main bearing housing. There was an oil seal within this bore, and the spigot had a spiral groove to assist in preventing oil from entering the clutch housing. Clutch cooling was effected by a series of concentric ribs on the rear of the clutch body, and by air ducts in the housing.

Of conventional, all-indirect design, the gearbox had a top gear reduction of 1.3:1 and normally had five ratios (although four were used for certain circuits).

The complete engine/gearbox assembly was supported at three points in the frame: one each at front and rear of the lower portion of the crankcase, and the third at a steady point above cylinder level in the crankcase-half of the gear case. The frame was of the cradle type with a tubular extension to carry the racing seat and to provide anchorages for the rear suspension legs. On the works bikes, three different frame layouts were evolved to ensure that each rider could tuck himself away to the maximum advantage.

Pivoted-fork rear suspension, first seen on works BMWs in 1952, was employed, a feature being the enclosure of the drive shaft within the offside fork tube. Likewise, an Earles-type front fork first appeared for the 1953 season, replacing the telescopic fork which BMW had done so much to popularise. Front and rear suspension legs were similar in design and embodied two-way hydraulic damping; variations in road conditions or riders' weights could easily be met by fitting legs with the appropriate spring and damper characteristics.

Both brakes were cable-operated, the front one being of the two-leading-shoe pattern. BMW stated that the new fork improved front wheel braking by eliminating 'dip' when the brake was applied. The 1954-specification works Rennsport produced significant power from around 6,500rpm, with a maximum output of 58bhp at 8,500rpm using injectors, and 52bhp with conventional carburettors.

Besides the factory machines, a batch of 25 Rennsports was manufactured in 1954 for sale to private customers. These engines, together with the factory units, were not only to be used in solo racing BMWs but, as the next chapter will reveal, also to achieve unparalleled success in the sidecar class.

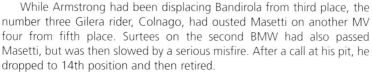

While Armstrong had been displacing Bandirola from third place, the number three Gilera rider, Colnago, had ousted Masetti on another MV four from fifth place. Surtees on the second BMW had also passed Masetti, but was then slowed by a serious misfire. After a call at his pit, he dropped to 14th position and then retired.

Meanwhile Duke and Zeller were circulating so fast that the German in second place was 90 seconds in front of third man Bandirola by half distance. So it remained until the end, with the two leaders pulling even further ahead of the field. For Zeller to have displaced all but one of the Italian multis must rate as one of the best, if not the best, of the performances by a post-war BMW rider.

A month later at the end of July, almost a quarter of a million spectators invaded Solitude to witness Walter Zeller and Willy Faust give BMW a popular double victory in the 500 and sidecar races. Zeller's race winning time was an improvement on Geoff Duke's record, but his best lap of 4 minutes, 42 seconds (a speed of 91.04mph) still left Duke in possession of the lap record for the circuit at 91.35mph.

Though BMW was not having a full attempt at the world title, they certainly made up for it on the record breaking scene. Another 24 world records fell to BMW in the autumn of 1955. After unsuitable weather had foiled record attempts by the company during the last week of September, a return was made to the Munich-Ingoldstadt autobahn on Tuesday 4th October, where two dozen records were set. These included 18 in the sidecar classes, for capacities of 500, 750 and 1,200cc, and six in the solo classes for 500, 750 and 1,000cc.

Weather conditions were absolutely ideal, with a gentle breeze over the autobahn and just sufficient moisture in the atmosphere to let the engines develop maximum power.

Zeller out testing, circa 1955.

Whereas Willy Noll's fully enclosed 500 sidecar (basically a strutted wheel!) used an unsupercharged engine with fuel injection and was reputed to rev to 10,000rpm, Walter Zeller's solo was a conventional road racing Rennsport carrying frontal streamlining only. Over 10 kilometres he averaged 145mph, whilst over the 10 mile distance Zeller managed to increase this to a shade over 150mph.

For 1956, BMW made two major changes on the road racing front. First, to fit full streamlining to their solos, and second, to sponsor ex-world champion and former Moto Guzzi team manager Fergus Anderson on works machinery.

Then aged 47, Anderson had begun motorcycling on a Douglas back in 1923, making his competition debut four years later in a grass track event on a Levis borrowed from his sister. His first road race was in 1932 at the Spanish Grand Prix, and in 1938 he had ridden for NSU, switching to DKW in 1939.

After the war he rode a Velocette, and then began a long association with Moto Guzzi. As related in my book *Mick Walker's Italian Racing Motorcycles* (Redline Books) 1998, Anderson then chalked up a vast array of successes on Mandello machinery. But a dispute with the Italian factory late in 1955 led to his alliance with BMW, after testing the three-cylinder DKW two-strokes.

Fergus Anderson campaigned this factory-supported Rennsport during spring 1956. The former Moto Guzzi world champion was killed on the machine at the Belgian Floreffe circuit on the 6th May that year.

His first appearance on one of the Munich twins came at Imola, Italy on Easter Monday 1956. Then came the Circuit de Mettet International in Belgium on 29th April, where Anderson came home third behind winner Surtees and Lomas in second place. There had been some teething problems, but with the machine sorted out, he took the BMW to Floreffe in Belgium on the 6th May. Opposition included John Surtees on an MV four. plus Bill Lomas and Dickie Dale on works Guzzi singles. Anderson put up a fine performance with a meteoric ride on the straight where his machine was visibly faster than Surtees' MV four. But tragedy struck a few miles from the finish line. There on an s-bend, Fergus Anderson, one of the great riders of his generation, crashed and was killed instantly.

Following the tragedy, BMW's solo effort was understandably overshadowed. But it had at last succeeded in producing really competitive solos. The latest flat twins were faster than they had ever been, and with it came improved handling and reliability. The speed that had been visible at Floreffe was demonstrated again by an impressive performance the same month by Zeller at Hockenheim, where he built up a 25 second lead over the Gilera four of Reg Armstrong.

The resurgence had come about thanks partly to new engine tuning, but mainly to streamlining, which now completely enveloped the frontal area of the machine. The speed was claimed as over 150mph.

Following the untimely death of Fergus Anderson, BMW fielded two solo riders, Walter Zeller and new boy Ernst Riedelbauch, but only Zeller was entered for the Isle of Man TT. During practice, he used full streamlining, but chose a naked bike in the race - this may have been a wise decision as on race day gusty conditions prevailed. At the end of the first lap Zeller lay sixth, but by the end of six laps he had moved up to fifth. Then with Guzzi rider Lomas in trouble to open up another place, the seventh and final lap saw Zeller move up to finish a creditable fourth behind race winner Surtees' MV four and the Norton singles of Hartle and Brett.

Following the Isle of Man, the Dutch TT at Assen a couple of weeks later saw Ken Kavanagh come to the start line aboard one of the sensational new Moto Guzzi V8s, whilst Bill Lomas rode one of the Italian marque's fleet singles. Surtees on the MV four made a lightening start, followed by Zeller on the solo factory BMW in second place. With several retirements including both Guzzi riders and Umberto Masetti on another MV four, Zeller maintained his runner up spot to the end to gain a rostrum finish. Another BMW (a production Rennsport) piloted by Ernst Hiller came home sixth.

The following week, Zeller made it a carbon copy result with another second behind Surtees in the ultra-fast Belgian Grand Prix at Spa Francorchamps. With a host of four-cylinder models in attendance, ridden by the world's finest riders, this result was superb. Referring to his move up to second when Duke's Gilera retired, *Motor Cycle* said of Zeller's performance; 'riding brilliantly, he was never passed'. His average speed for the 15 lap, 131.6 mile race was 113.34mph. At the same venue, Noll won the sidecar race, with the next BMW, Hillebrand's, in fourth place.

Then came the important German round held at Solitude. BMW's star, Walter Zeller, was on the front row of the grid together with Duke on a Gilera four, Lomas on a Guzzi V8, Armstrong and Monneret on Gileras, and finally Masetti, who formed the MV challenge in the absence of John Surtees, who was hurt in the previous day's 350 race.

At the end of the first lap, Zeller was sixth, and gradually pulled up to fourth by dint of some superb riding, thus splitting the Italian exotica. This effort, however, proved to be just too much for the BMW's engine, which clanked miserably as the bike pulled into the pits, its race run. With it went Zeller's chances of leading the world. But if the 500 was a disappointment, not so the sidecar event, with a BMW 1-2-3-4 from Noll, Hillebrand, Fath and Schneider. In the process, Noll succeeded in breaking both the lap and race records.

August brought the Ulster Grand Prix, where Zeller made the journey with vital points at stake, but he retired with clutch trouble. Noll once again won the battle of the chairs, while Hillebrand retired. And so the circus came to the final round at Monza in Italy on 9th September. But this was not a good day for the German team.

Earles-fork models

After a production span of 15 years, which lasted from 1955 until 1969, the last of the famous Earles-fork BMW twins were constructed in the summer of 1969 - the final motorcycles to be built at the Munich works. The 500 R50 and 600 R69 featured Earles-type front forks and full swinging arm suspension, closely related to that pioneered on the factory's racing models campaigned by Walter Zeller, and had set new standards when they debuted at the 38th International Brussels Salon, which opened to the public on Saturday 15th January 1955.

The treatment of the rear section of the frame was very unusual, bearing a marked resemblance to the old plunger design, with main loops that extended down and rearwards almost as far as the wheel spindle. Instead of the rear frame carrying top and bottom mounts for the old-style plunger boxes, however, the rear shocks were supported from the middle by the upper portions of the loops. A welded bracket extended rearwards to form the base of a top shroud for the spring damper assembly, which was secured in place from the top by a threaded alloy boss. The upper section of the shrouds also formed the rear mudguard mountings. This arrangement provided for an extremely rigid frame and was of great benefit in the design's suitability for sidecar duties.

A Gilera won the sidecar race and Zeller finished down in sixth place following a hurried pit stop. Three other BMWs finished, with Klinger ninth, Hiller tenth, and Riedelbauch eleventh.

The final positions in the 1956 World Championship, with Zeller's 16 points against Surtees' 24, gave BMW's star second place - and no doubt he thought that except for mechanical problems he could have been world champion. It was the nearest a BMW solo rider was ever to get to the title.

The 1957 season opener was the Circuit de Mettet in Belgium on 5th May, where, despite atrocious weather conditions, Hiller came home second in the 500 race behind Dickie Dale's Guzzi single. There were several retirements in this event, notably John Surtees' MV four and Keith Campbell's V8 Guzzi.

The following week, at the non-championship Austrian Grand Prix held at the 3.25 mile Salzburg circuit, on 11th May, the 500 solo event caused most surprise. Riding a production Rennsport, Austrian champion Gerold Klinger came out top after a close tussle with BMW team leader Walter Zeller, who led after the Austrian crashed on lap 7 of the 15 lap, 47.71 mile race. Remounting, Klinger caught Zeller on the last lap and won by a few lengths to the great excitement of the home crowd.

The official World Championship commenced at Hockenheim on Sunday 19th May. Zeller rode superbly to finish a gallant third behind Liberati and McIntyre on Gilera fours, but he was in front of Dale on a Guzzi, Terry Shepherd on an MV and Hiller in sixth place on another BMW.

1953 Earles fork .

Saturday 25th May was the start of official practice for the 1957 Isle of Man TT - the Golden Jubilee of the event. BMW had only entered one man - Zeller - but as *Motor Cycling* reported; 'The large crowd of watchers at Quarter Bridge seemed to agree that Walter Zeller took a lot of beating for speed combined with ease'. His fastest time for this first session was 25 min 14.8 seconds at a speed of 89.67mph.

However, following this excellent start, things did not go quite according to plan. On Monday 27th, the BMW rider struck mechanical trouble at Glen Helen, followed the same evening by a crash at Laurel Bank on wet tar. But in typical see-saw pattern, Zeller topped the morning practice session again two days later on the 29th May with a lap at 96.91mph - impressive stuff!

For the same reason, the front forks had dual mountings for the swinging bottom link and suspension units, allowing trail to be adjusted with relative ease. The rear suspension pre-load could be varied simply by turning a handle built into the base of the unit.

The rear swinging fork pivoted on taper roller bearings from a pair of adjustable stub spindles screwed into each side of the frame, just behind the gearbox where previous BMWs had always employed an exposed final drive shaft. This was now contained within the offside leg of the swinging arm assembly, which was bolted to the rear bevel drive casing.

The ohv engines were built in two sizes: 494cc (68 x 68mm) and 594cc (72 x 73mm). The R69 (and from 1960 the R69S) were notably successful in sports/endurance racing, their silent progress often masking their impressive track performance in such events.

On the 3rd March 1961 a four man team of Ellis Boyce, George Catlin, John Holder and Sid Mizen riding an R69S entered by London-based BMW dealers MLG, set a new 24-hour speed record of 109.24mph (176kph) at the French Montlhéry circuit just outside Paris.

590cc BMW R69S at Snetterton, October 1964.

In the race itself, Zeller and the BMW seemed set for glory as at the end of lap one they came through holding third place behind Bob McIntyre's Gilera and John Surtees' MV. These positions remained unchanged as the leaders completed the third lap. But then came disappointing news when the loudspeakers announced 'Zeller retired at Ramsey'. The cause was dead ignition, and Zeller's racing was over for the day.

There were some surprising mechanical details associated with all the 1957 TT machines. The successful sidecar crews, and Zeller on his solo, all used Dell'Orto carburettors. In two cases, these used 'home made' float chambers and dash pots, whereas Hillebrand opted for two float chambers. BMW stated that the 1957 flat twins were capable of 9,500rpm and had excellent torque at low speeds - hence their particular suitability for sidecar duty.

Perhaps the strangest aspect of BMW's 1957 TT machines was the use of streamlining on Zeller's solo mount. Fearing a wet and windy Senior race, Zeller had handed his machine over to the scrutineers prior to the race in naked form (after using a streamlined dustbin fairing in practice). But when race day proved fine, he somehow managed to fit the dustbin back on again within the allotted half hour. Even more surprising was the statement he made at the time that his streamlining made a difference of 35mph to his maximum speed. When questioned about this statement prior to the race and asked whether he surely did not mean 35 kilometres per hour, he shook his head and affirmed that he meant 35 miles per hour. Many observers could not really believe this was possible, but Zeller was adamant, and he should have known.

Next race on the Grand Prix circuit was the Dutch TT at Assen on Saturday 29th June. Zeller was another magnificent third, this time behind Surtees (MV) and Liberati (Gilera). Privateer Hiller did well again coming home fifth, a position which Klinger had held on another Rennsport until forced to retire.

At the Belgian Grand Prix a week later only seven of the 23 starters reached the finish. One of the earliest in trouble was Zeller, who tumbled at Stavelot on the first lap. Klinger was holding fifth spot by mid-distance - but then missed a gear, with resultant damage which forced him to retire two laps later. No BMW finished. It was a muddled race where even the winner Liberati was denied victory when he was excluded from the result for taking over Geoff Duke's entry and not informing the organisers.

Zeller was not to score any more world championship points that season, even though he retained his national title. Hiller and Klinger proved successful in international non-world title races, for example taking several victories in Czechoslovakia, Holland and France as well as in Germany.

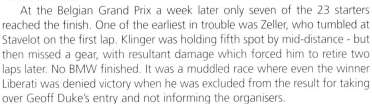

Meanwhile, on the commercial front, BMW was in deep financial trouble, and serious cuts in the competition budget had to be made. This first manifested itself when the company decided it could not take part in long distance trials, and there was thus no factory presence in the 1957 ISDT.

However, if it was a difficult period for BMW's competition department, there were still plenty of privateers to fly the BMW flag. One was Jack Forrest, who had stamped his authority on Australian road racing that year. After winning several small events, he took part in the important Queensland TT races at the 2.7 mile Lowood airstrip-cum-road circuit near Brisbane on 16th June. Riding a fully-streamlined BMW 500, he set the fastest lap of the day in the Senior race, but then crashed while well in the lead. At the time he was reported to have suffered severe abrasions and a fractured leg, but he was back in action in October on the rebuilt BMW - and in sensational style. Forrest raised the Australian speed records for 500, 750 and 1,000cc to 149.06mph at Coonabarabran, New South Wales.

Walter Zeller finished runner up in the 1956 500cc world championships, eight points behind winner John Surtees. He is pictured here during the 1957 Senior TT.

Ernst Hiller taking part in the ACU British Road Racing Championship meeting at Thruxton, near Andover, Hampshire, on August Bank Holiday Monday, 1958...

For 1958, BMW decided to continue in road racing, even though commercially it was still fighting for its corporate life.

In the solo classes, the surprise news was that the ex-Norton and Gilera star, muti-world champion Geoff Duke would race a factory-backed Rennsport of the type used so successfully by Walter Zeller over the last few seasons. Zeller had decided to retire from competitive motorcycle sport. Later in the year, as a token of its appreciation of his efforts, the company presented Zeller with a specially-built 589.5cc (72.2 x 72mm) supercharged racer in road trim to mark his retirement. The machine's engine came from the sidecar outfit which Max Klankermeier had campaigned in the 1949 600cc German sidecar championship.

Backing up Duke in international events were ex-Guzzi star Dickie Dale, Australian Jack Forrest, Gerold Klinger and Ernst Hiller. Despite Zeller's retirement, on paper at least, this was BMW's strongest-ever team. This might have seemed odd at a time when BMW was in the depths of its worst financial crisis. But there was an important external factor. Just a few months before, in October 1957, both Gilera and Moto Guzzi had announced that they would not be entering works machines during 1958. Apart from the ageing British singles, this left MV Agusta and BMW as effectively the only contenders for the world crown. No doubt it was this alone that brought BMW and Geoff Duke together.

The first benefits of the partnership were seen on 17th April at the BMCRC (British Motor Cycle Racing Club) 7th International Silverstone Saturday. As *Motor Cycling* put it, 'What a day to remember!' Held in fine conditions it brought an immense crowd to see Duke making a bid to prove that he was still 'the Master' after almost two years away from week-in, week-out competitive racing.

Riding a Manx Norton in the 350 race, Duke did not disappoint, winning in fine style. But the keenest race of the day was the 500, for which Duke brought his dolphin-faired works BMW on to the front row of the grid. This was the flat twin's first outing since it had been collected in Munich a couple of days before. Reputed to be an ex-Zeller machine, the BMW had not been handling too well in practice and now sported a pair of completely untried Girling rear shock absorber units... It was wait and see, and the crowd held its breath as the flag dropped and the riders pushed their machines into motion.

Forty-three starters snarled and weaved away in a close-knit bunch, with Duke among the initial leaders. But this early promise was soon to be dashed when at the end of the first lap Duke and the BMW came past the packed grandstands opposite the start and finish line in eighth position with, as *Motor Cycling* commented, 'the BM's acceleration making no visible impression on the majority of the singles.' Next lap and Duke was down to eleventh place. And three laps later he halted a silent BMW just past the start line, with what were reported later as 'unspecified gremlins in the transmission.' It was not a promising start.

Meanwhile, things were going a little better for Hiller, he started his season at the non-championship Spanish Grand Prix. It was raced around the twisty Montjuich circuit near Barcelona where he finished fifth in a race won by Surtees on an MV four.

In the Austrian Grand Prix, again non-championship, BMWs showed up well again. Klinger led from the start but had to retire early with gearbox trouble. The race was won by Hiller, with Forrest third, Dale fifth, Huber sixth, Jaeger seventh and Duke eighth.

A week later, with less than a month to go to the Isle of Man Senior TT, Geoff Duke at long last got to grips with his mount. In one of the closest and hotly-contested races of his career, he scored a superb win on the fast 4.8 mile Hockenheim circuit at the annual International Rhein Pokal Rennen. Duke headed Ernst Hiller over the line by little more than four lengths.

... Hiller pushed the 500cc race winner, Derek Minter (Norton), hard and impressed many spectators in the process.

BMW presented Walter Zeller with this 600cc supercharged racing machine, in road-going trim, to mark his retirement in November 1958.

At the start, the only non-BMW on the front row was a Norton ridden by Australian Harry Hinton Jnr, who took off at a savage pace with Duke, Hiller, Dale and Forrest in hot pursuit. At the end, Hinton made third, ahead of Huber and Klinger on BMWs and another Norton ridden by 1957 350cc world champion, Keith Campbell in sixth place.

The first classic of the season was the Isle of Man TT. Commenting on his choice of a BMW for this event, Geoff Duke offered some personal views in an article in *Motor Cycling* for the 22nd May 1958: 'When I was a child my family frequently took me to the Isle of Man, but I was 16 before I saw my first TT race there. This was in 1939, when Georg Meier, on a German BMW, won the Senior at 89.38mph and achieved the fastest lap of 90.75mph. I am accepting this as a happy omen - because, unfortunately missing the TT for two seasons, I am, in June this year, returning to what I regard as the world's greatest event on a BMW. If 19 years ago, as I stood amazed and thrilled by Meier's performance, someone had suggested that one day I also would be riding a works entered BMW and in the fabulous TT too... well, I would have just told them that they were quite mad!'

Both Duke and Dale were entered for the Senior TT. Although both showed up well in practice, the race was another matter. First Dale was reported as motoring slowly at the end of lap one. This was followed soon afterwards, by Duke pulling into his pit shaking his head ruefully as he talked to his mechanic and after a careful examination decided to retire. The cause was front brake trouble. Dale at least kept going, finally finishing in tenth place at an average speed of 92.46mph, in a race won by John Surtees' MV.

Hiller during this time had chalked up important wins in Helsinki, Finland and Chimay, Belgium. It was Hiller who performed best for BMW in the next classic, the Dutch TT, where he scored fourth and Dale sixth. Duke once again suffered problems with his front brake, even though it had been relined since his Isle of Man retirement.

Seven days later at the Belgian Grand Prix, however, Duke at last seemed to have beaten the problem when he finished fourth, one place ahead of Dale. Duke's average speed for the 15 lap, 131.42 mile race was 113.59mph, compared to winner Surtees' 115.32mph.

Next came the German Grand Prix at the Nürburgring, where despite another victory for Surtees, the home crowd had at least something to shout about as the new national hero Ernst Hiller led for the first few miles, finally finishing fourth ahead of Dale.

At an international meeting at Thruxton early in August, Hiller came very near to taking the victory from British champion Derek Minter, but had to settle for the runner-up spot. At the Ulster Grand Prix, Dale was sixth, then at the final round in Italy, he rode superbly to clinch fourth, splitting a quartet of MV Agusta fours. Even Duke on his Norton could not match Dale at Monza in seventh spot. Two laps adrift, Klinger and Hiller filled ninth and tenth places respectively. It was enough to give Dale third place in the 1958 championships, followed by Duke, who had ridden both BMW and Norton, in fourth.

Ernst Hiller competing at the Thruxton circuit, August 1958. BMW Rennsport.

Away from the Grand Prix scene, John Lewis and Peter James brought an R69 into fourth place overall in the Thruxton 500 Mile production machine race. The men behind the venture were partners in MLG Motorcycles of Shepherds Bush, London - Vic Motler and Charlie Lock. Both were very much long-term BMW enthusiasts. It was a more impressive result than the mere statistic might suggest, as borne out by *Motor Cycle's* report of 26th June which said; 'So unobtrusive that its high placing surprised many onlookers, a 594cc BMW R69 was ridden into fourth place. Quietly, smoothly and cleanly the German flat twin, one of the most ordinary looking (read standard) models on the course, circled with admirable regularity, calling at the pits only for fuel and change of riders, never for oil or repairs.'

A sister machine to this Rennsport was raced by ex-works star (with Moto Guzzi and MV Agusta) Dickie Dale, towards the end of his career during 1958 and 1959.

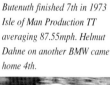

The following year, 1959, was a poor one for BMW, with the company escaping bankruptcy by the skin of its teeth, and although the 1958 sidecar world champions, Schneider and Strauss, won again, Dickie Dale was unable to maintain his 1958 form in the 500cc world championship series, with only two fourth places in France and Holland to show for his efforts. Huber was the only other BMW solo rider to score points, with a sixth at Hockenheim.

One bright spot in an otherwise moribund 1959 season, was when the American rider John Penton checked in on his R60 at the Western Union office in Los Angeles, on 10th June. Penton had covered the 2,833 mile transcontinental journey from New York in a motorcycle record time of 52 hours, 11 minutes and 1 second, an average of over 50mph.

Another high point was when John Lewis, partnered by Bruce Daniels, rode to an impressive victory in the 1959 Thruxton 500 Mile event. Lewis then left for Spain where he teamed up with Peter Darvill to win the Barcelona 24-hour race.

Hans Otto Butenuth was one of the first riders to race the new R75/5 which had been introduced in late 1969. He is seen here competing in the 1973 Isle of Man TT.

The sixties saw mixed fortunes for BMW's sporting achievements. The new decade started with the amazing prospect of a Japanese rider, Fumio Ito, campaigning a Rennsport in the 500 Grand Prix series, but after a superb sixth in the French Grand Prix during April 1960, he could not sustain his form. Later, in 1963, he finished third in the 250 World Championship on a Yamaha. He even won in Belgium, before returning to Japan.

The factory's last solo world championship points came in the 1961 German Grand Prix at Hockenheim, where Jaeger was third, Hiller fifth and Lothar sixth.

Early in 1961, a specially-prepared R69S established the first of a series of successes for the model in record breaking and production racing. The 12 and 24-hour records fell to an Anglo-German effort with a BMW entered by MLG Motorcycles. Although pipped to the post by Velocette for the honour of being first to complete 24 hours at over 100mph, the BMW shattered the week-old record by almost 10mph. Over the bumpy French speed bowl at Montlhéry, Ellis Boyce, George Catlin, John Holder and Sid Mizen completed the first 12 hours at an average speed of 109.39mph and went on at a barely reduced speed to turn in 109.24mph for the complete 24-hours. The total distance covered was 2,621.77 miles and fuel consumption worked out at 34mpg.

Fitted with a specially-made Peel dolphin fairing, the R69S carried a Marchal headlamp to supplement the track lighting during the hours of darkness. Other preparation consisted of stripping off any unnecessary equipment and fitting special high-compression Mahle pistons, long, shallow-taper megaphones (fitted with silencers), a Smiths 8,000rpm magnetic rev counter, a racing seat, reversed foot controls and a pad over the rear of the tank enabling the rider literally to 'lie' on the machine for considerable periods.

Butenuth finished 7th in 1973 Isle of Man Production TT averaging 87.55mph. Helmut Dahne on another BMW came home 4th.

German National Championships, Nürburgring 1964. BMW R69S.

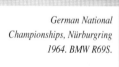

In March 1961 this R69S, prepared by London dealers MLG, broke the 24-hour speed record at Montlhéry with a team of riders comprising Ellis Boyce, George Catlin, John Holder and Sid Mizen. The squad averaged 109.24mph, a distance of 2,621.77miles.

38

Martyn Sharpe taking the Gus Kuhn R90S production racer to victory at Mallory Park, mid 1970s.

At the end of the marathon, the engine was stripped and found to be in perfect condition - the only problem having been a slight misfire at high revs around a quarter distance, which vanished as mysteriously as it had come. When tested later by *Motor Cycling*, the MLG R69S was certified at the MIRA test track as having a top speed of 118.3mph with the rider crouching behind the screen.

At the time, it was little known that MLG had made an earlier attempt on the 24-hour record at Montlhéry using another R69S. But this attempt, in October 1960, had ended in tragedy when 25 year old Bill Sawford piloting the machine went over the banking and sustained a broken leg and broken pelvis, as a result of which he died. The accident happened on the first lap of his opening stint. Before it, Bruce Daniels, Sid Mizen and Phil Read had done an hour apiece, each averaging between 106 and 108mph in darkness.

Following the successful record bid came more successes in 1961 at Thruxton, Barcelona and Silverstone - where a BMW won the 1,000 kilometre race. After this, MLG cut down its racing activities at the end of 1962, but BMW management took up the challenge, entering Helmut Hutten and Karl Hoppe in the 1963 Coupe de Europa endurance series. I can well remember seeing this pair perform at Thruxton, where they maintained steady, trouble-free progress to finish seventh in their class and 10th overall. Completing 216 laps (against the winner's 288) Hutten and Hoppe had an average speed of 65.1mph.

An interesting development, out of the main stream in the late 1960s, was the work of Dutch BMW dealer and enthusiast Henny Van Donkelaar, who had grown tired of waiting for Munich to produce a 750cc twin. So using 80mm bore (as opposed to the standard 72mm of the 594cc engine) light alloy cylinders with cast-iron liners from West German specialist Wolfgang Kayser, he began converting customers' R60 and R69S models to 730cc. The machines were offered with various forged Mahle pistons. These yielded a range of compression ratios from 7.5 to 9.5:1. These engines were used not only on the road, but some were raced with considerable success in long distance trials and even sidecar motocross in the late 1960s. Meanwhile, in Germany, several R50 type engines were converted to 700cc.

BMW R75/5 Isle of Man Production TT, 1972.

Dahne's bike at the TT, circa 1974.

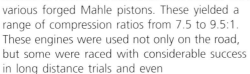

The best known of all the European riders who campaigned BMWs in production events during the 1970s was Helmut Dahne, seen here in the Production TT.

Dahne (seen here after a TT race) was a tyre tester for the Metzeler company.

Not since the 1950s and the days of Walter Zeller had BMW enthusiasts been able to claim their very own solo racing hero, but in 1967 a man who was to emerge as the BMW solo rider par excellence of the next decade, took part in his first road race. He was Helmut Dahne, and he had served his apprenticeship with BMW as a mechanic.

But Dahne was also an enthusiastic private rider - a real privateer, who prepared his own bike in his own time. Almost the only occasion on which he had official works help was after winning the Sudelfeld Bergrennen classic in 1968 in the face of strong opposition. His mount for the occasion was a home-built R69S special, but after the race, his boss Alex von Falkenhausen lent him a works engine. Almost overnight the young mechanic converted it to a 500. Dahne won first time out with the new power unit, with the result that von Falkenhausen gave him the works engine!

Later, after progressing to chief tester, Dahne quit BMW to work for the tyre giants Metzeler. But the parting was on good terms, and Dahne continued to campaign BMW flat twins. Still very much a privateer, his mentor was Helmut Bucher, who looked after the engine while Dahne concentrated on the chassis. He received a little support from the factories to whose fame he contributed, since Metzeler allowed him time off to race and paid all travelling expenses, and BMW assisted by supplying limited quantities of spare parts.

To some extent, it could be said that Dahne limited his career because of his loyalty to 'his' factory - BMW. For this reason Dahne never really got involved with the Grand Prix circus, as quite simply, BMW had no suitable bike. Because of this, he concentrated his efforts on the long-distance production machine races and real road circuits. The Isle of Man mountain circuit was his first choice, while the Nürburgring ran a close second. He believed that both of these were 'natural' courses and difficult to learn.

Why class Dahne with such luminaries as Zeller or Meier? Just his Isle of Man exploits, crowned by victory in the 1976 1,000cc Production TT are enough to guarantee his claim to this honour.

BMW would not have been able to chalk up the famous victory without Dahne's tenacity as demonstrated at the end of practice for the 1976 TT, when a loose valve seat caused an exhaust valve to break. The result was a badly damaged cylinder head, but Dahne had no spare bike or engine. So, he had to cannibalise another person's machine to repair his own engine.

'Sheer power was not the most important factor,' he once said about his racing success. Dahne was a man of few words, but was firmly of the opinion that modern Grand Prix two-strokes should have been banned, because as he put it, 'they represent a waste of energy and create pollution.' As the 1970s came to a close, even Dahne was forced to accept that no four-stroke was competitive any longer - certainly not one with only

Braun-Cobas K100 endurance racer

After several years of development begun during the late 1970s, BMW finally introduced to the public the first of its new K-series four-cylinder models, in October 1983, in the shape of the unfaired K100.

Designer Josef Fritzenwenger was assisted in the K589 (as the four-cylinder project was designed at the Spandau, Berlin factory) by a development team headed by Stefan Pachernegg. The result of their efforts was to be a power unit, comprising the engine/gearbox/shaft drive unit patented as the BMW Compact Drive System. The CDS was extremely light (for a 1-litre roadgoing engine and drive system). Chill cast - a sophisticated form of die-casting in an aluminium alloy containing magnesium and silicon, there were no cast-iron liners in the cylinders (a feature shared with the later flat twins), and this kept the dry weight of the standard unit down to 76kg (168lb). Instead, the bearing surfaces of the alloy cylinders were treated with a nickel-silicon carbide abrasion-proof coating, called Scanimet, which reduces friction, improves heat transfer and allows smaller clearances for quieter running and better lubrication. These

blocks cannot be rebored, but from actual usage have proved exceptionally long lasting (in excess of 150,000miles in some cases).

The 987cc displacement was achieved by the slightly long-stroke bore and stroke dimensions of 67 x 70mm. And in standard form the power output was 90bhp @ 8,000rpm for the five-speed dohc inline four.

One of the first to exploit the newcomers racing potential was Antonio Cobas, the internationally renowned Spanish chassis expert.

In late 1983 Cobas designed a spaceframe, utilising BMW's K100 Compact Drive System as a stressed member, with 40mm Japanese Kayaba teledraulic front forks and an almost horizontal monoshock, but retaining the standard BMW Monolever. In racing specification, twin floating 300mm Brembo discs with four piston calipers took care of the front end stopping power, whilst at the rear a single Brembo disc (a standard K100 unit) and twin piston caliper was to be found. Magnesium three-spoke wheels by Marvic, both using Michelin race rubber - a 16 inch at the front and an 18 inch at the rear - completed the rolling chassis.

Two machines were actually constructed. The engines were tuned by Eduardo Giro who was Ossa's chief designer at the height of that company's success. Power output was upped to 122bhp at 9,400rpm. And the complete Cobas-BMW K100 weighed (dry) 179kg (394lb); maximum speed was a very respectable 174mph (278kph).

Originally campaigned as JJ Cobas BMW K100RS, the bikes debuted in the 1984 Barcelona 24 Horas (Hours); that most classic of all long distance endurance events. But dogged by problems with the one-off computerised electronic ignition system, it was a debut to forget. However, this public humiliation directly led to official assistance from BMW, who had previously shown no interest. This in turn led to sponsorship by Braun, the giant German electrical company, through their Spanish subsidiary, Braun Espanola.

From then on the bikes were raced as Braun-BMWs and this vital backing enabled Carlos Cardus to win the 1984 Spanish Superbike title. In a country where motorcycle racing ranked second only to soccer this meant massive publicity at home, although largely unreported abroad.

two-cylinders. But for a period in the late 1960s and early 1970s, Dahne managed to defy the trend. Truly a great rider, it was a pity he had not lived in an earlier age.

Another notable BMW protagonist and special builder was the German Mike Krauser. Krauser had ridden BMW machinery in competition during the 1950s, and then ran a team of Rennsport sidecars in the 1960s. This finally led to his take-over of the works' sidecar racing effort in the mid-1970s when the bevel-drive dohc, 4-valve Rennsport engines were achieving 74bhp. At this point a combination of competition from the König and Yamaha 'strokers', together with the stringent FIM noise regulations, finally killed them off.

Krauser went on to make a name for himself as a producer of fine luggage and other aftermarket accessories from a factory based in Mering. During 1975 and 1976, he worked for BMW and was responsible for its endurance racing effort. By then the venerable boxer engine was beginning to feel its age as big bore Japanese multis gradually began to take over from Ducati, Moto Guzzi, BMW and other European marques.

In compensation for the Japanese lead in engines, chassis technology came to the fore for the Europeans. Frame rigidity and sure-footed handling were seen as the only way to make the most out of what was basically an outdated power unit which the Germans were committed to.

Riders for Krauser's BMW team at this period were Freddie Habfeld and Peter Zettelmeyer. Zettelmeyer was involved in engineering research at the University of Munich. He designed the fully-triangulated, lightweight chassis which formed the basis for the endurance racer, and would also later spawn Krauser's own 'production special'. However, while the new frame certainly proved a notable improvement over the standard production version, it was not enough to stem the tide of Japanese power. BMW's official racing effort was shelved after Habfeld was injured at Barcelona in 1976.

Dahne awaiting the start of a race.

Dahne with his R90S-based machine, 1975 TT.

Even so, March 1976 saw BMW triumphant again on the race-track at Daytona, USA. A headline of the time could not have hit it harder, 'Production one-two for undisputed BMWs.' Californian Steve McLaughlin riding a Butler and Smith prepared R90S, snatched victory from under the nose of team-mate Reg Pridmore in the 50-mile Superbike road race for production roadsters.

In fact, the specially-prepared flat twins had looked set to take the first three places until favourite

Martin Sharpe, 1975 Production TT at Union Mills, BMW R90S.

London dealership Gus Kuhn (headed by Vincent Davey) was deeply involved with racing BMWs during the mid-to-late 1970s, both in production and endurance events. One of the latter machines is seen here in 1976.

Gary Fisher, who had set the fastest qualifying time the previous day, struck engine trouble with only three of the 13 laps to go.

Only one other man could keep up with the flying BMWs - Cook Nielson, editor of *Cycle* magazine. Riding his own Ducati 900SS, time and again Nielson split the battling BMW riders as the lead changed half a dozen times per lap. In the elbow to elbow contest, continuing right round the 150mph banking, the crowd in the massive Daytona grandstand were on their toes with excitement.

Fisher, Nielson, McLaughlin and Pridmore all held the lead at some stage in the race and despite Fisher's retirement, the battle continued all the way to the finish line. British-born Pridmore looked to have a slight edge over team-mate McLaughlin, as the pair hurtled around the steep banking at over 140mph towards the chequered flag - but McLaughlin found the last ounce of power and took victory with only inches in it. Both BMWs had the same winning average of 99.714mph, which would easily have qualified them for the full Daytona 200 event that year. Nielson finished third a long way behind, followed by Californian Wes Cooley, who sweated it out all the way with a bucking, headstrong Kawasaki Z1 900.

In the same period, there were other production machine successes for British riders, both at home and in the Barcelona 24-hours and Bol d'Or marathon. Among the riders were Dave Potter, Gary Green, Graham Sharp, Ray Knight, John Cowie and Bernie Toleman.

An R100RS at a French endurance race in 1977.

Krauser Four Valve

During the early 1980s, the Krauser company (famous for their motorcycle luggage) produced a four-valve cylinder head conversion kit for the conventional two-valve BMW flat-twin engine series. Later, they also produced a complete motorcycle for twins type racing events.

The original aim of the Krauser Four-Valve Cylinder Head conversion was not only to raise the maximum power output, but also improve features such as flexibility, economy and reliability. Also the maximum output was produced without exceeding BMW's own limit. The chief advantage of the Krauser Four Valve Head came from developments in efficiency, rather than radical alteration.

Mike Krauser was a great enthusiast who had close involvement with 50/80cc solo and sidecar racing at world level.

The cylinder head was manufactured from hardened aluminium, low pressure die-casting alloy, thermo-shock resistant with shrunk valve seat rings, produced in special centrifugal casting, and valve guides of special bronze.

Gus Kuhn, R90-based endurance racer with John Cowie in the saddle.

During 1978, BMW dealer Werner Fallert created what may rank as the most technically interesting 'private' BMW ever, provided the factory racing effort is ignored. His dream was that the ultimate flat-twin BMW would be like the works Rennsport racing engines of the 1950s, boosted to 1,000cc. The result, based on the pushrod R100 production engine, was the FM1000. It was the most powerful BMW flat-twin of all, with a top speed of nearly 160mph.

1980's Stuik BMW special chassis. Le Mans 24 hours, 1985.

Very little of the original engine was left after Fallert had dispensed with the cylinder heads, camshaft and valve gear, and replaced them with new ohc four-valve heads with bevel gear drives on the top of the crankcase. The factory-fitted oil pump was retained, but the oil filter was now a replaceable paper element type. Capacity was enlarged to 999.8cc by using oversize 94.95mm pistons, and with special 45 choke Dell'Orto carburettors, the engine developed an incredible 110bhp at 8,500rpm. Drive was through a special six-speed gearbox manufactured by Wolfgang Kayser. The complete engine unit was mounted into a purpose-built tubular frame which was the work of Werner Dieringer, chief designer at the Kreidler factory.

1976 Krauser BMW endurance racer.

Perhaps the most amazing aspect of the whole machine was that it was not in reality a flat-twin at all. In an attempt to provide better ground clearance, each cylinder had been angled by five degrees from the horizontal - making it actually a 170 degree v-twin.

In 1979, ex-BMW endurance racer Habfeld, now recovered from his 1976 Barcelona injury, joined forces with Michael Neher and Franz Wiedemann, the latter a noted designer. Together, they developed a prototype road-going machine based on the layout of the ill-fated endurance racer. Mike Krauser was then asked if his company would sponsor the new space-frame BMW.

Compression ratio:	10.2:1
Maximum revs:	7,500rpm
Maximum output:	82 DIN at 7,300rpm.
Maximum torque:	83 Nn at 4,000rpm.
Weight:	0.5kg less than stock BMW version.
Rocker arm:	Chromium-molybdenum steel, drop forged, needle bearings.
Rocker arm spindles:	Inductively hardened.
Inlet valves:	Diameter 37mm, inductively hardened, 18 degree.
Exhaust valves:	Diameter 31mm, bi-metal nimonic, armoured, 21 degree.
Valve springs:	Double spiral adjustment by excenter rolls.
Piston:	Flat top.
Overall engine width:	35mm less than standard BMW R100RS engine.
Central plug:	10mm, Bosch W210.

Bearing of rocker arm spindles and cylinder head one piece.

Pushrod only one half of the standard BMW version, separately guided in the cylinder head, of austenitic sphere casting and finished by electronic rays.

Air-cooling between shafts of inlet and exhaust valves.

Paul Iddon warms up the L&C sponsored 1,000cc Krauser BMW at Brands Hatch, April 1984. This machine featured four-valve heads.

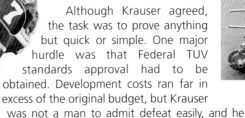

JJ Cobas K100-based four-cylinder racer (7) was one of two identical machines built for endurance events in late 1983 by Spanish chassis supremo Antonio Cobas.

Krauser MKM1000 'birdcage' space frame, early 1980s.

Although Krauser agreed, the task was to prove anything but quick or simple. One major hurdle was that Federal TUV standards approval had to be obtained. Development costs ran far in excess of the original budget, but Krauser was not a man to admit defeat easily, and he maintained his backing.

Finally, in 1980 the machine was unveiled and went into production as a prestigious sports tourer, the MKM1000. As the supreme accolade, the model was even offered with a full BMW factory warranty. While it used many standard parts, including the R100RS engine, plus wheels and forks, it was truly a hand-built special constructed around Zettelmeyer's latticework frame. It also sported striking bodywork by Zettelmeyer finished in brilliant white, with orange, pink and blue stripes. This paint scheme included fairing, seat and tank cover. Fuel was actually held in an alloy tank concealed underneath.

Production was strictly limited. The initial batch was 200, but even at their high price (£6,500 in Britain) there was no shortage of customers. Perhaps the biggest disappointment was that the machines lacked one of Krauser's own accessories as a standard option. This was his four-valve head kit which he marketed as an aftermarket fitting for standard BMWs. Not only did it offer a substantial power increase but it was actually narrower than the original BMW two-valve units. However, thanks to BMW's warranty, it could only be offered as an accessory kit for the MKM1000 from 1982 onwards.

At least one MKM1000 was constructed purely as a racing machine. This was campaigned by Englishman Paul Iddon in the 1984 Battle of the Twins series, sponsored by L&C of Royal Tunbridge Wells, Kent. Besides usual race tuning, the L&C machine featured the four-valve heads, an oil cooler, larger discs and three-spoke wheels. In pure speed, it proved a match for anything on the track, but its handling was not up to that of the Ducati v-twin. It finished the year in second spot in the series.

A different kind of BMW special continued to break records into the

Another K100-engined racer was constructed by the German concern VV Motorradtechnik. This employed their own hub-centre steering and fabricated frame. The power output was 110bhp at 9,500rpm, giving a maximum speed of over 155mph.

The main components of the four-valve Boxer engine - modern in every way, but holding true to BMW's flat-twin heritage.

Racing a four valve R1100RS

One of the most interesting and significant chapters in the long-running history of BMW's flat-twin family of motorcycles came in the spring of 1993, when the German marque unveiled its long awaited replacement for the conventional air-cooled pushrod, two-valves-per-cylinder Boxer; powered by the all-new R259 four-valves-per-cylinder Boxer engine. This had a capacity of 1,085cc (99 x 70.5mm), a two-piece crankcase (one-piece on the 'old' engine), oil and air-cooling, high camshafts (chain driven by short pushrods), Gilnisil coated alloy cylinders, one-piece crankshaft, two oil pumps and connecting rods manufactured of sinistered and forged steel (categorised into no less than seven weight groups). In addition, for the first time on a motorcycle design, the connecting rods of the new four-valve Boxer were made using the fracture (or 'crack') technology first introduced on BMW cars. This sees the large con-rod eye intentionally fractured, and not simply sawn in half. The advantage is that both surfaces along this intentional fracture fit together perfectly when subsequently re-joined.

The first model with the new engine was the R1100RS, and like subsequent additions to the range, this employed Bosch Motronic fuel injection, Telelever front suspension and BMW's patented Paralever rear end.

Soon the new engine was finding its way into racing (notably in Germany, but also Holland and even Great Britain) mainly through its use in endurance type events.

In 1997, an R1100RS finished 2nd in the Twins/Triples/Singles category of the British Endurance Championship series (held over five rounds). Entered by the G-force BMW team, it was the brainchild of Pat Keenan, then working as a technician for Heathrow BMW. Together with the rest of the team, a salvaged crash-damaged stock R1100RS was painstakingly converted into a circuit racer.

Changes to the original specification began with a race-type 2-1-2 exhaust system, a one-off 351 aluminium fuel tank, and a programmable engine management system. Other items including a Premier refuelling kit, and a pair of beautifully crafted Harrison six-pot

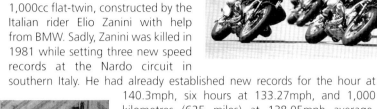

1980s. This was a 94bhp streamlined 1,000cc flat-twin, constructed by the Italian rider Elio Zanini with help from BMW. Sadly, Zanini was killed in 1981 while setting three new speed records at the Nardo circuit in southern Italy. He had already established new records for the hour at 140.3mph, six hours at 133.27mph, and 1,000 kilometres (625 miles) at 138.05mph average, when a gust of wind caught him out.

For several years (the last event was held in 1997) BMW ran a Legends race series at the annual Daytona Speed Week in March. At first, as this 1992 photograph shows, the machines were identical R100R, two-valve Boxers, but with the introduction of the four-valve models, R1100RS machines were used.

1991 Enzinger BMW BOTT racer. Dutch Nico Bakker alloy frame, single-sided swing arm and 17in Marvic wheels.

Another Italian was involved with a noteworthy BMW flat-twin special of the early 1980s. The MB2 was the work of former MV Agusta race chief Arturo Magni, and used an R100 power unit, making its debut at the Cologne Show in September 1982. Described in detail in my book MV Agusta (Osprey Publishing), it was marketed, unlike the Krauser machine, as a complete chassis into which the customer could slot his own engine. Frame, forks, wheels, brakes, tank, fairing, seat and other cosmetics were all Italian.

Although BMWs were hardly ever seen on the race circuits during the early 1980s, they made their authority felt in a new, challenging form of motorcycle sport - the ultra-demanding Paris-Dakar marathon. The organisers billed it as 'The World's Toughest Race.' BMW took victory in 1981, 1983, 1984 and 1985. But after this record of four wins, and a poor result in the 1986 event, the factory announced its retirement from the rally towards the end of the year.

When BMW introduced their new four-valves-per-cylinder 'Boxer' range, beginning with the R1100RS in 1992, it heralded a new era for the company's long running flat twin concept. But as with the three- and four-cylinder K Series a decade before, it did not result in a serious return to racing. Although both the K100RS and R1100RS have been raced in sports production races, such as the Isle of Man and more latterly the KRC (Kent Racing Combine) British Endurance Championships, there has been no official entry from the German factory itself.

Herbert Enzinger-tuned 979cc two-valve boxer engine; 11:1 compression ratio, twin 40mm flat-slide Mikuni carbs, 105bhp.

Following its car technology, BMW intentionally separated the connecting rod boss of the 1990's four-valve Boxer engine, a world first in motorcycling.

Pat Keenan, British Endurance Championships 1997. BMW R1100RS.

brake calipers followed. A special lightweight sub-frame was constructed, and this was mated to a fibre-glass seat unit adapted to suit the sub-frame and the standard RS's original fairing. The original fuel tank had its base cut away and fitted over the new alloy component, whilst the ABS system was removed to shed weight, and the original battery was axed in favour of a smaller, lighter one, which was re-located under the seat tail-piece to ensure easy access.

Finally the roadster's headlight was removed and its place taken by an Emerald programmable fuel and ignition ECU, and the fuel pump, fuses and so on. This 'compartment' was then covered by the regulation race number-plate.

After testing and dyno work, the initial target of 100bhp was achieved, making for a competitive, and unusual, race entry.

Scuderia RO

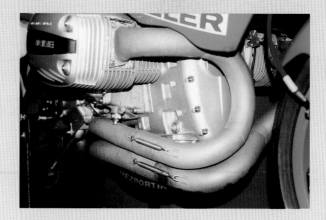

What do most race engine tuners do these days? They use every available electronic device available, fit fuel injection, juggle the 'chips' and more... but not Rudy Ottenhoff, Amsterdam-based Dutch BMW dealer and constructor of some of the most rapid BMW twins ever built. Instead he removed all the electronics and fuel injection when results didn't shake up during the 1995 season. So what started as an almost stock R1100RS roadster has, over the last four years become something of a rocketship. Instead of the standard bike's Bosch fuel injection and engine management system came a pair of 44mm Bing Gold Cup carburettors - and conventional ignition. The result was immediate and surprising, generating 123bhp from the original 1,085cc (99 x 70.5mm) and later upped to 1,192cc (102 x 71.5mm) to give a massive 147bhp @ 9,000rpm; which in road speeds means in excess of 175mph!

Rudy Ottenhoff headed up the RO team, with rider Scott Richardson and mechanic Roy Jensen, to contest the 1999 Sound of Thunder World Series.

Specification 1999 RO2 R1200RS

Engine:	Air-cooled, four-valves-per-cylinder, hi-camshaft horizontally opposed twin.
Capacity:	1,192cc.
Bore & stroke:	102 x 71.5mm
Comp ratio:	12:1
Carburation:	Two Bing 44mm Gold Cup carburettors with integral float chambers.
Connecting rods:	Carillo
Camshaft:	RO2
Pistons:	Mahle-Wahl
Exhaust:	Nico Bakker
Ignition:	KOVA
Lubrication:	Wet sump; oil Castrol
Gearbox:	Six-speed
Clutch:	Dry, Luftmeister Turbo
Primary drive:	Gears
Final drive:	Shaft
Frame:	Steel, weight 3.8kg.
Suspension:	Front: Inverted, White Power Rear: Monoshock, Öhlins
Tyres:	Front and rear 17inch, Metzeler
Brakes:	Hydraulically operated triple discs, Carbone Lorraine manufactured.
Brakelines:	Goodridge, braided steel.
Fuel capacity:	22 litres
Weight:	162kg (including 10 litres of fuel)
Wheel base:	141.5cm
Max power:	147bhp @ 9,000rpm
Max speed:	175mph+

Four-Valve Single - The F650

Launched in November 1993 the F650 Funduro, and its derivatives, has been one of BMW's major success stories of the last decade; at least as far as its two-wheel operation is concerned. It has also been the company's first major European joint venture in the motorcycle market, involving the German company, the Italian Aprilia concern and the Austrian engine constructor, Bombardier Rotax. Up to the end of 1997, over 45,000 examples had been sold worldwide.

The project originally stemmed from BMW's wish to introduce an entry-level model on to the market, in the shortest possible time span and at minimum cost.

Digi Power (German) igmition system.

Following initial discussions with potential partners during the late 1980s, the idea slowly materialised into a fully fledged project and by the 5th of June 1983, a contract was ready for signature in Munich, and announced to the public by a press release shortly thereafter.

The press release outlined that BMW would be responsible for the new machine's styling, and for its technical concept, and that development would be undertaken by Aprilia at its ultra-modern plant at Noale, in north eastern Italy, not far from Venice. Power was to be provided by a four-valve Rotax engine displacing 652cc (100 x 83mm). Developed jointly by BMW and Rotax, the new liquid-cooled engine developed 48bhp at 6,500rpm in standard form.

Oil tank, RS Honda forks, Tigcraft frame, 17 guage seamless chrome moly tubing.

Other features of the F650s engine unit included chain driven dohc, a balancer shaft, twin 33mm Japanese Mikuni carbs, twin spark ignition and a five-speed gearbox. There was dry sump lubrication, with the engine lubricant being carried in the upper section of the tubular steel frame. The F650 also broke new ground by being the first BMW motor cycle to feature chain, instead of shaft, final drive.

The success of the F650 on the street has been mirrored by an equal amount of glory on the race circuits of Europe and as early as the winter of 1993 competitors were eyeing up the new arrival for a track debut the following year. BMW's reputation was something of a quality guarantee. It wasn't just in the homeland that this interest arose, with the popular European Supermono racing championship now in full swing, it meant that there were also national championships in many countries scheduled for 1994 season, including Germany, Great Britain, France and Italy. In Italy Superbike specialists Bimota decided to enter production with suitable machines in both street and circuit guise, called appropriately Supermono.

Strangely, Bimota of all people were destined to be one of the least successful of all those who employed the BMW four-valve single cylinder power unit. This was not helped by a disastrous attempt to produce a six-speed gear cluster (which didn't work!) and a fuel injection system which gave less performance than the carb version. Finally, Bimota gave up and sold all its remaining Supermono bits to German specialist Gottfried Michels (trading under the Pami name) who is based in the town of Triers, a few kilometres from the Luxembourg border.

BMW F650 four-valve single, dohc, new standard engine.

720cc (105.5mm). This obviously means a special piston (often an Omega). Incidentally, there is also a longer stroke conversion for sidecar motorcross (popular in mainland Europe), which using the 102mm bore size gives exactly 700cc. In Germany there is even an eccentric crankpin conversion to provide a shorter or longer stroke than standard. To withstand the bigger bore sizes and the increased rigours of racing, the stock con-rod is changed for a Carillo assembly. Other racing requirements include different cams, crankpins with an extra oil hole and a tighter fit. The cylinder head is modified with larger valves: 39mm inlet, 34mm exhaust (36 and 32mm respectively, standard).

Except for Bimota's attempt, there has not so far been a six-speed conversion, but the British-based Novo-Dyson concern produced new gears to raise 1st and lower 4/5th, which proved quite successful in 1994. This was followed in 1995 by a close-ratio box manufactured by engine builders, Rotax. There is also a different oil pump available giving a higher output return; the feed remaining unchanged.

As standard, the cam chain tensioner is originally oil pressure fed, but a change to mechanical operation gives an increase in oil pressure from 30 to 90psi. Special racing exhausts are another tuning aid. Gary Cotterell specialises in the manufacture of these, his systems being hydraulically formed. Usual carb choice is a pair of the ultra-expensive 37mm flat slide Keihan CR instruments.

Instead the racing development of the four-valve BMW engine has been left largely to men like Michels and Englishman Gary Cotterell (GRC) of Downham Market, Norfolk.

The standard 652cc displacement with its 100mm bore has been increased to either 676cc (102mm) using the stock barrel, or using a special cast cylinder, up to

F650 tuning kit; 105mm barrel, close-ratio gearbox, special cams, Carillo rod, modified crank pin, piston, valve-gear gasket (alloy-one-piece).

Tigcraft BMW, F650.

Finally, the stock ignition is dumped in favour of a more suitable racing assembly. Gary Cotterell recommends Digi Power. This is digital and reprogrammable with no less than eight different curves available in the power box. Another benefit is that it can be plugged into a computer and read by the rider's race technicians.

The choice of chassis is also vitally important. For example, during the 1994 season the Harris-framed machine ridden by Carl James (prepared by his ex-racing father, Mick) suffered a spate of engine problems centring around failed big-ends and camshafts. This was ultimately discovered to have been no fault of the engine; instead the cause was to be found in the layout of the oil reservoir in the frame. Under heavy braking the oil surged up the frame tubing and became trapped thus starving the engine. Harris soon worked to remedy this glitch.

Besides Harris and Bimota, the other notable frame builder was Tigcraft. The latter concern, run by Dave Pearce based in Farnborough, Hampshire is also responsible for supplying frames to the controversial German re-born Norton single, masterminded by Joachim Seifert. Gary Cotterell is the man responsible for the racing version of this interesting addition to the ranks of the European Supermono championship series.

Another well known BMW racing entry is that of Dave Morris with his Team Chrysalis machine. He won the Single Cylinder TT in three consecutive years. But perhaps his most famous victory was in June 1998 when the Englishman spoilt Honda's 50th Anniversary celebrations by winning, and thus preventing the Japanese giants making a clean sweep of the series that year.

Father and son team. Former racer Mick James (left) and his son Carl with their Harris-framed BMW F650-based racer, Monza, Summer 1996. Carl had just finished 6th in the European Supermono race, a support series to WSB.

R1100S Racer Project

Taking a stock R1100S (launched by BMW in 1998) Bernie Wright and Martin Jones set about creating their own Sound of Thunder racer.

Wright and Jones became friends whilst working for Tooting (South West London) BMW dealer RGS Motorcycles, where the former is workshop foreman.

The plan was to produce a competitive machine using as many standard components as possible, and with this in mind the pair have been successful. Basically, at the time of writing the engine remains in standard tune, complete with the original R1100S Bosch electronic fuel injection system. But there have been subtle changes to the rest of the machine.

For starters, a full race exhaust has been supplied by Mark Hill Performance of Chessington, Surrey, which like the original (and for that matter Carl Fogarty's World Super Bike winning Ducati) sees both pipes exiting through mufflers under the seat. The seat too has a Ducati connection, being in fact a fibreglass replica 916 moulding.

To update the brakes braided hoses have been fitted all round, and

there are also fully adjustable AP racing master cylinders. BMW have supplied their optional Sports Suspension, which has the main advantage of being slightly longer, thus lifting the engine further away from the ground - which almost solves the problem of grounding rocker covers. BMW have also provided the team, which is sponsored by RGS, IMCA (leathers) and Laser (helmets), with spare wheels and discs.

The rider is 35 year Bernie Wright who has worked on BMWs virtually non-stop since leaving school. Besides RGS, he has also seen spells with Gus Kuhn (South London) and Eddy's (Leeds).

Prior to the fuel injected R1100S, Bernie rode an ageing R75/5 in Classic racing events during 1997 and 1998. Riding the R1100S racer is like the roadster, all about rhythm. It's a thinking man's machine requiring smoothness, which will then repay the rider by proving just how unruffled and deceptively quick a modern four-valves-per-cylinder BMW can be. An eighth first time out at Snetterton proves the potential against a host of Ducati and Suzuki v-twins, which on paper should be much more competitive.

BMW Sidecars

3

1954-55 BMW sidecar-factory model.

Although beaten by Fraust in the 1955 title race, Noll was busy that year amassing a large number of new three-wheeler speed records for BMW. He is shown here in December 1954 preparing to carry out some testing on the Munich-Ingoldstat autobahn. Also in the picture, left to right: Georg Meier, Wiggerl Kraus, Ernst Henne and BMW engineer.

Phenomenal is the only word for the overwhelming success of the double-overhead-camshaft, BMW flat-twin engine in the Sidecar World Championships of the two decades from the mid 1950s to the mid 1970s. In the 21 years from 1954 until 1974 inclusive, BMW-engined outfits took the title on 19 occasions!

As recorded in the previous chapter, except for the immediate pre-war period, when the Munich factory's supercharged machinery ruled supreme,. the German flat-twins had not been particularly successful. However, having once realised this, BMW switched much of its effort into the sidecar class where its subsequent dominance emphasised the engine's greater suitability for the three-wheel sector of the sport.

In sidecar racing, the engine's width was no disadvantage, nor for that matter, was its shaft drive, while its silky smoothness and great engine torque were a positive boon. The engine could be slung ultra-low for faster cornering, while the cylinders were cooled effectively. Another great advantage was the high standard of engineering quality and its resultant reliability. The 180-degree crankshaft was extraordinarily robust, as were its other major components.

The dashing Swiss star Florian Camathias (with passenger Hilmar Cecco) finished second in the 1958 Isle of Man Sidecar TT. The machine's fairing was originally fitted to one of the factory FB Mondial lightweights.

Until 1954, the world of sidecar racing had been dominated by the British driver Eric Oliver, who raced a series of outfits powered by the venerable single-cylinder Norton engine. During this period, the highest BMW-powered sidecars had finished in classic races since the instigation of the new World Championship in 1949, were the third positions gained by Kraus and Huser in the 1953 Belgian GP, and Noll and Cron in the Swiss GP the same year.

Otto Kolle, Rennsport sidecar, Cadwell Park International, September 1962.

Oliver had started his championship defence in his usual winning style, taking the first three rounds of the 1954 series in the Isle of Man, Ulster and Belgium. The next round was scheduled to be staged on BMW's home ground at the Solitude circuit, near Stuttgart. However, a week prior to this, both Oliver and his passenger, Leslie Nutt, were injured when their outfit skidded off a wet track at a non-championship meeting near Frankfurt in mid July. In the accident, Oliver broke his arm, while Nutt injured a shoulder. Without the four-times World Champion, the German Grand Prix was a walk-over for the pair of factory BMW outfits driven by Noll and Cron and Schneider and Strauss.

Although Oliver bravely rode in the next round in Switzerland, Wilhelm Noll and Fritz Cron put an end to the English supremacy, taking the title with three straight victories (Germany, Switzerland and Italy), as many wins as the Oliver/Nutt combination but their superior finishing positions in the other three races made all the difference. BMW finished the year with not only Noll and Cron as champions, but Schneider and Strauss fourth, with Hillebrand and Grünwald fifth in the title chase.

In 1955, the title went to Willi Faust and Karl Remmert, who won three of the six rounds in Spain, Germany and Holland. However, the pair crashed their works BMW outfit during a practice session at Hockenheim later in the season, and the brilliant partnership was broken by the death of Remmert. Faust recovered after a long period in hospital, but never raced again.

Max Duebel's world championship winning BMW sidecar outfit, circa 1962-65.

Former Luftwaffe fighter pilot Fritz Hillebrand (passengered by Manfred Grünwald) were the World Champions of 1957, with victories in Germany, the Isle of Man and Holland. Later that year, Hillebrand was fatally injured in a racing accident in Spain.

Wilhelm Noll with BMW press officer Carl Hoepner on 4th October 1955 after annexing no fewer than 18 sidecar records on the Munich-Ingoldstat autobahn. But Noll's outstanding performance was to recapture for Germany the world's flying kilometre sidecar record at 174mph - beating the previous holder Bob Burns (Vincent) by 12mph.

On 4 October 1955, Wilhelm Noll broke a total of 18 sidecar world records when he rode a specially prepared, fuel-injected flat-twin fitted with a streamlined shell that featured an enclosed cabin and a rear stabilizing fin. The sidecar wheel was also streamlined. The records broken included: flying kilometre at 174mph; mile at 174mph; five kilometres, 168.5mph; and five miles at 165.5mph; standing-start kilometre, 86.5mph; and mile at 103mph.

Noll's efforts had recaptured the world's fastest three-wheel record for Germany, his speed of 174mph being some 12mph quicker than the previous record held by Bob Burns with a 998cc Vincent v-twin. He then went on to cap an outstanding personal effort by winning a second world title to add to the one he had won in 1954. In 1956, he and passenger Fritz Cron became World Sidecar Champions once more. They won in Belgium, Germany and Ulster, and finished second in Holland. After this, Noll announced his retirement. In 1957, he tried his hand at car racing, but without success.

Next in the line of world sidecar champions came the former Luftwaffe pilot, Fritz Hillebrand, and his passenger, Manfred Grünwald. After dominating the 1957 title series with wins in the first three rounds (Germany, Isle of Man and Holland) and a third position in Belgium, the team suffered a terminal blow when they were involved in a serious accident after becoming champions.

At an international meeting in Bilbao, on 24 August 1957, their outfit crashed, killing Fritz Hillebrand. Manfred Grünwald sustained only minor hand injuries, but decided to retire.

After a drastic fall-off in sales of its production models, BMW only supported one sidecar crew for the 1958 season. This was the pairing of Walter Schneider and Hans Strauss, who had finished as runners-up in the previous year to Hillebrand and Grünwald.

Camathias and Hilmar on their victory lap after winning the British Sidecar race at Thruxton on Monday, 4th August 1958.

Sidecar Racing

Sidecar racing made its first hesitant steps during the early 1920s when racing pioneers, such as Bert Le Vack, added a third wheel to their racing machines to add additional spice to racing at the world's first purpose built circuit, at Brooklands in Surrey. The first sidecar event at the Isle of Man TT came in 1923 when 14 outfits lined up to do battle. Eight different marques took part, Douglas being the most prolific with three machines, while Norton, Scott and Sunbeam fielded two each.

Three laps around the 37.75 mile (60.73km) mountain circuit was the test and Freddie Dixon (Douglas) emerged the victor. The same man was also destined to go down in the record books four years later as the only rider to win both a solo and sidecar TT.

Sidecar entries declined the following year to only ten, but the future looked bright enough in 1925 with an entry list of 18, with no less than 11 different makes on the sheet. The revival did not last, however, and sidecars were deleted from the TT programme in 1926, when not enough entries were received to stage a race. They did not return for another 30 years, when in 1954 Eric Oliver won on a Norton outfit. By then, sidecars had benefited from the considerable prestige of being included from the start in the world championships, which had been inaugurated in 1949.

Future double champion Fritz Scheidegger, 1960 Isle of Man Sidecar TT. He finished 11th, at an average speed of 72.28mph. The race was won by Helmut Fath on another BMW.

However, if the works pair thought that they were in for a walk-over, they could not have been more mistaken. The privateers Florian Camathias and Hilmar Cecco, on a home-tuned Rennsport outfit, gave them a fight in every one of the four rounds of the title series. In fact, the Swiss pair (who both raced solos as well) won the Dutch TT at Assen.

Another serious contender for honours that year was Helmut Fath, who displayed his future potential for the first time to a wider audience.

Schneider and Strauss retained their title in 1959 when, once more, their biggest challenge came from Camathias and Cecco, whom they beat by a mere four points. In the five-round series, the Germans won three races, the Swiss the remaining two.

Schneider and Strauss decided to call it a day and retire after winning their second title. Like Noll, Schneider tried his hand at motor racing, but also without success.

Many expected Camathias and Cecco to become the next champions. However, things did not pan out that way, for Cecco split with Camathias and joined his rival, Edgar Strub.

- how it evolved

British machines and drivers (not riders!) dominated the early years of the world championships, with Eric Oliver and Norton proving a virtually invincible combination.

But then BMW arrived on the scene and although Oliver caused a sensation when he debuted a comprehensively streamlined Norton-Watsonian 'Kneeler' during practice for the Belgian GP in 1953, even this major innovation in the evolution of the racing sidecar could not stave off the challenge from the German manufacturers the following year.

Phenomenal is the only word to portray BMWs success from the mid-1950s to the mid-1970s. In 21 years from 1954 until 1974, the BMW outfits took the title on no fewer than 19 occasions. Breaking their hold in 1968 came Helmut Fath, who created history by not only winning, but doing so on a four-cylinder engined sidecar of his own design (see chapter 5).

Next came König (see chapter 7), whose watercooled four-cylinder outboard engine was transformed into a championship-winning sidecar racer, which took the title in 1975 and 1976.

After this the likes of Yamaha and Krauser came onto the scene, and also the Swiss engineer/rider Rolf Biland who created the 'worm' concept outfit which relied heavily on Formula 1 car technology.

With a new passenger, Camathias had a poor season, his best placing being a second at Solitude in the final round. He finished the season down in fourth place in the final ratings. So who finished in front of him? The answer is Fath, Fritz Scheidegger and the Englishman Pip Harris.

In 1957, the pairing of Fritz Hillebrand, a Luftwaffe fighter pilot, and his passenger Manfred Grünwald became champions. They are seen here on their way to victory in the Isle of Man TT. Their average speed was a record 71.89mph.

World Champions in 1959, Walter Schneider and Hans Strauss are seen here winning the Belgian Grand Prix at Spa Francorchamps.

Winners of four of the five Grands Prix contested in 1960, Helmut Fath and Alfred Wohlgemuth dominated the three-wheel category that year. However, as recounted in Chapter 5, a serious accident at the Nürburgring in 1961 halted a very promising career. Wohlgemuth was killed and Fath spent many months in hospital. He eventually returned with his own four-cylinder engine in 1966 after BMW had refused to provide backing for a comeback.

Not only had Fath been sidelined, but Camathias too. Intent on a serious crack at the world crown in 1961, the diminutive Swiss star had joined with his old 'ballast', Hilmar Cecco, and much was expected of them. However, at a meeting at Modena, Italy, in mid May, Cecco sustained fatal injuries when the pair crashed their BMW. Camathias was also badly injured - to the extent that he did not race for the remainder of that season.

This tragic turn of events threw the championship wide open. The factory-supported pairing of Max Deubel and Emil Hörner became champions, while the privateers Scheidegger and Burckart were runners-up.

If luck had favoured them in 1961, it was skill and determination alone that brought Deubel and Hörner their second title in 1962. They gave their challengers, Camathias and Scheidegger, little chance of glory. These three teams dominated the series, except in the Isle of Man where all three retired, leaving victory to a grateful Chris Vincent and Eric Bliss with a specially prepared, twin-cylinder, pushrod, BSA roadster-engined outfit.

For the next two years (1963 and 1964), Deubel and Hörner retained their championship laurels, their only real challenge being the outfits of Scheidegger and Camathias. However, this run of success came to an end during 1965 and 1966 when the Deubel/Hörner partnership was unseated by the newly-formed pairing of Scheidegger and Robinson. They then retired from the sport at the end of 1966, Deubel to run his hotel in Muhlenau, and Hörner returning to his former occupation of car mechanic.

The 1963 champion Max Deubel at the non-championship international meeting at Oulton Park in August 1963.

Fritz Schiedegger and passenger John Robinson, 1964 Dutch TT.

Scheidegger, together with his fellow Swiss Camathias, had brought to an end the long supremacy of German sidecar drivers. Once again, however, fate was to strike at the very top of the sidecar world, as first Camathias (Brands Hatch, 10th October 1965) and then Scheidegger (Mallory Park, 26th March 1967) were involved in fatal accidents. Both were caused through mechanical failure, rather than rider error. The deaths of the two Swiss stars, and Deubel's retirement, benefitted the up-and-coming partnership of Klaus Enders and Ralf Engelhardt. They won five of the eight events to lift the 1967 championship crown.

In 1968, Helmut Fath stunned the racing world by becoming the first man to win a world championship with a machine he had built himself. However, with Fath striking mechanical problems, Enders and Engelhardt, with BMW backing, won their second title in 1969.

With a new passenger, Wolfgang Kalauch, Klaus Enders took his third championship in 1970. At the end of the year, aged 33, he decided to retire moving to four wheels. This let in Horst Owesle and Peter Rutherford who (as recounted in Chapter 10) took the title for the Münch team in 1971.

Englishman Pip Harris and R Campbell, BMW, 1963 Oulton Park

Pip Harris (3) leads Colin Seeley and Bill Boddice on his way to victory in the 1963 Easter Trophy meeting at Oulton Park. With a world-class field there was a record breaking 60,000 spectators.

For 1972, three-times champion Klaus Enders arrived back on the scene. His four-wheel career - still with BMW - had not achieved the level of success to which he was accustomed. Consequently, he decided to don his leathers once more and re-enter the sidecar-racing arena.

Passengered by his old chum, Ralf Engelhardt, Enders proved that he had made the right decision by winning his fourth sidecar crown. This put him on level pegging with those other two great three-wheel legends, Eric Oliver and Max Deubel.

Like fellow Englishman Chris Vincent, Colin Seeley switched from British power (in this case Matchless) to BMW in the mid-1960s.

This success spurred Enders to even greater effort. In 1973, he not only became the first man on three wheels to win five world titles, but he won all of the seven rounds that he contested!

It was perhaps fitting that Enders should be the man to win BMW's last sidecar championship in 1974, and so create a record which still stands. However, this final year was not the relatively easy series of victories to which he had become accustomed. Instead, there were problems with his new Busch-tuned engine, as well as the ever-increasing competition from the two-strokes, headed by König.

Enders decided to retire (for real this time) rather than race a two-stroke, having scored a record total of 27 GP victories - all on BMWs. Strangely, after that final championship year, no BMW-powered sidecar ever won another Grand Prix!

During the 21 seasons in which the BMW had been a serious contender for sidecar championship honours, the power output of the dohc, flat-twin engine had not altered, as lap times may have suggested. The engine remained almost the same as it had been in the mid 1950s. It was the chassis to which the engineers had turned their attention in an effort to raise the performance.

Camathias' BMW Kneeler. He once broke down on the M1 motorway on his way to race in the Isle of Man. Taking his machine out of the stranded van, he put all his tools and luggage onto the sidecar and continued his journey up to Liverpool to catch the ferry on this very outfit!

BMW Sidecar World Champions

1954	Wilhelm Noll/ Fritz Cron
1955	Willi Fraust/ Karl Remmart
1956	Wilhelm Noll/ Fritz Cron
1957	Fritz Hillebrand/ Manfred Grünwald
1958	Walter Schneider/ Hans Strauss
1959	Walter Schneider/ Hans Strauss
1960	Helmut Fath/ Alfred Wohlgemuth
1961	Max Deubel/ Emil Hörner
1962	Max Deubel/ Emil Hörner
1963	Max Deubel/ Emil Hörner
1964	Max Deubel/ Emil Hörner
1965	Fritz Scheidegger/ John Robinson
1966	Fritz Scheidegger/ John Robinson
1967	Kraus Enders/ Ralf Engelhardt
1969	Kraus Enders/ Ralf Engelhardt
1970	Kraus Enders/ Ralf Engelhardt
1972	Kraus Enders/ Ralf Engelhardt
1973	Kraus Enders/ Ralf Engelhardt
1974	Kraus Enders/ Ralf Engelhardt

From 1958, a major change had been introduced to the works BMW outfits (pioneered by Eric Oliver's Norton back in 1954). This saw the riding position transferred from the conventional sitting to a kneeling position. The resultant lowering of gravity provided much improved cornering abilities. The fuel tank was also moved. At first, it was split into two and lowered; later, it was joined again and housed in the sidecar.

Another development was the replacement of the telescopic front forks by a type of suspension that was more akin to that of a car than a motorcycle. In many ways, the same could be said about the wheels, brakes and tyres.

Streamlining was another aspect that played a vital role in the development of the modern racing sidecar outfit. The 'chairs' had not been affected by the revised FIM regulation which had banned full streamlining from solos after the end of the 1957 season.

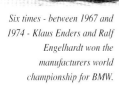

Six times - between 1967 and 1974 - Klaus Enders and Ralf Engelhardt won the manufacturers world championship for BMW.

Towards the end of its reign as World Sidecar Champion, the BMW factory itself ceased direct support. Its place was taken by several entrants, notably men such as Busch and Krauser - the latter would later win world-wide fame through his motorcycle luggage empire.

Thus, the curtain was drawn on a truly illustrious era, which saw BMW engines employed by all the leading sidecar exploiters of the day. They achieved a record number of championship titles in this branch of motorcycle sport which has yet to be equalled.

Klaus Enders and Ralf Englehart seen here winning the 1973 Czech GP at the Brno circuit.

DKW

4

1956 works DKW three-cylinder.

Together with BMW and NSU, DKW ranks as one of the major German companies that pioneered the motorcycle up to World War 2. Thereafter, it thrust its development to new horizons in the years now known as the 'classic' period.

The history of the DKW marque began with the birth of its founder, Jorgen Skafte Rasmussen, on 30th July 1878 in Nakskow, Denmark. The young Rasmussen moved to Dusseldorf, Germany, in 1904 and then in 1907, to Zschopau, 20 kilometres south of Chemnitz in Saxony (today called Karl Marx Stadt). Here, he was involved in several engineering ventures with a partner called Ernst, manufacturing and selling machines and tools ranging from boiler fittings to fire lighters and domestic appliances.

In 1916, inspired by the acute wartime fuel shortages, Rasmussen began to experiment with a steam car, the Dampf Kraft Wagen. Even though this was not proceeded with, it provided the first use of the now-famous DKW initials.

The next event of significance came in 1919 when Rasmussen produced an 18cc toy two-stroke engine (designed by Hugo Ruppe). This was known as Das Knaben Wünsch (the schoolboy's dream), and it led to engine production, the company's first full year in this sector of engineering being taken up largely with development and research. The first fruits of this effort came the following year, 1921, with the debut of the Ruppe-designed 122cc auxiliary engine. This sold extremely well (some 25,000 units had been sold by mid 1922).

Next came motorized bicycles, 'armchair' motorcycles (forerunners of the modern motor scooter), and finally full-blown conventional motorcycles. By 1926, DKW had manufactured its 100,000th engine assembly, while the motorcycle range included machines with capacities of 200, 250, 350 and 500cc.

1930's DKW 200cc single cylinder two-stroke.

The founding father of DKW, Jorgen Skafte Rasmussen. Born in July 1898, as a young boy Rasmussen moved from Denmark to Dusseldorf, Germany in 1904, and then in 1907 to Zschopau, 20 kilometres south of Chemitz in Saxony. He held a number of engineering posts and, after the First World War, formed his own company in 1919 - J S Rasmussen, the forerunner of DKW.

1954 DKW 350cc triple.

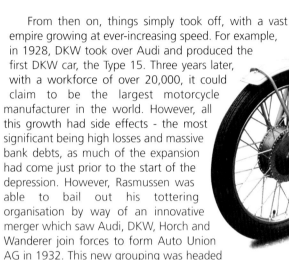

DKW were the first bike builders to employ a system of rubber bands as a springing medium for its inter-war racers; this is the 1935 design. This replaced the central spring usually employed on this type of girder fork.

From then on, things simply took off, with a vast empire growing at ever-increasing speed. For example, in 1928, DKW took over Audi and produced the first DKW car, the Type 15. Three years later, with a workforce of over 20,000, it could claim to be the largest motorcycle manufacturer in the world. However, all this growth had side effects - the most significant being high losses and massive bank debts, as much of the expansion had come just prior to the start of the depression. However, Rasmussen was able to bail out his tottering organisation by way of an innovative merger which saw Audi, DKW, Horch and Wanderer join forces to form Auto Union AG in 1932. This new grouping was headed by Dipl. Ing. Carl Hahn and underwritten by the State Bank of Saxony.

The new combine took as its trademark four interlinked silver circles, which continue today on the up-market Audi car range. The merger coincided with the gradual easing of the financial gloom which had swept the industrialised world during the early 1930s, with the result that it was a huge commercial success. Both its two- and four-wheel products sold well throughout the remainder of the decade up to the outbreak of World War 2 in 1939.

Of the four companies, only DKW made motorcycles. Besides its bikes, however, the Zschopau company was also very much a trend-setter on four wheels, typified by the hugely successful F series cars. Over 250,000 of these had been made by the time production was finally halted in November 1942.

No four-wheel racing enthusiast worth his salt does not know of the legendary achievements of the Auto Union racing team in the mid-late 1930s. On two wheels, DKW was almost as well known, both in Germany and abroad, during this same period.

Start of the 1937 250cc Dutch TT in late June saw DKWs finish first, third and fifth. Riders were Winkler (1), Kluge (3) and Hauser (12).

The 250 UL DKW racing engine of the mid-1930s.

As far back as 1925, DKW had entered the racing fray with 175 and 250cc machinery using, of course, two-strokes, but with intercooling and the Bichrome system of supercharging. However, it was not until 1931, when the Hermann Weber-designed split-single layout appeared, that the marque enjoyed any real success.

August Prussing, who worked in the DKW racing department alongside Weber, was also involved with the successful development. During the next few years, just about every one of Germany's top riders raced DKWs at one time or another. Riders such as Fleischmann, Herz, Steinbach, Klein, Müller, Ley, Rosemeyer, Wünsche, Kluge and Winkler all piloted the screaming 'Deeks'.

The first of the new generation of split-singles was a quarter-litre machine in which the supercharging piston operated in front of the crankcase. Models based on this machine went on to achieve a truly amazing haul of victories and lap records throughout, what were for DKW, the golden 1930s. Before long, DKW's track reputation had spread outside the German frontiers, and in their day, these machines were often winning in faster times than the 350s. DKW even ventured to the Isle of Man for the famous TT series - the very heart of the mighty British racing empire.

At the Berlin show in 1935, DKW debuted an 'over-the-counter' racer, the SS250. This was based on the all-conquering works machinery and used the same basic split-single, water-cooled power unit.

In 1938, Ewald Kluge (who had initially led the 1937 Lightweight TT) became the first German to win an Isle of Man race when he took his 250 DKW to victory.

The following year, 1939, DKW not only had the largest racing department in the world, with around 150 engineers, but also some extremely competitive machinery. This included the 250 US, a supercharged, double-piston twin that pumped out an impressive 40 bhp at 7,000rpm, and a similar 350 producing 48 bhp. These bikes also had the dubious honour of producing the world's most ear-splitting sound, their exhaust notes drowning every other machine on the circuit!

Twin piston layout of the supercharged DKW racing engine.

Six versions of DKW's pre-war blown split-single theme. One has a reed valve, another a cylindrical rotary valve. The two production versions have short-stroke charging pistons in the crankcase. An eccentric-vane compressor was employed with both parallel and opposed cylinders.

For the 1938 season DKW's racing designer, Arnold Zoller, introduced the ULd (replacing the ULe). Although the chassis remained much as before, the engine, was considerably updated.

A feature of the October 1937 record attempts was this specially constructed streamlined helmet worn here by Ewald Kluge. On the left is team mate Walfried Winkler. Both men also raced the Grand Prix bikes.

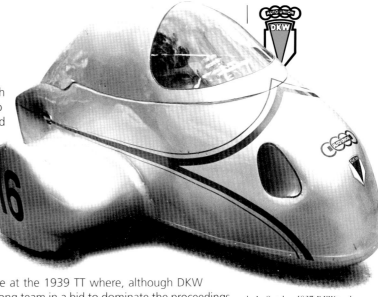

One example of each engine capacity was also specially prepared for speed record attempts, and running on alcohol fuel, they produced 49 and 60 bhp respectively. These machines were the last for which the brilliant Hermann Weber was responsible (he was to die in Russia after the war).

In October 1937 DKW took part in its first ever record attempt. Staged on the Frankfurt-Darmstadt autobahn both solo and sidecar (shown) were used.

A disappointment came at the 1939 TT where, although DKW fielded an extremely strong team in a bid to dominate the proceedings in both the 250 and 350cc races, the best it could achieve was a second (Kluge) behind the lone Benelli single of Mellors in the Lightweight.

However, on the Continent that year, the 'Deeks' were dominant, gaining victories in Holland, Sweden and Germany.

Then, in early Sepember, at the outbreak of war, for six long years competitive motorcycle sport was shelved while an altogether more deadly game was played out.

If wartime had brought its problems, then peace, when it finally came in May 1945, was traumatic to say the least, for the DKW marque. Not only had all four of Auto Union's main factories been severely damaged by Allied bombing, but they were also in the Russian sector when Germany was partitioned. (The former DKW plant went on to make motorcycles for the Eastern Bloc countries, first under the name IFA and then MZ - see Chapter 11).

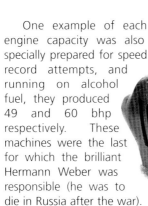

A series of drawings showing the various components of the twin-piston split single DKW (Ladepumpe) racing engine, 1937-1939.

Auto Union elected to move West. For the company's rebirth in the new West Germany, DKW selected Ingolstadt on the River Danube, in Upper Bavaria. Here, the first post-war business conducted was the servicing of ex-military vehicles, rather than the manufacture of any new machinery. However, 1947 saw the formation of Auto Union GmbH which, initially, was engaged in the manufacture of spare parts for pre-war DKW cars and motorcycles. Currency reforms in the summer of the following year allowed some of the pre-war Auto Union management to raise enough capital to relaunch vehicle manufacture. In effect, this move refinanced the Auto Union company.

1939 350 US specification included 48.5bhp at 7,000rpm, plunger rear suspension and rearward facing exhaust.

1939 RT125 designed by Hermann Weber, this lightweight motorcycle was powered by a 122cc (52 x 58mm) piston port two-stroke engine. Besides being one of the most copied designs of all time, it went on to be raced post-war by both IFA (MZ) and DKW themselves.

The first project by the new organization was the introduction of an improved version of the piston-ported RT125 roadster. However, even before this, DKWs had appeared on the race circuit once again.

As early as 1947, some of the pre-war works bikes had been given an airing. Remarkably, some had survived the war in barns, cellars, and in at least one case, actually buried!

Ewald Kluge (left) and Siegfried Wünsche rebuilding a 250 ULd. This photograph, taken in 1950, shows engine and frame layout to maximum advantage; note massive radiator and large head/cylinder casting.

The 1951 DKW works team with one of the new air-cooled 250 parallel twins. Left to right: Wünsche, Kluge and Müller.

Then, in May 1948 at Hockenheim, a racing version of the RT125 appeared. This made quite a respectable showing against the mainly NSU opposition. Later, ridden by Kluge, Wünsche and Müller, it was raced in modified form with rear-facing twin exhaust, high-level megaphones, magneto ignition (the original had battery/coil), nearside-mounted carb, rev-counter, plunger rear suspension, oil-damped telescopic front forks and a larger-diameter, full-width front stopper.

By 1949, both the racing 125 and the pre-war supercharged, double-piston twins were becoming the quickest machinery in German Lightweight racing events. Just how competitive they were was illustrated by the leading racer of the day, the Scot Fergus Anderson. He was also a part-time journalist who, writing in his 'Continental Chatter' column in the 17th November 1949 issue of *Motor Cycling* said: 'Most memorable incident at Cologne: I was doing a little training on my 500cc Gambalunga (Moto Guzzi) just in case the powers-that-be said "yes", and had it wound up to maximum revolutions in the biggest gear - when a machine came creeping inexorably past me in the middle of a long straight. It was Walfried Winkler on the four-piston 250cc DKW!'

Obviously, one has to take into account that unlike 'foreign' manufacturers, DKW, together with other German marques such as NSU and BMW, was able to use blowers, whereas in other countries supercharging had been banned by the FIM in 1946. Nonetheless, DKW was still top dog in the Fatherland, 'Siggi' Wünsche taking the 350cc German Championship title.

This state of affairs was not to continue, as not only were DKW's rivals developing new machinery, but in the spring of 1950 came news that Germany was to be re-admitted to the FIM in time for the 1951 season.

DKW, together with the other major producers, responded by announcing that it would be entering the international fray with new normally-aspirated 'strokers' in both the 125 and 250cc categories. Its team was to comprise Kluge, Müller and Wünsche - all competitors of considerable experience and ability.

Post-war, DKW relocated to the West and a new home at Ingoldstat in Upper Bavaria. Their first racer of the new era was this 125 ridden by Karl Doring at Hockenheim, 8th-9th May 1948.

Former DKW star Sigfried Wünsche pictured in the Isle of Man during the 1988 TT period with one of the pre-war factory 250 racers.

At the first meeting of the 1951 road-race season, the Eilenriede-Rennen at Hanover on 29th April, DKW debuted its latest machinery, as did its principal rivals, BMW and NSU. The Ingolstadt company's offering included an all-new 247.3cc parallel twin. The cylinders were inclined slightly forward from the vertical, each having its own Dell'Orto carb.

The sparking plugs were placed centrally for maximum efficiency, while the ignition was taken care of by a Bosch flywheel magneto. The clutch ran in an oil bath and was mounted on the nearside with chain primary drive. Suspension was taken care of by an oil-damped telescopic front fork and a swinging arm at the rear with twin, hydraulically-damped shocks. The frame was of the all-welded, tubular, full duplex variety.

Setting off the bike was a massive, hand-beaten, alloy fuel tank. The combined rear mudguard/ number plate and the front mudguard were also in the same material. Some machines were fitted with a small fairing, again in alloy.

The designs of the all-new 250 twin and the revamped 125 single were the responsibility of Dipl. Ing. Erich Wolf. He had made his reputation as a private tuner of the earlier DKW engines, together with the Austrian Puch split-single, before joining the Ingolstadt factory. Number two in the DKW design team was another young engineer, Dipl. Ing. Jacob.

Although Wolf increased the power output of the new twin from its initial 20 to 23 bhp, he could not succeed in making it competitive against the top four-stroke 250s of the day, such as the Italian Benelli and Moto Guzzi machines.

In their attempts to extract more power, Wolf and Jacob not only tried numerous induction systems with different discs, pistons, cylinders, heads and the like, but also carried out an extensive weight-pruning exercise. Eventually, the works 250 'Deek' became the lightest machine in its class. Although these changes resulted in a superior power-to-weight ratio, they also led to mechanical and structural unreliability, which proved counter-productive.

The 348.48cc (53 x 52.8mm) DKW three-cylinder as it was in 1952.

The 250 parallel-twin showing the frame, swinging arm, hand beaten aluminium tank and early expansion chamber-type exhaust. Swiss GP, May 1952.

Thus, it was not until the following year, 1952, that any real results were seen from the team's work. The 250 parallel-twin was significantly improved by the fitment of a Bosch magneto in place of the flywheel magneto, a single Dell'Orto carburettor and, most important of all, a change in the design of the exhaust system. The latter had a pair of expansion chambers in place of the original noisy, but largely ineffective, megaphones. This was one of the earliest, if not the first, motorcycle to be so equipped in Germany, possibly the world. Moreover, as Wolf discovered, this relatively simple move enabled the DKW design to gain a relatively large increase in power output.

The first appearance of the latest DKW twin was at Hockenheim in mid May. The team now comprised the veterans Kluge and Wünsche, plus two newcomers Karl Hofmann and Rudi Felgenheier. Müller had left to ride for Horex (and later NSU).

However, the most interesting news of all at Hockenheim was the appearance of a three-cylinder 'Deek'. This had come about purely by chance. In an attempt to solve ignition problems, Wolf had modified the 250 twins by fitting the magneto (and also the inlet disc) in front of the crankcase. It was this that had given him the idea of actually fitting a third cylinder in place of the magneto at the front of the crankcase, to create a 350. In this way, one of the most innovative racing designs of the 1950s was born.

The Erich Wolf-designed 250 twin featured square (54 x 54mm) bore and stroke dimensions, together with rotary-valve induction. This is the 1952 version.

Both the 125 single and 250 twin DKWs featured square 54 x 54mm bore and stroke measurements, but for the new three-cylinder model, in order to restrict the swept volume to 350cc, the bore of each cylinder was reduced to 53mm and the stroke was fixed at 52.8mm. This gave each cylinder a capacity of just over 116cc - totalling 348.48cc. The two outer cylinders were inclined slightly forward at 15 degrees from the vertical to assist the cooling of the rear of the air-cooled cylinders, resulting in an included cylinder angle of 75 degrees.

To produce the desired 120-degree firing interval between the cylinders, DKW employed offset crankpins, the central 17.5mm big-end leading the nearside one by 165 degrees and trailing its offside partner by 45 degrees. In addition, the Ingolstadt engineers reverted to piston-port induction, with a 28mm Dell'Orto SS1 carb for each cylinder (using their own specially designed float chambers).

A six-cylinder-type magneto, from a BMW 328 car, was fitted to the offside of the crankcase and driven at half engine speed by a spur gear off the crankshaft. As this 'new' engine was fitted into the rolling chassis of the 250 twin, on paper, it had an excellent chance of achieving outstanding power-to-weight ratio figures. However, the initial power output was a disappointing 31 bhp. The prototype made its classic debut at the 1952 Swiss Grand Prix, but Wünsche was forced out on lap 12 with engine trouble, after holding fifth spot.

In its final form the 350cc triple was fitted with a fully streamlined alloy dustbin fairing.

The next outing came at the home round, in front of a hugely partisan crowd of 400,000 spectators. Two of the new triples were entered, ridden by Kluge and Wünsche; both created drama at the Solitude circuit near Stuttgart.

On lap 12, Kluge caught up with the leading Nortons at the front of the field, only to fall. With his shoulder blade broken, he retrieved the DKW, remounted and came home in sixth place, but was rushed straight to hospital. Meanwhile, Wünsche had ridden most of the race without his nearside footrest, to finish a hard-earned 11th - a popular result with his many fans in the vast crowd.

In the 125 race, all the DKWs retired, but in the 250 event, Rudi Felgenheier (a last-minute substitute for the injured Kluge) scored the factory's first postwar GP victory.

Generally, however, classic outings that year were severely limited by the time needed to sort the bugs out of the new three-cylinder model, but progress was being made. The most important modification that year came in August with the introduction of a new lubrication system. Right from its first race, the triple had been prone to piston seizures as a result of using a straight petroil mixture. This was supplemented at first, and then replaced entirely by direct lubrication to cylinder walls and main bearings. The oil was carried in the top frame tube and fed by gravity through a multiplicity of small pipes and needle valves.

1953-54, DKW 350cc triple showing carb, cylinder and magneto. Later models had battery/coil ignition.

The Ingolstadt factory announced its team in early 1953, the riders being unchanged (Kluge, Wünsche, Felgenheier and Hofmann), but the 125 had been dropped. Wolf and Jacob had spent much of the winter working on the 250 twin. The problems of the single rotary valve and its single carburettor, which led to unequal inlet tract lengths, were tackled by simply turning the rotary valve through 90 degrees and relocating it between the cylinder barrels so that it ran fore and aft, parallel to the wheelbase. The single carburettor was at one end and the forward-facing magneto at the other. This change, together with more work to the exhaust, increased the power to 22bhp - enough to help Wünsche and a new works rider, August Hobl, to several leaderboard placings that year in the quarter-litre category. Even so, the Ingolstadt models were not quick enough to match the class-leading Moto Guzzi and NSU four-strokes.

The prototype three-cylinder DKW which caused a sensation when it was first wheeled out at Hockenheim in early May 1952. Unfortunately, its original performance left much to be desired, but no-one could deny it was an ingenious design.

At the Italian GP at Monza, in September, one of the 250 twins sported rearward-facing exhausts and twin carbs. However, although this was used in practice, it did not make the race.

Meanwhile, the three-cylinder model had received limited improvements to its power unit, aimed at increasing reliability. As before, great effort had been expended upon paring the dry weight of the machines to a bare minimum. This meant that the frame tubing was of the narrowest gauge thought practical, while the brakes were just adequate. So seriously was the weight-saving issue taken that there were four sizes of aluminium-alloy fuel tank (interchangeable between the two engine capacities). These held 12, 22, 28 and 32 litres.

The Isle of Man TT was the first of the 1953 classics. Prior to this, in May, team leader Ewald Kluge had suffered a broken leg when he had crashed at the Nürburgring during a German National Championship event. Many observers believed that this would stop the DKW team from honouring their entries, which had been made before the Kluge accident.

However, the DKW equipe duly arrived in Douglas (but not until half-way through practice week) with Siegfried Wünsche and the substitute for Kluge, Rudi Felgenheier, accompanied by race chief Wolf and a couple of mechanics. They had a major task in front of them if they were to qualify, as there remained only two practice periods for both the 250 and 350cc races. Dipl. Ing. Wolf conducted much of the testing himself. He was actually seen out on the mountain section of the circuit one morning, prior to breakfast, in shirt-sleeve order and with trousers rolled up to just below the knees, testing one of the triples at well over 100mph - and with no crash hat!

After Wünsche and Felgenheier had successfully completed their initial laps and qualified, disaster reared its ugly head - young Felgenheier crashed heavily whilst returning from an unofficial course-learning trip. This left only Wünsche to race. Although he retired on the larger model, on the 250 twin he put up a creditable performance - both in terms of speed and reliability - to finish third, at an average speed of 81.34mph.

By the next round in the World Championship, in Holland, modifications had been made to the cylinder finning on the three-cylinder models. The fins were now square on the two upright cylinders, and much deeper than previously on all three pots. The outer head fins on the upright cylinders had been cast at an angle to assist the passage of air through the finning. After completing practice, however, it was decided not to contest the race.

So it was for the majority of the 1953 season, with more retirements and non-starts than finishes. The only bright note was the excellent riding of new boy Hobl.

However, as a company, DKW had done well on the commercial front, and by the beginning of 1954, the workforce had more than doubled compared with 1950, 10,000 workers being employed on all aspects of two- and four-wheeled production. Therefore, the company was on a much stronger financial footing, which meant that there was more support available for the race shop.

'Siggi' Wünsche with the improved 350 triple during the 1953 Junior TT near the 33rd Milestone. Although he retired on the larger bike, with the 250 twin he put up a creditable performance - both in terms of speed and reliability - to finish third, at an average of 81.34mph.

Moreover, in early 1954, a man was to appear on the scene who was to have a considerable influence upon future events at the Ingolstadt company, on both the production and racing fronts. His name was Robert Eberan von Eberhorst. Originally a student of the Vienna Technical College and a genuine motorcycle enthusiast during the late 1920s, he later joined Auto Union at Chemnitz in the 1930s, becoming an assistant on the development side to the legendary Professor Ferdinand Porsche. After the war, von Eberhorst went to work in England, where his appointments included periods at the Aston Martin and BRM car organisations. In late 1953, however, he decided to return to his homeland where he joined DKW as Technical Director. He was also given responsibility for the racing programme, and the resultant changes showed what a wise move this was.

Quickly deciding to concentrate efforts upon the 350 three-cylinder model, von Eberhorst scrapped the 250 twin. He also opted to reorganise the racing development team and put Dipl. Ing. Helmut Gorg (who had first joined DKW in 1930) in charge of the day-to-day running of the racing section.

One of Gorg's first tasks was to dismantle a complete triple and fully redraw the original blueprints! The redesign which followed showed a host of changes, including a strengthened crankcase, minus the fins which had previously made a section of it appear like an additional cylinder. Another alteration was a redesigned cylinder liner.

The crankshaft, pressed together from six separate sections, was truly a work of engineering brilliance. To avoid wasted space and achieve the required crankcase compression, there were extremely narrow clearances for the slender, highly polished connecting rods and full-circle flywheels for a higher degree of pumping effect. As an example of the extra efficiency, Wolf had obtained a 48-percent balance factor, but Gorg managed to increase this to 62 per cent.

Both big- and small-ends comprised caged needle bearings, and the forged, two-ring Mahle pistons were made of Sintal with American steel rings. The depth of these rings was originally 0.75mm, but Gorg increased this figure to 1mm. It had been found that the ultra-thin rings had tended to become caught on the ports and, in addition, had a tendency to flutter (vibrate). Also in the Wolf era, deflector-type pistons had been used, but Gorg immediately turned to the more-or-less flat type which today are standard ware for the modern two-stroke. To match these, he adopted new cylinder heads incorporating a squish area.

A trio of SS1 Dell'Ortos supplied the fuel. Those feeding the pair of vertical cylinders shared a common float chamber, while the horizontal cylinder's carburettor had its own. In fact, together with the correct shape and length of expansion boxes, the positioning of the float chambers was discovered by Gorg to be the most critical of all the engine's performance factors.

Close up details of the 1956 350cc triple, showing: heads, barrels, carbs, float chambers and ignition.

During early testing with the 'new' engine, Helmut Gorg soon discovered that, although the result of his redesign had generally been successful, the horizontal cylinder still refused to generate as much power as either of the vertical pots. To cure this, its designer burned a considerable amount of midnight oil before the output was up to the required level.

The debut of the Gorg 350 came at a German national meeting at the Nürburgring in late May. Compared with the Wolf engine, maximum rpm had been reduced from around 12,000 to a shade under 10,500 in order to gain piston reliability. There were now five, instead of four, gear ratios, larger and more powerful brakes, and leading-link front forks. The frame itself remained largely unchanged. Even though a trio of the revised bikes (ridden by Hofmann, Hobl and new boy Bodmer) took the first three places, their race speeds and lap times did not match those of the NSU Rennmax twins, which dominated the 250 category. Helmut Gorg decided, therefore, that more development was needed before making an entry into the classic arena.

350 three-cylinder 1956

Engine:	Air-cooled, three-cylinder two-stroke, in v-formation (two vertical cylinders and one horizontal). Piston ported.
Capacity:	348.48cc
Bore &stroke:	53 x 52.8mm
Comp ratio:	12:1
Carburation:	Three Dell'Orto SS1 carburettors with remote float chambers.
Ignition:	Battery/coil; with 3 contact breakers (earlier bikes had magneto ignition).
Lubrication:	Petroil mix, 25:1 ratio.
Gearbox:	Five-speeds.
Clutch:	Wet, multi-plate.
Frame:	Steel, tubular, double cradle.
Suspension:	Front - leading link. Rear - swinging arm with teledraulic dampers; needle bearings for swinging arm pivot.
Brakes:	215mm drums on each wheel, hydraulically operated.
Tyres:	18 inch front and rear.
Dry weight:	145kg (320lb), with streamlining.
Fuel tank:	Four sizes: 12, 22, 28 and 32 litres.
Max power:	46bhp at 9,700rpm.
Max speed:	140mph (with dustbin shell)

Compact nature of control layout. On the left (nearside) handlebar is the choke control, with an individual lever for each of the three cylinders.

A new 125cc single also made its debut in 1955. This is the original prototype.

This was made at the Belgian GP in early July, where the machines showed considerable modification. In an attempt to reduce weight, the heavy six-cylinder, car-type magneto, fitted since the original prototype of 1952, was discarded in favour of battery/coil ignition, with a triple contact-breaker assembly driven from an extension of the off-side end of the crankshaft. The three carburettors were now equipped with air slides which operated separately through cables from a tiny, triple-lever cluster mounted close to the handlebar clutch lever.

Of the three 'Deeks', only the machine ridden by Wünsche survived the race to take third place, showing that the design lacked the outright speed and reliability of the latest Moto Guzzis. In fact, the most notable feature of the DKW in Belgium, was the controversy which surrounded the weird-looking number plate-cum-streamlining. This was deemed illegal by FIM officials, who said it contravened existing regulations. Although the race officials allowed them to be used, they were banned the following week in Holland, where the only DKW finisher was Hofmann in fifth spot.

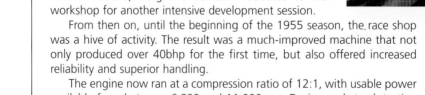

The 'cockpit' of the 1955, 125cc single. Note battery mounted in front of rev counter, behind screen.

After that, none of the Ingolstadt bikes raced that season. Instead, Gorg and his team retreated to their workshop for another intensive development session.

From then on, until the beginning of the 1955 season, the race shop was a hive of activity. The result was a much-improved machine that not only produced over 40bhp for the first time, but also offered increased reliability and superior handling.

The engine now ran at a compression ratio of 12:1, with usable power available from between 6,800 and 11,000rpm. During early track testing with the revised power unit, it had been discovered that even when changing down, with the engine revolutions soaring to around 15,000rpm, nothing had fallen to pieces. This led Gorg to realise that his basics were right, but he needed to create and harness usable power -

which is exactly what he achieved. Another move was to make the engine run cleaner - the earlier Wolf motor employed a 16:1 petroil mixture, but Gorg steadily decreased this to 25:1, through better engineering and the use of a heavier grade of lubricant.

Although the actual weight of the power unit remained the same, the whole machine now weighed 145 kg (320lb) with streamlining. Now considerably heavier than previously, and weighing more than the competition - for example, the 1954 championship Guzzi weighed 118 kg (260lb) - the latest DKW was preferred by its riders over the earlier models. This was not only because of improved power characteristics and reliability, but also because the extra weight had solved several problems which had been features of the earlier, ultra-lightweight triples.

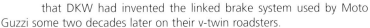

Works star August Hobl with the triple in 1954.

Finally, there were now much larger, stronger and more powerful hydraulically-operated brakes on both wheels. The earlier 'stoppers' had not only proved borderline in their ability, but the drums had been prone to cracking. The new brakes were 215mm in diameter, and each wheel had two separate units back to back. These were connected to a master cylinder operated by the foot pedal, which applied both and automatically supplied the correct bias to the front and rear wheels. A hand lever enabled the rider to increase the braking effect on the front wheel if required. It could be argued that DKW had invented the linked brake system used by Moto Guzzi some two decades later on their v-twin roadsters.

Another problem which had finally been eradicated was that of high-frequency vibration. During 1953 and 1954, the life of a rev-counter on one of the racing triples had often been a mere 20 miles! After careful investigation, Gorg discovered that the problem centred around certain vibrations which were being transmitted from the engine to the frame. He finally solved this by increasing the quality of the crankcase material and strengthening the crankshaft, but it was also found that the extra weight of the machine and modified crankcase supports combined to defeat what had formerly been one of the design's major drawbacks. As might be imagined, few riders wished to race a two-stroke vibromassager with a super-narrow power band and no rev-counter!

Considerable time was also spent with the INA bearing company, who came up with more robust needle bearings for both the small- and big-ends. Gorg even took this a stage further, using needle-roller bearings in the swinging-arm pivot from 1955.

Little and large. August Hobl's works DKWs at Monza in September 1955. The 125 single on which he came 4th is on the left; on the 350 triple (right) Hobl was 5th; excellent results when looking at the number of works entries from the likes of FB Mondial, MV Agusta, Gilera and Moto Guzzi.

Another problem was crankcase sealing, and much time and energy was to be expended before a satisfactory solution finally evolved. This included the use of double-lipped seals in place of the original single-lipped components.

Other changes took place in the cylinder heads, porting, timing and, most importantly of all, the exhaust system. Gorg employed a flat type of expansion chamber and, after many exhaustive bench tests, ascertained the optimum length and size. He was able to gain a relatively high increase in the mixture induced at certain engine revolutions - up to an amazing 80 per cent at certain points!

Another aspect of the development cycle was the use of streamlining, which the Ingolstadt team found, like Moto Guzzi and NSU, could add up to 10mph to the maximum velocity, depending on the circuit. Well over 100 different shells were tested in a wind tunnel. However, unlike the other two marques mentioned, which raced four-strokes, DKW not only had air resistance, but also the effective cooling of three cylinders to consider.

Helmut Gorg also built a single-cylinder version of the engine, initially to provide additional data on the behaviour of the horizontal cylinder, but later he decided to use

The 1956 DKW triple with its fairing removed...

it in a 125-class racer. This did not make its debut until midway through the 1955 season, when it won first time out at the Sachsenring circuit, in the eastern sector of Germany.

That year, the DKW team comprised Wünsche, Hobl and new man Hans Bartl. It was Hobl who made it a much better year for the Ingolstadt equipe by taking third place in the World Championship. This was thanks to a big leap in both speed and reliability, rewarded by second places on such demanding circuits as the Nürburgring (stamina) and Spa (speed). An additional encouragement was the performance of the new 125 machine. At its classic debut at Monza, in September, Hobl came home fourth, with team-mate Wünsche fifth.

Hobl also took the 350 German National Championship on the redesigned triple, to give DKW its most successful season yet in post-war racing.

This success did not stop further development, however, and Gorg again spent the winter months on painstaking work to further refine both the 350 triple and 125 single. By the beginning of the 1956 season, the larger machine provided a reliable 46 bhp at 9,700rpm, which meant over 140mph, while the 125 offered 17 bhp at 9,700rpm - 110mph out on the road. Obviously, the full 'dustbin'-type streamlining played a vital role in achieving these speeds.

Also in early 1956, the former Moto Guzzi rider and team manager, Fergus Anderson, tested the 350 DKW at Monza. Although Gorg was highly impressed with the Scot, nothing ever came of this, as Anderson was killed at Floreffe in Belgium before the classic season got under way.

However, another British rider did join DKW that year. This was the 1952, 125cc World Champion, Cecil Sandford. Unfortunately, probably due to the massive down-turn in sales of DKW's production roadsters at the time, neither Sandford nor Hobl rode in all six rounds of the 350cc world title series.

That said, the team still put in some impressive performances in a number of events, including the Dutch TT, Belgian GP, German GP and the Italian GP. DKW's sole entry in the Isle of Man TT was Sandford, who came home fourth, proving how reliable the triple had become.

At the season's end, Hobl repeated his third place in the 350cc championship table, with Sandford fourth.

The final round of the 1956 World Championship took place in early September at Monza, Italy. Nobody knew it at the time, but this was to prove DKW's classic swan-song—never again were the screaming triples or, for that matter, the tiny horizontal singles to appear in a Grand Prix. However, it was not the team's final appearance. This came later that month at the international Avus races, held over the steeply-banked Berlin circuit on Sunday 16th September.

Hobl made it an event to remember with pride by giving DKW victory in the 350 race at an amazing average speed of 116.5mph. Thus, the curtain came down on one of Germany's truly great racing motorcycle marques.

...note the massive air scoops to direct cooling air onto the cylinders.

FATH

Helmut Fath was born in 1930, and his first motorcycle purchased in 1946, was a well-worn, pre-war BMW 250 single. In those days, Fath was living just outside Mannheim, working at an experimental laboratory where research into high-altitude aviation was undertaken. He had begun there at the age of 14 in the dark days of 1944, when the whole of Germany was under great strain with the Allies attacking on all sides.

When the war finally came to an end in the following year, the young Fath was kept on at the plant after it was taken over by the Allied forces. Serving an apprenticeship as a precision engineer, he stayed on until he was 18. By that time, Helmut Fath had been converted to the ranks of motorcycle enthusiasts and had owned a string of machinery. This interest led him to quit the aviation industry and go to work (for less money!) in a motorcycle dealership. With his precision engineering background, Fath was soon given the more specialised jobs, such as building up BMW crankshafts and inserting valve seats.

The following year, 1949, he took part in his first competitive event. This was a trial in which he rode a twin-piston German

Fath URS Rickman Metisse solo racer.

Fath URS four (solo).

Triumph (TWN) two-stroke. With money in short supply, his real interest - road racing - had to wait. It was to be three long years before his ambition on this front was finally realised. This came in the shape of a standard, roadgoing, BMW pushrod flat-twin, which was tuned and fitted with a sidecar. This effort proved two things; the machine was simply not fast enough, and neither was its pilot!

For 1953, the BMW chassis was retained, but the engine was subjected to a vast amount of tuning work. Having several years of experience on this type of unit was a distinct advantage, but the problem of finance, or lack of it, remained. As he was only able to race in his holidays, Fath took part in only three meetings that year. However, a victory was taken at each of these, with the result that the name Helmut Fath joined the Senior category in German classification. This meant that although Fath could only race within the German borders, he was able to take part in international meetings.

His new status posed another problem, however - the home-tuned pushrod BMW, although quick enough to win races in the Junior class, was totally outclassed among the superior opposition which he now faced.

Therefore, taking the chance to sell his original outfit, Helmut Fath ordered one of the small batch of Rennsport BMWs that the Munich factory was building at the time (see Chapter 3). Unfortunately, a financial hiccup prevented him from obtaining his overhead-cam BMW, with the result that he did not compete in a single race during 1954.

Helmut Fath (right) with his passenger Alfred Wohlgemuth. Hockenheim, 1960.

However, in December that year, he finally managed to obtain a solo Rennsport model, one of the 1954 batch and set about converting it to sidecar use. This included building a special frame, converting the brakes to hydraulic operation and constructing a superbly-crafted aluminium fairing.

For the next four years, it was a case of steady and ever-improving form, and in 1959, Helmut Fath finally launched himself as a serious contender for the World Sidecar Championship when he finished the season in fifth spot, partnered by Alfred Wohlgemuth on a BMW Rennsport outfit.

The year 1960 was full of glory, for the duo totally dominated the title series, winning four out of the five rounds, and placed second in the other, the Dutch TT. Typical of the man behind the name, Fath not only won the Isle of Man TT, but also helped his rival, Pip Harris, to gain second place. Harris had blown his BMW engine in practice and, to his surprise, Fath had waded in and completely rebuilt the Rennsport engine, using new spares, pieces from Pip's old engine and parts from Jack Beeton's BMW engine. The work took the best part of two days, and Helmut's only reward was Pip's second position - true sportsmanship, indeed.

The following year, 1961, Fath and Wohlgemuth looked all set to retain their world title, following a runaway victory during the first round in Spain when they lapped the entire field.

Helmut Fath 500 BMW. 1960 sidecar TT.

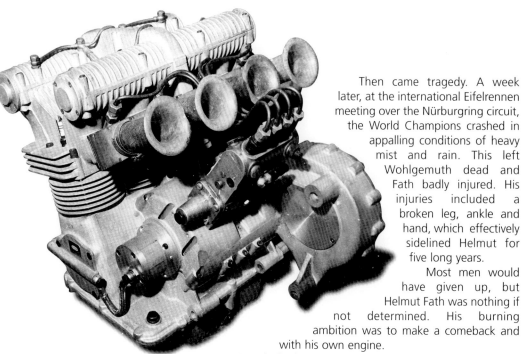

Rear view of Fath's original prototype 498cc (60 x 44mm) dohc, four-cylinder, fuel injected racing engine.

Then came tragedy. A week later, at the international Eifelrennen meeting over the Nürburgring circuit, the World Champions crashed in appalling conditions of heavy mist and rain. This left Wohlgemuth dead and Fath badly injured. His injuries included a broken leg, ankle and hand, which effectively sidelined Helmut for five long years.

Most men would have given up, but Helmut Fath was nothing if not determined. His burning ambition was to make a comeback and with his own engine.

Once he had recovered from the effects of the accident that had claimed his passenger and friend, Fath set about designing, building and finally testing his own across-the-frame, four-cylinder, double-overhead-camshaft racing engine. This was known as the URS, after the village of Ursenbach where he had made his home.

The URS design was really a pair of side-by-side parallel twins, coupled together by a countershaft driven from the crankshaft between cylinders 2 and 3. The firing order was 1-4-2-3, and the engine featured a central timing chain. The crankshaft ran on six main bearings, with caged roller big-ends and phosphor-bronze small-ends in the titanium con-rods. The lubrication system included a combined oil cooler and filter. The bore and stroke measurements of the new engine were 60 x 44mm, the ultra-short-stroke unit giving useful power between 8,000 and 13,500rpm. Even from the first prototype, the URS was a very high-revving unit, and it was a remarkable technical achievement to be able to control the valves up to 15,000rpm with a conventional two-valves-per-cylinder layout.

Credit for this went to Fath's partner, Dr Peter Kuhn (formerly a lecturer at Heidelburg University). He had designed the cam profile and valve spring rates to match the special Swedish wire used for these springs, which was later supplied by Fath for use in various other engines.

The valves themselves were large in size - 34mm inlet, and 30mm exhaust - and were splayed at 67 degrees. As a result, twin 10mm sparking plugs were fitted in each cylinder and, unusually, these were mounted vertically, as otherwise there was not enough room for the valves.

Fuel was injected directly into the ports by a Bosch injector mounted between the wide-angle upper frame tubes, above and behind the engine unit. The injector had come from a 1.5 litre Borgward car, and a divided cable from the twistgrip moved the single flat throttle plate to regulate the fuel supply. Although contemporary press reports claimed 80 bhp for the engine, Fath laughed at this and said he alone knew the dyno reading - and he was keeping it a secret!

Fath's prototype four-cylinder made its first public appearance in May 1966.

FATH

Helmut Fath and passenger Alfred Wohlgemuth totally dominated the 1960 World Championship series. The following year they looked set to repeat the performance, but a horrific accident at the Nürburgring left Wohlgemuth dead and Fath badly injured.

Fath made his comeback in May 1966 at the West German Grand Prix, staged at Hockenheim. His reappearance five years after the Nürburgring accident, along with the new engine, created a sensation. Unfortunately, he retired after just three laps when lying sixth. This was the start of a series of problems which its creator discovered with the URS engine during that first season. In fact, Fath hardly finished a race.

At the beginning of 1967, it appeared to be the same story, the URS seeming not to have enough power. However, at the West German GP at Hockenheim, Fath took an instant lead from the start, but despite building up a four-second lead over Klaus Enders' BMW, he was forced out near the end with a broken gearbox selector mechanism.

It was also during that year that the URS engine was first considered for solo use, with the news that John Blanchard was considering racing one mounted in a frame built by Colin Seeley. At the time, Blanchard stated: 'I think the engine may be better for a solo than a sidecar, and is now giving good power.' Unlike the sidecar power unit, the solo engine was fitted with carburettors and had magnesium-alloy, instead of aluminium castings.

By the time of the 1967 TT, Helmut Fath's homebuilt, four-cylinder URS outfit was outspeeding the fastest short-stroke BMWs - no mean achievement. Furthermore, it appeared that if he could achieve reliability and improve handling, he would once again dominate the class.

It was then revealed that although the engine had repeatedly suffered from fractures of the long bolts clamping the crankcase halves to the central driving sprockets, some of Fath's engine failures had been due to the inability of the battery/coil ignition system to cope with the unorthodox crankshaft layout. Therefore, to stabilize the ignition, Fath had reverted to a magneto.

Englishman John Blanchard on the Fath URS at the Ulster GP, 19th August 1967.

The difficulty had been due to his choice of crankpin spacing. Instead of having all four in one plane (two up, two down), Fath had spaced them like the points of a compass to achieve smoother running. This gave firing intervals of 90, 180, 270 and 360 degrees. However, at the peak power point of 14,000rpm, the 90-degree interval had given the contact-breaker precious little time to do its job. It was hoped that the new system would solve this problem.

Both Fath and Dr Kuhn spent time in England with John Blanchard at the Seeley works in Belvedere, Kent. Late July saw the Seeley-framed Fath four solo racer completed, and a particularly neat effort it looked, too. Many of the cycle parts - except the full duplex cradle frame - were the same as used on the production Seeley 7R and G50 ohc single-cylinder racers.

Fath and Blanchard both appeared with their respective fours at the Hutchinson 100 at Brands Hatch on 13th August. Two weeks later, the duo appeared at Scarborough on Saturday 26th August, when Fath and his passenger, Wolfgang Kalauch, scored an impressive win over the World Champion Klaus Enders.

Blanchard, however, fell at Mere Hairpin, putting himself out of the running. There followed a row, with Blanchard being withdrawn from the Snetterton and Oulton Park meetings in the remaining two days of the Bank Holiday weekend. This followed a stormy exchange between Seeley and Blanchard at Snetterton over the bike

Helmut Fath and passenger
Wolfgang Kalauch in action
Isle of Man TT - bike is a
four-cylinder URS built by
Fath who won the
World Championship, 1968.

being fitted with a Lockheed disc brake before Scarborough, without Seeley's permission. The result was that Blanchard was dropped as development rider and would not be allowed to ride the machine any more that season.

A couple of weeks later, following discussions between Seeley and Fath, the prospects of work continuing on their four-cylinder racer brightened. However, Fath had elected to leave all decisions concerning the project to his partner in the design and development of the URS, Dr Kuhn.

In any case, the Seeley Fath co-operation didn't last beyond the end of the season, and for the future, the Fath team chose to use the Metisse chassis made by the Rickman brothers of New Milton in Hampshire. John Blanchard returned to ride the URS Metisse solo - and in a supreme irony, it was fitted with the very Lockheed disc brake set-up that had caused the rift between him and Seeley.

FATH

Blanchard gave the machine its first outing at Brands Hatch in January 1968, when he was principally concerned with testing the brakes and suspension, watched by Derek Rickman and Mike Vaughan of Lockheed. Afterwards, all decided that they were very happy with the machine's performance, but thought that a little more experimentation was needed to sort out the rear suspension.

More tests were carried out before Blanchard and the URS-Metisse were entered in the season's first classic, the West German GP at the Nürburgring. This was anything but a successful debut, as Blanchard crashed twice. The machine was then offered to John Hartle, who rode it at Hockenheim on 12th May.

If the solo plans didn't proceed as intended, Fath's own racing efforts certainly did. At the Nürburgring, he and Wolfgang Kalauch took the flag at the front of the field, Fath's first Grand Prix victory since his win in Spain in April 1961. What a sweet taste of success it was for a man who had not only made a successful comeback, but built the engine of his machine into the bargain!

Then came the Isle of Man TT and a fourth, followed by a fifth in the Dutch TT, a retirement in Belgium and then a couple of victories in Belgium and the final round at Hockenheim. The last event was to have taken place at the Italian GP at Monza, but as the sidecar event was cancelled, by FIM decree, it was contested at Hockenheim, with the final of the German National Championship in October.

Before Hockenheim, both Fath and Georg Auerbacher had gained 21 points each, while TT winner Siegfried Schauzu was four points behind, but still in with a chance. With so much at stake, Fath took a desperate gamble after official practice finished. Dissatisfied with his engine, he fitted a completely new short-stroke unit which had not been raced before, but which had been showing promising results on the test-bed. Would it last the race? Fath commented grimly before the start: 'The only way to find out is to use it.'

Helmut Fath and passenger Wolfgang Kalauch in action on the four-cylinder URS, winning the sidecar class of the 1969 Belgian Grand Prix.

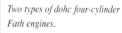

The gamble paid off. Before the first corner, Fath and passenger Wolfgang Kalauch already had a tremendous lead, and even the super-fast BMW of ex-World Champion Enders was unable to get a tow in the slipstream of the flying URS. A wet and slippery track failed to deter a determined Fath, then 39 years old, and at the end of the second lap, his lead was 6.6 seconds. This doubled in the next two circuits to take him out of reach of everyone - a lead which was maintained until the end. The 15 lap, 63.15 mile race was won at an average speed of 98.55mph, with a fastest lap (by Fath) of 100.72mph, breaking Enders' previous record.

Fath in action during his World Championship year, 1968 - the first, and only, man in histroy to win a motorcycling world title using an engine designed and built by himself.

Helmut Fath made history because, up to that time, nobody had ever won a world championship on a home-built machine. Strangely, when defending the title in the following year, the results turned out almost in reverse, with wins in France, Holland and Belgium, a third in the Isle of Man, and a retirement in Germany. With two rounds to go and leading the championship, he crashed in Finland, preventing his participation in the final round in Ulster where Klaus Enders took the title for BMW.

For 1969, Fath built a larger version of his four, initially for British short circuits, where it was popular to race larger-capacity outfits. the 68 x 51.5mm bore and stroke gave 748cc, compared with the smaller unit's 60 x 44mm. Much longer con-rods were used, together with different cylinders and larger valves. The aim was to produce an engine with tremendous low down punch, rather than power at high revs, and Fath hoped that a four-speed gearbox would be adequate. In this, he was proved wrong, as like the 500, the 750 needed at least five speeds.

Two types of dohc four-cylinder Fath engines.

At long last, however, the 500 solo racer began to shine. Ridden by veteran Karl Hoppe, the URS Metisse dominated many of the early season Continental Internationals. Perhaps his finest performance came just a week after his first victory - the Eifelrennen at the end of

FATH

April when Hoppe won the 500 class of the non-championship Austrian GP at Salzburg. Under ideal racing conditions, in front of a crowd of 28,000 spectators, no one could keep up with Hoppe, who shot away from the start and won as he pleased. Not only was his race speed a record, but he also shaved 0.7 seconds off Giacomo Agostini's lap record, which had been set on an MV Agusta four in 1967.

During the 1969 TT, the Fath URS sidecar was timed at 134.8mph - a full ten miles an hour quicker than the fastest BMW!

Then, to prove that his early form was no fluke, Hoppe finished a fine second in the West German GP at Hockenheim, behind Agostini's MV. Sadly, however, Hoppe did not contest the remainder of the classics. This was a great pity, as except for MV, 1969 saw the URS emerge as the most serious World Championship contender in the 500cc class.

Although there were several URS engines in existence, there were still only two machines: Fath's own outfit and the Metisse solo ridden by Hoppe. Fath had also received help from several British companies, including Reynolds Tubes, Automotive Products, Renold Chain, Duckhams Oil (the main sponsor) and Dunlop, who had developed a special 4.00 x 12 tyre for the outfit. Both types of the URS engine were now giving useful power between 9,000 and 13,000rpm, and transmission was via a Norton box with a six-speed Schafleitner cluster.

Two views of the 1969-series Fath URS dohc, fuel-injected engine. Side view showing clutch, ignition and fuel injection ...

The Bosch fuel injection on the sidecar engine now had twin air intakes instead of the single intake previously used. Moreover, a final solution had been found to beat the ignition problems which had remained, despite the adoption of a fully transistorized system. The answer was found by fitting a separate coil for each cylinder and making a special contact-breaker with four sets of points spaced at 45, 90, 135 and 180 degrees. Since each cylinder had two spark plugs, the coils were double-ended to furnish pairs of sparks simultaneously.

... front view with huge amount of finning for heads, cylinders, crankcases and sumps.

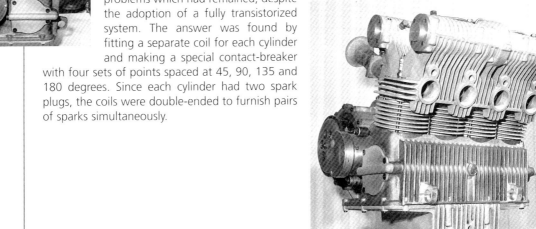

Karl Hoppe won the Austrian Grand Prix at Salzburg in May, 1969 on a URS Metisse. The spectators are suicidally close to the action.

Things looked bright, indeed, but then Fath broke his leg in Finland on 12th August. While he was recuperating, towards the end of the month, there came the news that the Fath team had been purchased by Friedl Münch with American backing, as related in Chapter 10. The Münch/Fath tie-up eventually took place in May 1970, and because all of his machinery had been taken over, it was not until much later that Fath resumed manufacturing. During 1970-1, he was strictly a tuner, although during 1971, he was said to be one of the top Yamaha tuners around - even the 250 World Champion was a customer.

In the middle of 1973 came the first news that Fath, then aged 43, was thinking of a possible comeback. At his forest hideout near Heidelburg, Fath was busy constructing a brand-new four-cylinder outfit. Furthermore, not only did he have plans for a racing return himself, but he hoped to have a spare engine for Billie Nelson to race in solo events.

This time, his design was for a water-cooled, disc-valve, two-stroke flat-four, which many wrongly considered at the time to be a development of the König. In fact, any resemblance began and ended with the flat-four cylinder layout. In any case, in the early 1960s, Fath's original scheme had been to build a water-cooled flat-four (albeit a four-stroke) before ultimately opting for the across-the-frame layout of the URS. The reason he had not built the original design was said to be the reluctance of BMW to provide certain parts, notably the transmission, on which the design depended.

A mechanic with one of the Fath flat four two-stroke engines in 1972.

Unlike the König, Fath's two-stroke had a longitudinal position for the crankshaft and an integral six-speed gearbox with the clutch at the rear of the crankcase, in a similar manner to the BMW design - but with a pair of bevel gears coupling the output shaft to the left-hand side-mounted sprocket for the chain final drive, turning it through an angle of 90 degrees. Another departure from König practice was the oil supply to the big-end which, on the Berlin company's engine, was by a direct shower of petroil. Fath devised a belt-driven pump, controlled by the throttle, which dribbled a supply of straight oil to the big-ends, main bearings and disc bearings. Caged needle rollers were used for both the big- and small-ends.

With a capacity of 495cc (56 x 50mm), the Fath four had aluminium-alloy cylinders with Nickasil bores. Originally, Yamaha pistons were used, but these were soon replaced by purpose-built units, carrying only a single ring each.

A unique feature of the Fath design was that each cylinder casting incorporated half the crankcase, so that the crank chambers themselves were also water-cooled. There was no water pump of the type fitted to many water-cooled 'strokers', but as on Bultacos and MZs, the thermosiphon system was used, with water entering the underside of the cylinders and leaving them at the top.

FATH

Fuel was supplied by a quartet of separate carburettors — 34mm Japanese Mikunis. Because Fath used four carburettors, this called for four small disc valves instead of the König's one, but like the König, the drive to these was by toothed rubber belt. Also unlike the König, Fath used four separate expansion chambers in an attempt to extract the maximum possible power output - 112 bhp at 12,200rpm. The exhausts ran from the top of the engine and back under the rider's legs. To prevent him from being burned, they were coated with a baked-on finish, and as Billie Nelson was to remark; 'It's really amazing. You can touch them and not get burned even after a long race.'

At first, the ignition was by a Bosch flywheel magneto, with the generator incorporating a pair of ignition coils, two pulse coils and three more for the water pump, fuel pump and tachometer. However, this system proved too heavy, and thereafter a battery was installed for current, and only a pulse unit was fitted to the front of the crankshaft.

At 44, Helmut Fath was not sure if he would race again, but May 1974 saw Fath's new four in action for the first time, at the West German GP at Hockenheim, in solo trim, ridden by Billie Nelson. Ready to race, but without fuel, the Fath weighed only 130 kg (286lb), some 25 kg (55lb) less than the comparable Yamaha or Suzuki 500 fours—but there were problems.

The power proved exceptional, but not so the handling. The frame had been constructed in only ten days, after the original builder failed to come up with the goods, and Fath freely admitted that he was not a frame specialist. The problems centred around the swinging arm, which was whipping so badly at Hockenheim that it caused Nelson's ultimate retirement. There were also early problems with the transmission system.

The Isle of Man TT was given a miss, and the machine's next outing was at the international meeting at Raalte in Holland, where again it showed a tremendous turn of speed. However, trouble with the throttle linkage slowed Nelson in the race, although he kept going to finish fourth.

The next race was the Dutch TT at Assen where, in the 350 race, Nelson clocked up a fourth on his Yamaha. At the start of the 500 race, however, the Fath four oiled a plug. By the time it had been changed and Nelson got started, the leaders had already come round to complete one lap. He followed them down the straight and, to his amazement, caught them up. He said afterwards that he could have passed them easily, but for two things. Firstly, he was not totally confident in the machine's handling on the very fast curve towards the end of the straight, and secondly he himself hated people who indulged in what he called 'dicing with me when I'm lapping them.'

View of flat-four engine showing installation of carbs, exhaust pipes and gearbox.

The Fath flat-four for sidecar use, showing carbs, exhaust and final drive.

The riders whom Billie Nelson was in danger of catching in this way were none other than the trio of Barry Sheene (Suzuki), Giacomo Agostini (Yamaha) and Phil Read (MV Agusta)!

Besides the evident speed, Nelson was impressed by the smoothness of the engine, describing it 'just like a big electric motor'. He thought the wide spread of usable power from 8,000 to 13,000rpm was particularly impressive, and development continued apace throughout the summer of 1974, with an excellent understanding existing between builder and rider.

However, on Sunday 8th September, all this was shattered. Billie Nelson, the man who had once been known as 'Mr Consistency' on the Grand Prix circuit, died after he crashed during the 250 race at Opatija in

Englishman Billie Nelson on the flat-four Fath two-stroke leads Gerrit Veldink's TR500 Suzuki twin at the Dutch TT on 16th June 1974.

the Yugoslav Grand Prix. He crashed on a 125mph left-hander at one of the highest points of the closed road circuit on the Adriatic coast. The Yamaha went into the crowd and a spectator was seriously injured, while Nelson suffered severe chest injuries and died after an operation in hospital at nearby Rijeka.

The 33-year-old Nelson, from Eckington, Derbyshire, had begun racing in 1958 and made his Continental debut six years later in West Germany. He combined solo racing and sidecar passengering for several years. It was a crash while racing as passenger with Fath in 1969, during the Finnish GP, which ruined not only Fath's chances of retaining his world title, but also Nelson's hopes of taking the Bill Hannah-sponsored Paton twin to second place in the 500cc World Championship behind Agostini.

Fath and Nelson had been firm friends as well as colleagues, and his death was a cruel blow. Following the accident, Fath decided to make a return to the sidecar scene, the engine from Nelson's solo being built into a special three-wheeler for Siegfried Schauzu. However, Fath was far from happy with the outfit (it was not of his design) and, in May 1975, said: 'It is far too big and the width of the sidecar alone loses me 10-15 bhp.'

By then, Fath had almost completed a new engine which he said would produce even more horsepower, and he hoped that the rest of the outfit would be modified. Early results were far from impressive, however, with only one placing in the top ten at any of the Grands Prix that year, when the ARO-Fath finished at Hockenheim.

FATH

For 1976, the sidecar team consisted of two pairings: Schauzu and Kalauch, plus newcomer Heinz Schilling partnered by passenger Rolf Gundel. In the very first round at Le Mans, in France, Schilling managed a third place, with Schauzu coming home eighth. At the Salzburgring, in Austria, Schauzu came in third, although Schilling had to retire.

Displaying their greatly-improved reliability, both crews finished the punishing Isle of Man TT, Schauzu in fourth and Schilling in sixth place. Then, in Holland, Schilling was fifth, with Schauzu in tenth place, while the following weekend, in Belgium the ARO-Fath teams made it third and fourth - Schilling and Schauzu. Neither team competed in the Czech GP at Brno, and the season ended with a ninth for Schauzu at the Nürburgring. As a result, Schauzu and Kalauch came fifth overall in the year's championship table.

In the same year, Alex George, the Scottish solo racer, then based in Holland, rode Helmut Fath's four-cylinder 'stroker' solo in the Czech Grand Prix. George's Suzuki four had been sidelined with a broken idler gear, so he took over the Fath bike, the chassis of which remained untouched since Billie Nelson last raced it. He found the machine to be around 10mph slower than the all conquering (but at that time, none too reliable) Suzukis, and a match for them on acceleration. He led for most of the first lap, but gradually dropped back and retired when he grounded one of the plug caps.

For 1977, the ARO team was again reorganised. Schauzu left to race his own Yamaha, while Schilling was provided with a new ARO-Yamaha. Then, after the season had started, Werner Schwarzel (second in 1976 on a König) was brought into the team with passenger Huber and took over one of the vacant ARO-Fath outfits.

Siegfried Schauzu with the ARO Fath outfit at the 1976 Isle of Man TT.

This is the Fath flat-four engined Nico Bakker monoshock prototype of the mid 1970s.

Schwarzel's first finish was at the Dutch TT, with a third, after which he demonstrated his own superb skill and the full potential of the Fath engine by winning the next round in Belgium on the super-fast Spa circuit. He retired in Czechoslovakia, but won the final round at Silverstone to finish third in the world series. This was an amazing result when you consider that the team had only finished in three of the seven rounds!

This result was to prove the pinnacle of achievement by Fath's flat-four, even though it was not recognised at the time, and the man himself was still interested in both the sidecar and solo classes at world level.

At the end of 1977, South African Jon Ekerold, later to be 350cc World Champion in 1980 on a Bimota-Yamaha, was tipped to be rider of a new machine powered by a Fath flat-four. Fath had been so impressed with Ekerold's riding ability, when he saw him in action at the end-of-season Nürburgring International, that he offered to let him have one of his 500 engines and also to prepare Ekerold's 250 and 350 Yamaha power units.

Ekerold soon had a Nico Bakker frame with monoshock suspension constructed to house the Fath four, but in the end, he decided to concentrate on riding his pair of Yamahas. The Fath four was shelved, this time never to reappear. With the speed and reliability of the new breed of Japanese four-cylinder 'strokers', a private effort, even with as gifted a tuner as Fath, simply could not compete.

In the 1978 world sidecar series, Fath was to suffer yet more disappointment. Schwarzel still proved almost unbeatable, but his two victories at Assen and the Nürburgring, with a second at Mugello, in Italy, and a sixth in Nogaro, France, simply were not enough to stop Rolf Biland and his passenger, Englishman Kenny Williams, from taking the title with their Yamaha-powered BEO machine. What a machine it was, too - quite simply the most radical interpretation of the sidecar construction rules that had ever been seen.

FATH

It appeared to be a perfectly natural development of a line begun in the mid 1970s. Parallelogram suspension had appeared when sidecar racing constructors started using racing-car suspension and wheels on conventional, shortwheelbase outfits. However, this line of development, as racing outfits grew steadily more like three-wheeled racing cars, was speedily terminated when Biland produced his BEO tricar. It was so radical that it forced the FIM into creating two world sidecar classes for 1979: the B2A for conventional outfits, and the B2B for the new breed. Regulations were hastily redrafted to outlaw racing-car suspensions and steering systems, and this meant a total reappraisal for everyone connected with the three-wheel racing fraternity. The result was a new breed of long-wheelbase, fully-enclosed racing three-wheelers now commonly referred to as worms.

This was the last straw for Fath, who by now had not only given up the idea of making a return himself, but with the split championship in 1979, had finally decided to call it a day in his bid to be a combination of world champion and one-man motorcycle manufacturer.

It was the end of an era that had spanned 20 years, during which he had been World Champion in 1960, fought back from serious injury to win back the championship in 1968 with his own four-cylinder dohc engine, then had everything taken from him in the Münch deal in 1970, before coming back again with a completely new design to join the contest once more. In the process, some of his closest friends and racing partners had lost their lives through accidents, and it is unlikely that any other man in the history of motorcycle sport has ever suffered such peaks of triumph and depths of despair as Helmut Fath. In overcoming the setbacks, his character can be summed up in one word - fighter. Helmut Fath died in 1994.

Helmut Fath at work in his tent at the Belgian Grand Prix, 1978.

A rider who had the chance of racing Fath's Nico Bakker-framed 500cc GP solo race was the South African Jon Ekerold (later to win the 350cc world title in 1980 riding a Bimota-framed Yamaha).

Horex

6

Horex classic racer - 1950s Imperator ohc twin, with Münch brakes, hydraulic steering damper and megaphone exhaust.

Today, because of its association with the classic four-stroke single-cylinder roadster concept of the 1940s and 1950s, the Horex is widely sought after by enthusiasts and collectors alike in Germany. However, the Bad Homburg company also had another side - both before and after World War 2, it took part, with varying success, in road-racing events throughout the Fatherland and abroad.

The founder of Horex was Friedrich Kleeman who, together with his son Fritz, showed considerable entrepreneurial skills in a number of successful business ventures during the early 1920s. Kleeman senior was also the main shareholder of the Columbus Motorenwerke in Oberusel, which manufactured auxiliary engines for bicycles, as well as larger units for motorcycles.

In 1923, the father-and-son team founded another company, with the intention of designing and building complete motorcycles. This enterprise was centred on a former manufacturing company owned by the Kleeman family. It was given the name Horex from the first two letters of Homburg and the brand name Rex, which the previous company had used.

The first Horex motorcycle appeared in 1924. Not surprisingly, the new firm chose a Columbus engine, a 248cc pushrod single, with hand-operated, three-speed gearbox. The frame was typical of the era with its simple tubular steel construction, flat tank and sprung saddle. The front fork employed a rocker arm, which was suspended on a central spring and incorporated a single friction damper absorber.

Not only did these early Horex machines sell well to the public, but they were raced with considerable success, too. The interest in motorcycle sport stemmed from the fact that Fritz Kleeman was also a well-known racing motorist and motorcyclist, and with the new 248cc ohv single, suitably tuned and stripped for action, he soon had Horex competing in races throughout Germany. There was a trio of works riders - Phillip Karrer, Henry Veit and, of course, Fritz Kleeman (in true pioneering spirit).

Horex designs soon proved successful, not only in racing, but also in long-distance trials. Perhaps the greatest success of the original trio came in the first race ever staged over the legendary Nürburgring circuit in the late 1920s. Fritz Kleeman finished third on a 596cc Horex, the cylinder of which had been bored out to give 675cc, against the might of factory teams from the likes of Norton, Harley Davidson and New Imperial.

By 1930, the Bad Homburg marque was established on a firm commercial footing, with both production and profits soaring. Columbus engines were also doing well, not only being used by Horex, but also by other German marques, such as AWD, Tornax and Victoria.

In the early 1930s, Horex and Columbus merged their interests by moving engine production from Oberusel to Bad Homburg. This heralded even greater success, for the new grouping employed the brilliant designer Hermann Reeb.

It was Reeb who created a sensation in 1932 when he designed a pair of large-capacity vertical twins of 598 and 796cc with chain-driven ohc. The drive to the overhead camshaft was on the offside of the engine, enclosed in a large alloy casting which dominated that side of the power unit. This led to the design's one major disadvantage - the spark plug on the timing side was obstructed by this vast housing.

There had been vertical twins before, of course, but not like this. Far be it for me to claim a first for the Bad Homburg factory, but although Triumph and Edward Turner are today universally credited with the conception of the modern vertical twin, perhaps Horex and Hermann Reeb could have argued that they were there some four years earlier . . .

On the racing front, Horex had continued to participate with success. In the late 1920s, Franz Islinger and Josef Klein garnered considerable success on the 248 and 498cc singles. Then, at the 1929 German Grand Prix at the Nürburgring, expatriate Briton Tommy Bullus rode so effectively on one of the larger machines that only a retirement with just a few miles to go was to rob him and Horex of a famous victory. In the 1930s, Karl Braun used a supercharged version of the ohc twin to win many sidecar events, including victory in the 1935 German Sidecar Championship. Many of Braun's victories came with an engine enlarged to 980cc.

Fork developed by Roland Schnell and Hermann Gablenz late 1953. Originally intended for the Schnell-Horex racer but used on Horex roadsters.

Prototype dohc, 349cc (60 x 61.6mm) Horex twin, designed by the Austrian engineer, Ludwig Apfelbeck. Although it displayed considerable potential, its fate was sealed when the factory quit GP racing towards the end of 1954.

In the immediate post-war period, Horex traded under the Horex-ColumbusWerke KG Fritz Kleeman banner. Their first new machine in this era was the 342cc (69 x 91.5mm) ohv Regina. This racing version made its debut at the Eilenriede Rennen meeting near Hanover, on 30th April 1950.

During the mid and late 1930s, Horex continued in a leading position, both on the race circuit and the street. Not only did it refine existing models, but it also introduced brand-new 500 and 600cc four-valve singles.

However, as with other manufacturers, the demands of the Third Reich's war machine had largely taken over by the end of the decade. The result was that, by the outbreak of war in September 1939, the Bad Homburg production facilities had been turned over totally to the needs of the military (but not to the manufacture of motorcycles).

Horex survived the conflict in far better shape than any of its rivals and, therefore, was able to resume volume production without many of the difficulties encountered by the remainder of the German motorcycle industry. Allied to this, it was doubly fortunate in being the first company to gain permission from the occupying forces to build a machine with a capacity of over 250cc. At the time, several outsiders claimed that the Kleeman family had more than a close relationship with certain powerful Americans . . .

Horex traded under the title Horex-ColumbusWerke KG Fritz Kleeman in the years immediately after the war (although from 1953, the Columbus part was removed). In the late 1940s, Horex was authorized to build machines for police and other official duties.

This, in turn, led to the development of the best-selling Regina. It used an entirely new 342cc (69 x 91.5mm), semi-unit-construction, ohv single with a four-speed gearbox and simplex chain primary drive. In standard trim, the Regina produced 15bhp at a lowly 3,500rpm. It may come as a surprise, therefore, to learn that the first post-war Horex racer was one of the 350 Reginas with a specially-tuned engine that pumped out 25bhp at 5,500rpm, a close-ratio gearbox and several other modifications, including alloy rims and lightweight mudguards.

1950 Horex 350 Regina roadster.

The race-modified roadster made its debut at the Eilenriede Rennen meeting near Hanover in April 1950. However, its performance was not competitive against the pukka racing singles, such as the ohc Norton and AJS 7R 'Boy Racer', and the project was abandoned shortly afterwards.

The evident limitations of the pushrod, single-cylinder design in this new role led Horex to design a new flagship machine, one which could be used on both race track and road.

For this task, the factory's development staff opted for a twin - the first such Horex since Herman Reeb's trend-setting machine of 1932. Called the Imperator (meaning Emperor or General), the new bike first appeared in public during the spring of 1951, when a racing version appeared at the Waiblinger Dreieckrennen road races. At the time, Horex stated that the Imperator was competing solely as part of its development programme and that design work was not complete, nor indeed had the final specification of the machine been definitely decided.

Compared to Reeb's twin, the 1951 version was much wider. Although bulky, its lines were business-like, with the drive to its ohc by chain, which ran between the cylinders. Furthermore, a lavish (for the era) use of aluminium for its generously-proportioned, unit-construction engine kept the weight down.

Also, when compared to the earlier Horex design, the new unit's symmetry of layout had the advantage of offering more equal cooling for each cylinder and allowing the designer to fit the spark plugs in the normal position. The central camshaft drive allowed the cam itself to be shorter, thus avoiding the possibility of flexing with its obvious effect upon valve timing.

On the debit side, however, the 1951 engine had three factors. Firstly, a four-bearing crankshaft was essential on account of the central timing valve gear; secondly, the timing chain was more difficult to assemble; and thirdly, the air passage between the two cylinders was greatly reduced.

The running gear also displayed a number of innovative features for Horex. Rather than relying on the engine unit as a stressed member (which its full unit-construction layout would have allowed), the frame was a full duplex cradle affair that enclosed the engine. However, as if to make the point that it was a prototype, the telescopic front forks and full-width alloy brake hubs appeared to be standard production Regina components. I say appeared, as in reality, the hub diameter had been increased to 190mm on both wheels.

In place of the plunger rear suspension, which the production Horex models employed at that time, the Imperator prototype featured an entirely new and bang-up-to-date full swinging-arm system. This incorporated twin, hydraulically-damped suspension units.

There was no oil tank, as the engine used wet sump lubrication. A large 20-litre alloy fuel tank, sponge-rubber saddle, hand-beaten alloy tail fairing, and a chromed exhaust system with short cobby megaphones, rising slightly at the ends, completed the specification.

With only 30 bhp and a claimed 95mph maximum, the 1951 racing overhead-camshaft Imperator twin was clearly a development prototype, as the factory claimed, rather than a serious racer. Towards the end of that year, the new twin appeared in roadster form. This closely followed the lines of the racer in its basic engineering format, both as regards the power unit and cycle components.

The next Horex racer was this prototype sohc 497cc (65 x 75mm) parallel twin which appeared in May 1951, viewed from the nearside...

...and a close-up of the engine from the offside.

Then it was revealed that the bore and stroke measurements were 65 x 75mm, giving a capacity of 497cc. Although commentators at the time expected it to enter full-scale production, in fact, this did not happen (although smaller 392 and 452cc Imperator roadster twins did appear later). Instead, 1952 saw Horex hard at work on various versions of its bestselling Regina single.

That year also saw the Bad Homburg factory become committed to a full racing programme, with not only the introduction of a revised 500 parallel twin, now with double overhead camshafts, but also new 250 and 350cc singles. Although the singles had full works backing, they were the work of the gifted engineer/rider Roland Schnell, who had previously worked wonders with his super-quick Parilla specials.

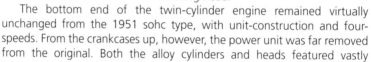

All three of the new racers made their debut at Germany's early-season Dieburger race meeting on 6th April. Interest naturally centred around the half-litre twin, two examples of which were wheeled to the line by Friedl Schon and Hugo Schmitz. As on the Schnell 250 and 350cc singles, the frames closely resembled the trend-setting Norton Featherbed type, except that on the Horex models, the bracing tubes did not cross over near the steering head.

In 1952 a revised 500 Horex twin was brought out. A major change was to dohc. A distinctive feature was the tail fairing assembly.

The bottom end of the twin-cylinder engine remained virtually unchanged from the 1951 sohc type, with unit-construction and four-speeds. From the crankcases up, however, the power unit was far removed from the original. Both the alloy cylinders and heads featured vastly increased finning and, of course, the central chain drove twin overhead camshafts. Two valves (although some pundits had suggested four) per cylinder were featured, together with exposed hairpin valve springs. Carburation was taken care of by twin 29mm Dell'Orto SS1 racing instruments with a single, remote, central float chamber. The carbs themselves were quite steeply inclined at 45 degrees. Ignition was provided by a twin-spark, crankshaft-mounted magneto.

Transmission was taken care of by a clutch which had been modified to a dry type, with a massive air scoop on the offside of the crankcase. Interestingly, although the gearbox was housed within the crankcases, the engine was not of true unit-construction. In fact, the gearbox was contained in a separate, cylindrical casing which was free to rotate within its housing. As its mainshaft was off centre, turning it to a new position provided adjustment of the duplex primary chain. The cycle parts were largely unchanged from the previous year, except for the frame itself. However, there were subtle improvements.

Introduced to Horex by the gifted engineer/rider Roland Schnell, Hermann Gablenz is seen here on one of the Schnell-Horex dohc 250 singles, in April 1952.

Works rider Friedl Schon with the 'new' Horex dohc, 6th April 1952, at the German early-season Dieburger meeting.

For example, the forks not only sported rubber gaiters, but also a strong front fork brace/mudguard support, while the rider was provided with an additional pair of foot-rests, set further to the rear. These were fitted in such a position on the rear spindle, aft of the rear units, that the pilot could lay almost flat (a scheme pioneered by Guzzi star Fergus Anderson) along the fast straights. In the days before streamlining, this stance was often worth an extra 5mph to the maximum speed.

As for the smaller bikes, Roland Schnell had certainly waved his magic wand to create a pair of highly interesting Horex 'specials'. However, the 250 and 350 were so alike that the observer needed to inspect the respective model closely to identify exactly which one it was - the only real give-away was the background colour of its racing plates.

The dominant feature of each was the massive casing for the drive chain to the inlet camshaft, which gave them a similar appearance to the works AJS three-valve model. On the nearside of the camshaft housing, there was a further chain drive to the exhaust cam. Again, there were exposed hairpin valve springs, and two sparking plugs were fitted (one on each side of the head), although quite often only one was actually employed. Ignition was by a Bosch magneto, and the rev-counter was driven off the exhaust cam.

As with the twin, carburation was via a steeply inclined Dell'Orto SS1 instrument. An unusual feature was the very extensive finning on the crankcase. This was not an oil container, because the lubrication was dry sump, an alloy tank being fitted below the nose of the racing seat. There was a separate, four-speed, close-ratio gearbox.

The first classic appearance of the new team came at Berne, where the 1952 Swiss GP was staged over the tree-lined 4.5 mile Bremgarten circuit on 18th-19th May. Before this, in a non-championship race on Sunday 12th May, at Hockenheim, Friedl Schon had shown what the new double-knocker twin was capable of by taking it to a sensational victory in the Senior race, at an average speed of 99.73mph. Unfortunately, the venture into Switzerland was to be rather different...

The meeting was staged in hot, sunny weather, and there was a large number of works entries, not only from Germany (BMW, DKW and Horex), but also Italy (Moto Guzzi, Gilera, MV and Parilla) and Britain (AJS and Norton). In the 250 race, a Horex, ridden by Hermann Gablenz, came home eighth (and last). On the 350, Schnell himself could finish no higher than 16th out of 20 finishers, and in the 500cc event, both Horex twins retired ignominiously.

Engine and gearbox assembly from a 350 Schnell-Horex 500 single, August 1952.

A couple of months later, for the German Grand Prix at the Solitude circuit on 22nd July, Horex made a bid for classic honours once more. The Bad Homburg factory even signed up the leading British Continental circus star, Bill Petch, in an attempt to gain honours. However, whilst practising, Petch had a valve drop on the 500 dohc twin and was a non-starter in the race. Even so, he was reported as having been impressed enough to ride the bike later that season. If this was not bad enough, another Horex rider, Kurt Mansfeld, had injured his back after crashing another of the twins in practice.

However, in the 250cc race, Horex enjoyed some consolation to these problems when Gablenz took one of the dohc singles to a magnificent third place behind race-winner Felgenheier, on a works DKW twin, and leading Guzzi privateer, Thorn-Prikker.

At the end of the season, persistent rumours concerning the poor performance and reliability of the 500cc twin were finally confirmed when it was announced, in October, that the machine was being scrapped. If Horex fielded a twin the following year, it would be completely redesigned, possibly with gear-driven camshafts.

This proved to be accurate information. When the 1953 racing season commenced, although the Schnell singles were virtually unchanged from 1952, this certainly did not apply to the larger-bore parallel twin. As forecast, the engine had received a considerable amount of extra tuning, although it still retained chain drive to the overhead camshafts.

1952 Horex 500 Imperator twin.

The gearbox and clutch had been completely redesigned and repositioned, while the clutch had been transferred to the rear offside of the engine - to the position formerly held by the gearbox. This, in turn, had been fitted in a more conventional position within the centre of the crankcase. The gearchange pedal was now on the offside.

A revised, much smaller, housing was fitted in front of the exposed clutch in place of the crankshaft generator assembly, which had been replaced by a much simpler, total-loss battery/coil system. The carburettors had been mounted on much longer induction manifolds which carried them up to a position almost immediately beneath the seat.

Roland Schnell was responsible for creating a family of dohc Horex singles during 1952-1954. This is a 350cc in August 1952.

The frame, front forks and wheels remained unchanged, but the rear tail fairing had been deleted. A new seat, deeply-scalloped alloy fuel tank and an alloy fairing assembly had been fitted. Finally, a new exhaust system with shallow-taper megaphones, and rear shocks sporting exposed springs completed the facelift.

1952 Horex 350 Regina.

Although they took part in the German National Championships, the Horex equipe's main thrust in 1953 was in the classics. These got under way that year in the Isle of Man, but Horex did not join the fray until the second round in Holland. Unfortunately, the Dutch TT at Assen was not to prove a happy hunting ground that year, as not one Horex lasted the distance.

A week later came the Belgian GP over the superfast Spa Francorchamps circuit. Obviously, the pace did not entirely agree with the Bad Homburg machinery, Fritz Klager's 17th position in the 350cc race on one of the Schnell singles being the best result. A couple of weeks after this came the German GP at Schotten. This was destined to be a meeting beset with controversy.

Horex 350cc twin prototype 1954

Engine:	Air-cooled parallel twin with dohc, inclined cylinders and full unit construction. Bevel driven cams.
Capacity:	349cc.
Bore & stroke:	60 x 61.6mm.
Compression ratio:	9.5:1
Lubrication:	Wet sump, gear driven pump.
Gearbox:	Five-speeds.
Clutch:	Dry, multi-plate.
Frame:	Backbone, steel. Engine assembly hanging underneath with no front downtube.
Suspension:	Front leading link with forks; rear pivoted swinging arm with twin shocks.
Brakes:	200mm drums front and rear.
Tyres:	3.00 x 19 front, 3.25 x 18 rear.
Dryweight:	155kg.
Max power:	38bhp @ 9,000rpm.
Max speed:	119mph.

First of all, the majority of foreign riders on works machinery refused to take part on the grounds that the ten-mile circuit was too dangerous for the latest 350 and 500cc Grand Prix machinery. This came after numerous trees had been felled in the vicinity of the more difficult corners.

Then the status of the 250cc race was affected when Enrico Lorenzetti fell from his machine while entering the pits during practice and injured his foot; his team-mate, Fergus Anderson, announced that he had no intention of racing. Thus, Montanari rode the only factory Moto Guzzi in the event. German riders, perhaps because of their familiarity with the circuit, expressed no concern about it.

The Schotten track wound through the picturesque Vogel mountains, some 2,400ft above sea level, the road abounding in steep gradients and sinuous turns. It was lined by trees for almost its entire length.

Towards the end of the lap, the road dropped steeply through a series of acute hairpin corners. In the main, the surface was of concrete, and where the concrete sections had broken up, repairs had been carried out with tar. Added to this was a poor safety record, including Geoff Duke's 1952 accident which had ruined his chances of retaining the 500cc World Championship that year.

With much of the significant competition not taking part, Klager did well in the opening stages of the 350 race, holding fifth position before finally retiring. In the 250 event, which followed, the other Schnell/Horex double-knocker single ridden by Georg Braun, finished ninth - not a bad result considering that there was a full complement of both NSU and DKW works machinery, plus Montanari's Guzzi.

However, the really outstanding result for Horex came in the Senior race. Here, the factory's new signing, H.P. Muller, riding an enlarged dohc single - not one of the twins - disputed the lead with the works BMW team headed by Walter Zeller. At the end, Muller was placed third - an excellent debut ride on a brand-new bike!

The Horex twin had its first race victory at the International Hockenheim meeting in May 1952. While all the other classes went to foreign entrants, Schon scored the only German victory in the 500cc race, leaving a gaggle of British Nortons far behind.

Unfortunately, this taste of glory was somewhat spoilt when the FIM decided that the results of the 350 and 500cc races would not count towards the world title. Thus, the points won were deleted. The results gained at Schotten convinced the Horex management to drop the ill-fated twin and concentrate upon the Schnell singles. This proved a wise move, with Schnell and Müller gaining some notable results that season in both the classics and the German National Championships.

Schnell also had a hand in some of the development work on the Horex production roadsters, including a new front fork assembly.

Horex continued its support of the racing programme into 1954, the season getting under way in promising fashion with victory in the 250 race of the Grand Prix of the Saar, run over the famous two-mile 'round-the-houses' St. Wendel road circuit. Riding one of the double-knocker singles, Georg Braun averaged 57.6mph (this should be compared with the 500cc class in which the winning speed was only 60.6mph!).

1953 Horex 350 Regina Sport.

The following week, Fritz Klager scored a superb third place against the cream of the world's riders in the 350 race at Hockenheim. With Müller now a full-time NSU works rider, Klager and Schnell, together with Braun, made up the Horex team. The machinery comprised the latest dohc singles in 250, 350 and 500cc engine capacities. The 1954 bikes sported streamlining that was based very closely on the 'bird-beak' type employed by Moto Guzzi on their 1953 works machinery. Like that of the Mandello team, this was in hand-beaten, polished alloy, the front mudguard and fairing being seen very much as one integral assembly. Some of the machines were equipped with the Schnell-designed front fork assembly, too.

Even better was to come, when later that month, Braun created a minor sensation by finishing second at the 17th international Eifelrennen on his 500cc Horex single. The race-winner was Norton works star Ray Amm. Braun also had the satisfaction of coming home in front of the entire BMW works entry.

It was Braun who, at the beginning of July, made more headline news when he debuted a brand new Horex during practice for the Belgian GP. This was another parallel twin, but one that owed absolutely nothing to the earlier overweight and unreliable examples. Although it was not actually used in the race, because of a minor lubrication fault, none the less, it put up some very respectable lap times.

Designed by the Austrian engineer Ludwig Apfelbeck (later employed by BMW for design work on its car cylinder heads), the impressive-looking newcomer employed a dohc engine which showed clear influence from the latest NSU Rennmax twin. The Horex power unit carried its oil in a massive alloy sump tank, under the engine's crankcase, and was nearly square with its 60 x 61.6mm bore and stroke dimensions, which added up to a capacity of 349cc. Power output was 38 bhp at 9,000rpm.

Drive to the rev-counter was taken from the offside end of the exhaust camshaft. Hairpin valve springs were employed, while the large-diameter valves were in a special material. Fuel was supplied by twin Dell'Orto carbs, and the ignition was taken care of by a Bosch battery/coil system.

The five-speed gearbox was built in unit with the engine, and a dry, multi-plate clutch was employed. Horex had chosen a backbone-type frame, with the engine assembly hanging underneath and no front

The Apfelbeck-designed prototype dohc 348cc Horex twin of 1954.

A 1954 Schnell-Horex 500 single, with fashionable 'bird beak' streamlining.

downtube. The rear portion formed the pivot point for the swinging arm. A pair of leading-link front forks were of a totally new design for the factory.

The cosmetic details were dominated by a fuel tank that was designed very much as a unit with the handlebar fairing and front mudguard, providing the maximum wind-cheating effect.

The new twin's only other classic outing was to be the 1954 German GP at Solitude where, in front of a vast half-million crowd, Georg Braun came home sixth, averaging 80.73mph for the 24-lap, 99.57 mile race. As a point of comparison, Klager, on one of the singles, finished way back in 17th place, a lap behind.

Friedl Münch, with Derek Rickman in 1969; bike is a Horex-engined Rickman prototype.

The Modern Era

Horex, as a motorcycle manufacturing concern, all but ceased to exist at the end of the 1950s. However, several enthusiasts throughout Germany continued to keep the name alive well into the sixties, by building machines from spares or rebuilding older bikes. One of these was Friedl Münch (see chapter 10). Another was Alfred Petith, the latter constructing a 700cc v-twin by grafting a pair of three-fifty Resident singles into a common crankcase. The resulting machine proved the star entry at the 1965 Elephant Rally.

Later still, in the 1970s Fritz Roth, Klaus Ibsen and Friedl Münch attempted to relaunch the Horex brand name. At first this centred around an enlarged Münch Mammoth Superbike, but these efforts, or at least those connected with the Münch machine were to come to little. However, Roth pushed ahead and subsequently marketed a number of machines, including Italian Testi's and Portugese SIS lightweights under the Horex banner.

But Roth had not given up his plan for larger capacity machines. So he contracted the Italian HRD concern to build a café racer, an enduro and even a pukka racing version, using the ohc Austrian Rotax single-cylinder engine, in either 503.91cc (89 x 81mm) or 562cc (94 x 81mm) capacities.

All three models had beautiful lines, but few had been manufactured before HRD failed in 1986. And even though Fritz Roth had other business interests (including the import rights for Ducati and Laverda at that time), this really was the end of the Horex rebirth. However, with the growth of the classic scene, Horex machines have become one of the most popular in Germany, with both collectors and enthusiasts alike; so the famous old Bad Hamburg marque lives on through nostalgia.

Unfortunately, this was to be the last occasion when Horex entered factory machines in a classic race, as by now the company had begun to feel the first effects of the approaching downturn in sales and subsequent wholesale depression and closures within the industry.

After this, it was left to private tuners to fly the Horex flag, which they did with some level of success into the 1960s, several years after the Bad Homburg factory had ceased motorcycle production in 1957. A notable entrant and tuner of Horex machines was one Friedl Münch (see Chapter 10), who built much of his early reputation with these machines.

König

7

König 500, ridden by Dutchman Dick Alblas in Grands Prix during the 1970s.

Early in 1969, Dipl. Ing. Dieter König, managing director and chief engineer of the König company, decided to build a 500cc-class, solo road-racing motorcycle for Rolf Braun.

Based in West Berlin, the König factory had built up quite a name during the 1960s, but not for motorcycles, for it was the maker of a successful range of multi-cylinder, two-stroke engines for powerboat racing. It was one of these modified production boat engines, a horizontally-opposed, water-cooled, four-cylinder two-stroke, that formed the basis of the bike engine.

Despite a lack of experience at the new game, König was not content to start at club or even national level, the new machine first appeared in the West German Grand Prix at Hockenheim on 11th May 1969. Even on paper, the König engine showed promise. Together with a Manx Norton racing gearbox and clutch, it weighed 55kg (110lb) less than a Norton engine without its gearbox. Usable power was available from 7,000rpm, and its peak power of 68bhp was produced at 9,000rpm.

In effect, the engine comprised a pair of flat-twins, mounted side by side in the common crankcase. The pressed-up, three-bearing, single crankshaft ran across the frame. Bore and stroke measurements of the four cylinders were classic 'stroker', 54 x 54mm, while each of the Mahle pistons had a single Dykes-type ring. A belt-driven pump circulated water through a small radiator and a reservoir under the engine.

For bike racing, the boat engine had been equipped with a pair of East German BVF carburettors to improve acceleration. Each of these supplied petroil mixture to one pair of 'fore-and-aft' cylinders, which fired at the same time, while induction was controlled by a single disc valve situated on top of the crankcase. The exhausts from the front and rear pairs of cylinders were siamesed and ran into a massive expansion chamber over the gearbox.

Designer and company boss Dieter König with his prototype solo racer early in 1969.

However, the first prototype was very much a development vehicle rather than a pukka racing unit, and Dieter König fully expected to encounter teething problems. His main fear concerned the cooling system, which he considered (correctly) would need a radiator of larger capacity. Essentially, 1969 wore on through a series of problem-solving exercises, rather than any real racing. However, 1970 saw the development process take a giant leap forward with the addition of the Australian continental circus star, Johnny Dodds as rider, and New Zealander Kim Newcombe as development engineer.

By the time the König was raced seriously in the Dutch TT at Assen that year, power was up to around 75bhp and the gearbox was a six-speeder comprising a Norton shell and Austrian Schafleitner internals. A Krober electronic tachometer was fitted, while a major revision to the breathing arrangements was the use of a pair of high-level expansion chambers.

Although the machine was fitted with an extra-large radiator, it was a non-finisher due to problems which again centred on ineffective cooling. Despite this, the two-stroke four had impressed with its straight-line speed and acceleration. The next move was to fit a smaller radiator and apply more attention to forced airflow. The smaller radiator also permitted a much narrower fairing, which helped the racer's penetration at higher speeds.

A new frame was promised once the engine had been perfected, but for the time being, it remained much as in the original 1969 design. However, the bottom frame rails were omitted and a square-section swinging arm was used in place of the old round tube one. Front forks were Ceriani, the rear Girling, and the racing brakes Fontana.

Also in the pipeline was a larger-capacity version, rumoured at the time to be of 800cc, but with similar external dimensions. This had already been used successfully on the other side of the Atlantic where, in the USA, König-powered midget racing cars were producing a claimed 120bhp on alcohol. In June 1970, Newcombe stated, 'On petrol, the figure should be around the 90bhp mark.'

Another view of the König prototype. It is difficult to imagine that this highly original unit had begun life as a racing outboard engine for powerboats.

König outfit making a nose first landing, Isle of Man TT.

101

Dodds continued as König's development rider through 1971, prompted not just by the engine's potential, but also by the earlier (and expensive!) failure of the Italian Linto four-stroke twin, which he and other circus riders had purchased. However, during the season, the Australian's only placing within a GP top ten was a tenth at Hockenheim for the 1971 German GP.

Over the following winter, a major redesign took place. For the first time, the original square engine dimensions were dispensed with, to be replaced by four cylinders with the short stroke of 50mm and a 56mm bore, giving 492.6cc. The crank was redesigned with two main bearings on the drive side, one at the opposite end, and a fourth in the middle. Lubrication was still by petroil (at a ratio of 16:1), and because the mixture was directed straight at the caged-roller big-ends, there was no need for the usual two-stroke slots in the con-rod eyes, providing additional strength. The small-ends were uncaged needle rollers.

By the time the Australian Johnny Dodds began to race this 500 König during the early 1970s, the engine was delivering around 75bhp.

Another major change was a 45mm twin-choke Solex carburettor, still controlled by a single inlet disc. The drive to this, from the right hand end of the crankshaft, looked impossibly weak. Not only did the toothed belt have to change direction from the vertical to horizontal, as it circled the pulleys, but the two rollers which effected the change required the belt to twist through 90 degrees each time to offer its smooth side to the rollers. In practice, however, the arrangement proved quite adequate, as did the similarly weak-looking pair of synthetic rubber bands which drove the water impeller.

However, a feature which did cause problems was the exclusive use of chains in the transmission system. The difficulty centred around the fact that it was still only an engine which its constructors had fitted with a gearbox and a clutch from another source. This usually meant the use of not only the secondary drive chain, but also as many as three triplex chains in the primary transmission, a fact which was to prove an embarrassment later.

The revised power unit made its debut at the 1972 West German GP, staged around the twists and turns of the difficult Nürburgring. By now, Dodds had left the team, to be replaced by Newcombe, who was doing his own riding, and German Ernst Hiller.

The line-up was formidable, with a pair of MV Agustas ridden by World Champion Giacomo Agostini and Alberto Pagani, works Kawasaki triples with Dave Simmonds and the Japanese rider Araoka, together with a factory Swedish Husqvarna ridden by Bo Granath. These were backed up by a host of leading privateers, including Jack Findlay and Billie Nelson.

Amazingly, the race not only proved that Newcombe's winter development had been spot on, but also that his riding talent was something special. The New Zealander was headed only by

Close-up showing the various belt drives on the König engine.

the pair of super-fast Italian multis and scored a brilliant third place ahead of Simmonds' Kawasaki. Then came Hiller on the second König, with the Husky sixth.

More development work meant that the team did not appear at every round, although Newcombe took another third at the Sachsenring, East Germany, behind Agostini and Rod Gould on a Yamaha. This was followed

König works rider and development engineer Kim Newcombe, Hutchinson 100, Brands Hatch, 5th August 1973 - a week before his fatal accident at Silverstone. Even so he was runner up to Phil Read and MV in the final World Championship points table that year.

by a fifth at Anderstorp, Sweden, and a tenth in the French GP at Clermont Ferrand. The Swedish result was truly something, as *Motor Cycle News* reported in their 26th July 1972 issue under the headline 'Impressive Kim'. The article reported, 'After the New Zealander had come through to fifth place after being last on the first lap, Newcombe said, 'I had to push to the first corner before it would fire, and then the clutch cable broke on the third lap and I was getting into slides on every corner.' The machine's performance proved that air vents he had styled into the fairing seemed to have solved previous overheating problems.'

A newcomer, Paul Eickelburg, had joined the team mid-season, gaining a third place in the Yugoslav GP and an eighth at the Dutch TT. He was also responsible for several non-championship continental internationals in which Königs performed even better.

Typical was the 500 race at Chimay, Belgium, on Sunday 9th July. Here, Kawasaki team leader Dave Simmonds had looked set for victory until the Englishman's engine seized after three laps. Then Hiller, on another Kawasaki, took over. However, with three laps to go, the slow-starting König rider, Eickelburg, got by to take the flag 35 seconds ahead of Hiller, followed by yet another König rider.

Perhaps the most impressive König performance of 1972, however, was when Eickelburg won the 500 race at an international meeting held over the Hengelo circuit in Holland on 27th August. In the process, he set a new outright lap record for the three-mile course at 91.28mph - 3mph faster than the legendary Jarno Saarinen had achieved in the earlier 350 race on his works Yamaha. Dave Simmonds had taken the lead from the start and was pursued by 350 Yamaha-mounted Chas Mortimer. Then, Simmonds had to pit-stop to wire up a loose expansion chamber, allowing Mortimer to take over. However, he could not match the speed of Eickelburg, who had made another slow start, but now passed him.

It was the New Zealander, Kim Newcombe, who turned the König into a competitive racer. He was gifted both as a rider and as an engineer. Seen here at the Dutch TT, 23rd June 1973.

In 1972 a 680cc version of the König four had also been introduced - while both 500 and 680 units had debuted in sidecar events. Here, both Rolf Steinhausen (with a fifth in France and a fourth in Austria) and the British Boret brothers, Gerry and Nick, (with a brilliant third in the Isle of Man) had proved the potential of the König for sidecar use at the highest level. As 1973 dawned, the König horizontally-opposed four was set to challenge BMW's long supremacy in sidecar Grand Prix racing.

König 'Wedge' of the Boret brothers, early 1973. Actually it was the handiwork of its constructor John Renwick of Renwick Developments.

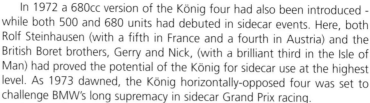

Its use for the sidecar class had both technical and economic attractions. Spares for the BMW Rennsport engine were becoming even more scarce and, therefore, highly expensive, while the machines fetched a price that almost no one could afford. In contrast, the Berlin outboard-based engine units were available at a reasonable price and, perhaps more importantly, with readily available spares at a fraction of the price being asked for BMW components.

There were problems with the König, however. Besides the transmission weakness mentioned earlier, the sidecar constructor also had to cope with the fact that the König had a total lack of engine braking compared to the BMW twin. So an outfit needed powerful brakes, either massive drums or a pair of the discs which were starting to take over from drums at the front.

The very first Grand Prix of 1973, staged at Le Castellet, France, saw König machines take honours in both the two- and three-wheel categories. In the solo class, Newcombe gained a fifth at the start of what was to be a year both of sweet success and bitter tragedy.

However, the chair-men really flew the Berlin company's flag that day, three of the first six outfits home being Konigs. Although World Champions Klaus Enders and Ralf Engelhardt kept their works BMW ahead, they were hard pressed for most of the race by the König pair, Jeff Gawley and Peter Sales. They were ahead of Schwarzel and Kleis on another König, with Steinhausen and Scheurer on yet another coming in fifth.

Gawley showed his form again with a repeat performance behind Enders at the next round, the Austrian GP at the Salzburgring. Following these early successes, many observers were tipping him as a future world champion. However, the lack of funds and mechanical problems meant that his championship thrust was all but over, his only other top-six placing being another second, this time in Belgium mid-season. The Englishman finally finished fifth in the world series.

Another König pair, however, came through to second in the world series. This was the team of Schwarzel and Kleis who, besides their fifth in the opener in France, scored in almost every round, the best of which was a second place at Hockenheim. Although König did not win a single sidecar GP, yet

The Renwick König in action at Snetterton, April 1973, with Gerry Boret at the controls and brother Nick in the chair.

another second from the Boret brothers in Holland (their only GP finish that year) meant that the flat-four 'strokers' had mounted a serious challenge to BMW's supremacy.

Confirming this were the speed-trap figures carried out during the Isle of Man TT, when the fastest 500cc sidecar was the Boret's König at 130mph, while in the 750cc class Gawley's 680cc König was fastest, screaming through the electronic eye at 136mph. This was a record for the chairs, beating the previous best of 134.8mph, set by Helmut Fath with his four-cylinder 500cc Münch URS in 1969.

In the solo class, 1973 saw the König reach its development peak, one man achieving worldclass results. This was Kim Newcombe, who not only scored the marque's only solo Grand Prix victory, but also gained the runner-up position in the World Championships, splitting the MV Agusta pair of Phil Read and Giacomo Agostini in the process. However, this excellent result was marred by disaster when the New Zealander was tragically killed on 12th August while competing at Silverstone, with only one round left to go at Jarama in Spain.

Technical details of the Renwick 'Wedge' showing engine, gearbox, frame, rear wheel, Krober electronic tacho and ignition. The steering and suspension owed more to car rather than motorcycle practice.

Jeff Gawley was the highest placed König in the 1973 Sidecar world title race with a 5th over all. His best results came at the beginning of the season with runner up spots in the first two rounds - France and Austria. Then he gained another 2nd midway through the year in Belgium. Note early use of hydraulically operated disc front brake.

Following his fifth in the season's opener in France, Newcombe had taken a third in Austria, victory in Yugoslavia, second in Holland, fourth in Belgium, third in Sweden and, finally, fourth in Finland. However, it was his Yugoslavian win at the Opatija circuit on 17th June which created the headlines; 'Newcombe takes the lead with first Grand Prix win,' as *Motor Cycle News* reported it. Newcombe summed up, 'I just can't believe I have won. We have been trying for so long to get the König over the line first and now all the effort seems worthwile.'

Following the New Zealander's death, much of the momentum seemed to go out of König's race effort, certainly in the solo class where there were virtually no successes on two wheels in 1974. History records that a König finished fourth in the 500 West German GP at the Nürburgring that year, but this was a hollow victory, as there were only four finishers after the race was spoilt by a mass withdrawal of star riders on safety grounds.

On three wheels, however, it was to prove a totally different story, with Konigs scoring three classic victories and securing second (Schwarzel) and fifth (Steinhausen) in the title chase. Added to this were four seconds, including George O'Dell and Barry Boldison's runner-up spot in the Isle of Man TT, so that it soon became apparent that Konigs had real championship potential for 1975.

Kim Newcombe leads the field on his König at a very wet Brands Hatch in 1973.

The chances of this had been greatly reinforced by two factors. The first was the engine's greatly enhanced reliability; the second was the withdrawal of König's major competitor. Many had said that the 1974 championship had only been retained for BMW by the highly-skilled riding of the victors, Klaus Enders and passenger Ralf Engelhardt, taking their sixth and fifth world titles respectively. Accustomed to winning easily, that year they had seen ever-increasing competition from König, which kept the title in dispute until the very last round. It may have been this which influenced the BMW team's decision to retire at the end of the season.

Enders' sponsor and tuner, Dieter Büsch, transferred his allegiance to Steinhausen and König for 1975, and this faith was repaid in full when Steinhausen and Josef Huber took the World Championship on the Büsch/König by winning three of the seven rounds staged. (An eighth, scheduled for Imola, in Italy, was not run due to organisational problems.)

In fact, except for the domestic West German event, which Rolf Biland won on a Yamaha, every round went to a König; Schwarzel and Huber won two rounds, and Schmidt and Matile another. As a result, König also took second and fourth places in the championship that year.

Rolf Steinhausen/Wolfgang Kalauch (500 Büsch-König) at Ramsey Hairpin during their successful drive to second place in the 1977 Sidecar TT.

At the start of the 1975 season, the success of the König engine had prompted the Austrian gearbox specialist, Michael Schafleitner, to build a batch of 20 special six-speed gear clusters for use in König powered sidecar outfits. He commented at the time, 'A closer set of ratios are needed than any of my previous designs, to make full use of the König's power output.' This was true, as although the solo König could make use of power from as low as 4-5,000rpm, the extra demands (and weight) of a racing sidecar outfit greatly reduced this ability so that the engine had to be kept spinning above 8,000rpm to produce its maximum output and torque. The Büsch-tuned König was rumoured to produce well over 90bhp, substantially up on the 1975-6 production racing engine, which turned out a claimed 85bhp at 10,000rpm.

1975 was the final year in which works-supported Königs were raced in the solo class. Early in the year, Frenchman Christian Leon, dropped by the French Kawasaki team, signed up to race the Königs used by the late Kim Newcombe. In February, he had tested both 500 and 680cc Königs at the Paul Ricard circuit and was reported to have been very impressed. On standard engines, he got round in 1 minute, 15.6 seconds, four-fifths of a second outside the lap record held by the late Jarno Saarinen. Leon had two 500s, plus two spare engines, and one 680cc, plus a spare engine. The 1975 version of the solo 500cc had the engine tuned to allow

Rolf Steinhauser's Büsch-König was the top three-wheeler at the Isle of Man TT, June 1975. He also won the Austrian and Belgium rounds on his way to becoming World Champion that year, passengered by Josef Huber.

*Rolf Steinhausen and
Josef Huber, World Champions
and TT winners for the second
time in 1976.*

the exhaust system to run under the seat, while the 680cc sported magnesium wheels, triple Brembo discs and Marzocchi front forks. The Leon deal was part of what was termed, at the time, 'a major factory effort'. Other Königs were scheduled to be raced in solo events that year by Horst Lahfield, former West German Junior Champion, but in the World Championships, the team was dogged by a series of retirements. Only three finishes in the top ten were made all season, with Lahfield taking a fine fifth at the Salzburgring in the Austrian GP and a sixth in the Finnish GP at Imatra. Leon's only placing was a seventh at Hockenheim.

In 1976, the solo effort was over. However, Steinhausen retained his world title, with victories in Austria, the Isle of Man and Belgium, while Schwarzel won at the Nürburgring. Many other excellent results were also gained by König-powered outfits at all levels, from club events to Grands Prix.

This reign, however, was to be very brief, for other, more suitable, engines were starting to appear - notably from Yamaha and Fath. Both of these power units featured an integral gearbox and clutch, something which the König never had. Thus, 1977 witnessed all of König's top contenders for championship honours defecting to other engines.

Steinhausen now had a Büsch-tuned Yamaha, while Schwarzel went with ARO-Fath power. The result was inevitable, although the previously unknown partnership of Venus and Bittermann took a fine second place at Hockenheim, the highest-placed König outfit in the 1977 World Series was Steinhausen's Büsch-König, which was sixth at the same event, before the team switched to Yamaha power. The challenge from the tiny Berlin factory was over.

A few 680cc Königs were raced solo at private level, and two of these were British efforts. One was the Crossier Special, ridden by Scotsman Bob Steel, while the other was owned by Roy Baldwin and ridden by Jerry Lancaster.

From 1977 on, however, virtually nothing was heard of König, the remaining machinery (both solo and sidecar) disappearing from the scene very quickly. Even though König's time at the top was short, none the less, it scored some excellent results at the highest level in the mid 1970s. Consequently, it has earned a permanent place in the history of motorcycle road racing, even though it never built a roadster or ventured into other branches of the sport.

Kreidler

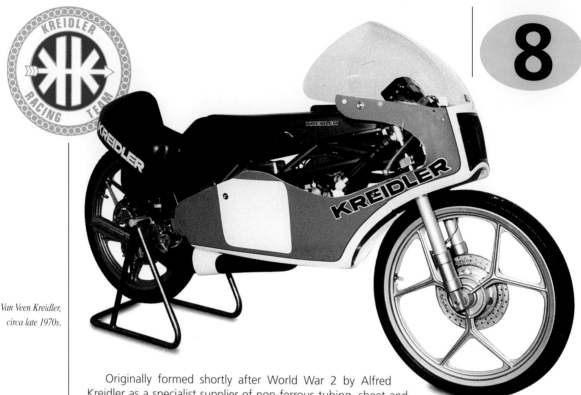

8

Van Veen Kreidler,
circa late 1970s.

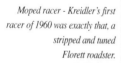

Moped racer - Kreidler's first
racer of 1960 was exactly that, a
stripped and tuned
Florett roadster.

Originally formed shortly after World War 2 by Alfred Kreidler as a specialist supplier of non-ferrous tubing, sheet and wire, Kreidler GmbH decided to enter the ranks of motorcycle manufacturing in 1951. The company's production facilities were situated at Kornwestheim, just to the north of the great city of Stuttgart, capital of Baden-Wurtemburg and the largest and one of the most beautiful cities of south-western Germany.

Dr. Kreidler's diversification centred around the design and manufacture of a 49cc moped, the K50. Built for reliability, the 38 x 44mm bore and stroke, piston-ported two-stroke soon became a firm favourite, and sales reflected this by rocketing Kreidler to the top of West Germany's booming ultra-lightweight market. Cheap and easy to run, the K50 attracted many a youngster to motorcycling, and it was only a matter of time before the first Kreidler was put to competitive use. This came in late 1958, initially off-road, but soon afterwards in road racing, as the first ranks of 50cc tarmac racers began to appear in the Fatherland.

Essentially, a group of enthusiasts at the Kornwestheim works decided to build a machine based on the recently-introduced Florett (Foil). However, even for this first prototype the project had to be authorised by the autocratic Dr. Kreidler.

In reality, this first racer was a standard Florett, with pressed-steel frame, Earles-type front forks, a mildly-tuned engine and a set of specially-made, close-ratio gears. Even the fan cooling of the Florett was retained, together with the road-going silencer. The Kreidler was the quietest, if not the quickest, machine in the race! Even so, it was surprisingly successful, which prompted Dr. Kreidler to take a more serious interest. The result was victory in the 1960 West German 50cc Racing Championship series.

Rudolf Kunz preparing for world
record attempts, Utah 1965.

A jubilant Hans-Georg Anscheidt with victor's laurels, after being proclaimed FIM Coupe d'Europe Champion in 1961.

For 1961, the sport's organising body, the FIM, decided to put 50cc racing on a firmer footing by instigating the Coupe d'Europe. In effect, this was a series of international races with a minimum duration requirement, run on rules which normally applied to the full Grand Prix events.

A total of eight race organisers staged Coupe d'Europe events during 1961 - three in Belgium, two in Germany and one each in Holland, Spain and Yugoslavia. Rather surprisingly, neither Italy nor Britain showed much interest, although the tiddlers had been popular in both countries for several years.

Though Kreidler did not contest all the rounds, it still came out victorious. This was due, in no small part, to the superb riding of one of its employees, Hans-Georg Anscheidt.

Born in East Prussia, at Konisberg, in 1935, Anscheidt had started his motorcycling career in off-road competitions during 1953. With the urge to go faster, he switched to grass, cinder and sand races. Between 1957 and 1959, he won a total of 21 races out of the 40 he entered.

Shortly afterwards, he became a works rider when he took his Kreidler to a gold medal in the 1960 ISDT, while employed in the factory's testing and development department. It was also in 1960 that he became a road racer and subsequently won the Hockenheim Motor Cup for his factory.

Although still based on the production Florett engine, the 1961 Coupe d'Europe winning machine had been modified to rotary-valve induction halfway through the season. It also featured twin Dell'Orto carburettors and a six-speed gearbox. With a claimed power output of 8bhp, the ultra-lightweight flyer was capable of around 80mph.

Hans-Georg Anscheidt rode this much more purposeful Kreidler in 1961 to win the Coupe d'Europe title. He is shown here during the Hockenheim round.

The machine upon which Anscheidt's Renn (racing) Florett was based continued to sell in ever increasing numbers. By 1962, an astonishing 50 per cent of all powered two-wheelers sold in Germany were of Kreidler manufacture.

On this basis, one could be forgiven for thinking that the Kornwestheim plant would have sported a lavish competitions department. However, this was not the case. The development team, led by Dipl. Ing. Johannes Hilber (who had joined Kreidler from the aircraft industry), all worked in the standard production research and development office and returned there each Monday morning. Not only this, but all the riders, including Anscheidt, were recruited from the factory's staff. At that time, it was an unwritten rule that you had to work for the company to get a works ride!

1971 Van Veen team bikes. In the foreground is Jos Schurgers mount with round cylinder finning, whereas Jan de Vries machine in the background had square finning. The photograph was taken at Assen in June that year.

Bits-and-pieces Four.

During 1965, German racing enthusiast Karl Reese stunned the national Junior racing scene by fielding his own home-brewed KRD four-cylinder special. Ridden by Koichi Shimada, a Japanese living in Hamburg, it was a superbly crafted machine which would not have disgraced a full factory effort.

Begun back in 1959, the KRD (Karl Reese Developments) four employed a quartet of Kreidler 50cc cylinder barrels and cylinder heads, with the cylinders bored to fit oversize 40mm pistons (giving an engine displacement of 208cc). The crankcase was specially cast, as were several of the other engine components.

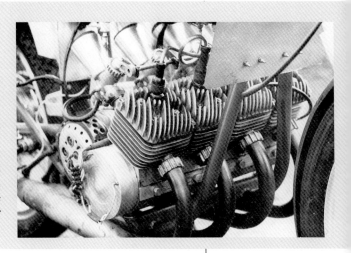

For 1962, the FIM introduced a full-blown 50cc World Championship series. In response to this, Kreidler set to and came up with a much improved machine to challenge the world.

Even before this, Kreidler realised that the conventional piston-ported, racing two-stroke, developed from the Florett roadster, was about at the end of its power line. Thus, in June 1961, during the later stages of the Coupe d'Europe, they had begun racing with a rotary-valve engine. Development continued through the winter months, with the result that the factory was ready to meet the Japanese onslaught when the first of the 1962 classics took place around the twists and turns of Montjuich Park, Barcelona, the scene of the Spanish GP in April 1962.

Like the Florett-based engine, the full GP unit employed a horizontal layout, the head pointing forward. To gain the maximum possible capacity, Hilber's team used a bore of 40mm and a stroke of 39.7mm to give 49.9cc. Amazingly, the crankshaft was taken directly from the production roadster, which spoke well of the reliability and engineering of Kreidler products. A special Mahle piston was used.

The cylinder barrel was cast in aluminium and finished with a 'pin-pricked' hard-chrome running surface. The idea was that the tiny holes would retain oil for improved lubrication, so important to a seizure-prone two-stroke.

In fact, Kreidler was the first German motorcycle manufacturer to use this system, which had been developed by Porsche for their high-performance cars. It should also be noted that another German marque, TWN (Triumph), had pioneered the chrome-plated cylinder bore on its production two-strokes in the immediate post-war period. There was also the use of magnesium for the outer engine covers.

For carburettors, Kreidler abandoned the Italian Dell'Ortos used in 1961 and fitted a pair of special Bings (one for each rotary valve) made to their specifications. The cost of these carbs was as much as the normal Florett sports moped!

The 1961 works Kreidler engine looked like this. Note rotary-valve induction, twin Dell'Orto UB carbs and comprehensive finning for head and barrel - 8bhp at 11,000rpm.

The cylinder heads were modified to provide a compression ratio of 11:1. Carburation was by four 20mm Bing instruments operated by a transverse shaft, with a single throttle cable. The carbs were fed by a pair of remotely mounted float chambers. Battery ignition was employed, with one coil per cylinder.

The four-speed gear cluster was in a special housing at the rear of the crankcase, with geared primary drive and a multi-plate, dry clutch. Housing the tiny four was a full loop duplex frame. The telescopic forks and front brake came from a Horex. Tyre sizes were 3.00 x 18 front and 3.25 x 18 rear.

On the test bench the KRD developed 26bhp at 10,800rpm - with a safe limit of 12,500rpm. This was enough to beat converted roadsters such as the Honda CB72 and Ducati ohc singles, if not pukka racers like the Aermacchi Ala d'Oro and Bultaco TSS.

The power was routed through a 12-speed gearbox. Actually, there were only four speeds, the other ratios being obtained by means of an external, three-speed overdrive controlled by a twistgrip on the handlebars. Even Hilber thought this excessive, but opted for it because the effective power only existed between 9,500 and 11,000rpm. For certain national events, however, including the German hill-climb championships, only eight ratios were used, simply because of the more-or-less constant gradients. The 12 ratios were intended solely for pukka Grand Prix action, not shorter courses.

Of course, the real problem with a highly-strung 50cc racing motorcycle was insufficient torque. As the power output and engine revolutions crept up, so this became even more apparent. Naturally, the Kreidler men did not use all 12 gears for each corner, nor even half of them, but they had enough gears to allow the right one to be selected for every corner on the circuit. Changing up was not a problem, the trick, according to Anscheidt, was 'remembering where you started on the down-changes.'

The 1962 racing Kreidler frame was manufactured from aircraft-quality, chrome-moly tubing. Unlike the 1961 version, this had a sort of parallel oval design, in which the two main tubes were one continuous unit, each running from the steering head down and back to support the engine and around and up to the steering head once more. They were cross-braced, not quite half-way back. A triangular pressing of steel was fitted at the rear of this twin-hoop system, furnishing the main engine mounting point, the swinging-arm pivot and a platform for the 6-volt, 7-amp/hour battery.

The Earles-type front fork used adjustable spring lugs, as in the previous year. Experience with racing these tiny machines had shown Kreidler that attention to the suspension system made up for any slight decrease in outright power output, compared to a rival who had a faster, but less well-handling motorcycle.

Anscheidt on the type of Kreidler used to contest the 1962, 50cc World Championship series.

Keeping the bike on the ground was one of the major problems with a dry weight of only 55kg (118lb). Riders had to weigh a minimum of 60kg (132lb), otherwise ballast had to be fitted to the machine to make up the difference.

The fairing itself was the result of a full winter's work. Using a Stuttgart wind tunnel, Kreidler put Anscheidt in the riding position and went to work, using a mesh fairing that could be covered with flexible plastic and bent in small increments until the most perfect form was found.

Braking was improved for 1962 with larger diameter front drums. Manufactured from Electron, these weighed no more than the smaller units fitted the previous year. The rear drums remained the same, except that they were now cast, rather than machined from a solid block.

To counter the might of Japan, Dr. Kreidler finally waived the rule which forbade non-factory employees from riding his bikes. This allowed the Dutch rider, Jan Huberts, to join the team, which also consisted of Anscheidt, Wolfgang Gedlich and Rudolf Kunz.

The first two championship rounds went to the West German factory, with team leader Anscheidt winning the inaugural Spanish GP, and Huberts taking the flag in France. However, even though the Dutchman won at the Sachsenring in East Germany, and Anscheidt at Monza, ex-MZ star Ernst Degner, riding a Japanese Suzuki, took the title. Anscheidt finally finished the year as runner-up in the championships, while Huberts was fourth.

Hans-Georg Anscheidt, Kreidler team leader during the 1964 Dutch TT at Assen; he finished 5th.

For 1963, a new duplex chassis, stronger (telescopic) forks and more powerful brakes were provided, together with more power at 12bhp. Even so, it was still not enough to stem the tide of the mighty Japanese. Anscheidt fought tooth-and-nail, right down to the final Grand Prix, but Suzuki and Hugh Anderson won the day, and with it the second 50cc world title.

Determined to achieve better results in 1964, Kreidler pulled out all the stops and came up with an almost totally new bike. The horizontal engine had seen a considerable amount of development during the winter, with a new, larger-fin cylinder, new expansion-chamber exhaust and beefier air-cooled clutch. Its 12 gears had been changed to six in the engine, with a two-speed, cable-operated overdrive. The new chassis was a notable improvement, and it held the now 100mph, 14bhp motor under a latticework of tubing, while up front, a pair of 30mm, leading-axle telescopic forks were fitted with an Electron, 170mm (7in), single-leadingshoe, drum front brake. Narrow and extremely light, the new Renn Florett, with rider Anscheidt, was ready to cross swords with the Japanese.

The season began with a fourth in the United States Grand Prix at Daytona raceway. Following hot on the heels of the Stateside event came a great result in Barcelona, where

Kriedler 50cc GP single 1964

Engine:	Air-cooled single-cylinder two-stroke with aluminium horizontal cylinder and twin rotary disc induction.
Capacity:	49.9cc
Bore & stroke:	40 x 39.7mm.
Compression ratio:	15:1
Carburation:	2 x Bing 26mm carbs.
Ignition:	Battery/coil, twin coils, condensers & CB points.
Lubrication:	Petroil mixture.
Gearbox:	six-speed in engine, with a two-speed cable-operated overdrive.
Clutch:	Dry, multi-plate.
Frame:	Duplex all-steel construction.
Suspension:	Telescopic 30mm front forks with leading axle; swinging arm twin shock rear.
Brakes:	Full width 170mm drums front and rear.
Tyres:	2.50 x 18 front and rear.
Dry weight:	58kg.
Max power:	14bhp.
Max speed:	99mph.

Anscheidt put it across the Japanese in no uncertain fashion to score a memorable victory. Unfortunately, this early promise could not be sustained and, yet again, Suzuki and Hugh Anderson took the 1964 50cc World Championship with the Japanese marque's latest featherweight racer, the rear exhaust RM64.

For 1965, Kreidler stuck with very much the same machine as the previous year with its horizontal, rotary-valve induction, single-cylinder motor and some 14bhp of puff. But it should have all been so different.

In 1963, a 50cc twin had been designed, but not built because of disagreement at boardroom level. Had that engine been authorised, it could well have been the leading entry in its class. As it was, Dr. Kreidler finally gave the go-ahead in early 1965, but by then it was too late. The Japanese had dropped their development into overdrive and simply blew the much smaller German company into the weeds, with machines such as the twin-cylinder RK65 Suzuki and Honda's jewel-like RC114 dohc twin. The best Anscheidt and Kreidler could do all year was a fourth place in the final round in Japan.

Anscheidt with Kreidler for a record attempt, November 1964.

Two works racers were used in November 1964, in an attempt to gain speed records.

This finally sealed Kreidler's fate, and its autocratic boss pulled the plug on the GP effort. The result was that Anscheidt upped and left, signing almost immediately for Suzuki, for whom he became thrice World Champion in 1966, 1967 and 1968. Furthermore, the long-awaited twin never made it to a Grand Prix start line.

Another blow to the Kornwestheim factory's pride came in May 1965, when its German rival, Zündapp, snatched Kreidler's 50cc speed records at Monza. However, that particular acid drop was not savoured for long. Soon, Dr. Kreidler sent his men into action to reclaim this honour, and several others, at the Bonneville Salt Flats, Utah, in October that year.

The rider for these record attempts was Rudolf Kunz. It was Kunz who had the honour of establishing the very first world record for the standing-start quarter mile, when his streamlined Kreidler clocked a mean time of 19.586 seconds, giving an average speed of 45.96mph.

The 1965 Spring Congress of the FIM in Moscow, had agreed to recognise standing quarter records from 31st May onward. At the same time, the mile, both for standing and flying starts, was reinstated as a record distance after a lapse of nearly nine years.

Kunz also took the standing-start mile record with a mean time of 53.506 seconds (67.28mph), handsomely beating Massimo Pasolini's 1956 Aermacchi average of 51.5mph.

Rudolf Kunz tests one of the works racers before leaving for the USA in 1965.

Local rider Francois Moisson appeared in the 1969 Belgian Grand Prix with his home-brewed 100cc Kreidler v-twin, in the 125cc event.

Kreidler's main goal was the 50cc land speed record, and in the specially prepared, streamlined projectile, Kunz sped through the electronic eye with a two-way average speed of 131.25mph to claim a new record for the German factory. The bike had a modified 12-speed GP engine, with an electric shift mechanism, that used special fuel and was cooled by ice.

During this period of uncertainty on the competitions front, Kreidler had been going from strength to strength in the sales of its standard production machines. By the mid 1960s, it had captured over 60 per cent of powered two-wheeler sales in Germany and neighbouring Switzerland. The company was doing almost as well in the Netherlands. So although the racing boys were far from happy, the reverse was true in the showroom.

At the Cologne Show in September 1967, Kreidler announced a new dual-purpose 50cc model, the Florett RS. The single-cylinder, piston-ported two-stroke was basically a roadster, but was sold with a special kit that converted the five-speeder into a fully-fledged racer.

The Kornwestheim factory claimed 5.3bhp for the RS in roadster trim, the race kit boosting the power output to over 9bhp, while maximum speed was up to around 80mph. The kit comprised a new cylinder, piston and head, Dell'Orto SS1 remote-float racing carburettor, a new induction stub, gaskets, cables, an air lever, racing spark plug, 14- and 15-teeth gearbox sprockets, and a full expansion-chamber exhaust system.

Several private tuners, both in Germany and abroad, soon found ways of making the roadster-based engine even more potent. In the late 1960s, these Kreidlers took over from the Honda CR110 production racer in club and national status events.

One of the first such machines was constructed by Anton Mohr of Koblenz. Whereas the factory obtained around 9.5bhp from its race-kitted Florett RS engine, Mohr, using modified roadster components, managed to squeeze 14bhp from his.

Later still, the Dutch-based Van Veen concern produced a cylinder which bumped this figure to over 16bhp. However, with the engine revving to over 16,000rpm, unreliability began to rear its ugly head.

Roadster motor converted to rotary disc induction with Van Veen cylinder and head. Notice bottom left of clutch casing, that's where the pedals came through on the moped type motor.

Anscheidt flat-out around Abbey Curve at Silverstone during the 1965 Hutchison 100 meeting.

Van Veen supported Dutch rider Alt Toerson who set three new world records at Elvington Airfield, East Yorkshire, in October 1968.

By 1970 the entire Kreidler race effort had been taken over by the company's Dutch importer, Van Veen. Jos Schurgers is pictured at the 1970 Ulster GP. He retired...

As a sign of spiralling costs, which the would-be 50cc private racer had to face for this extra performance, the cost of the Van Veen cylinder often exceeded the total cost of a complete factory race-kitted Florett engine unit! However, riders still coughed up for the most competitive bike outside Grand Prix racing.

In 1969, the FIM had restricted 50cc GP machines to only one cylinder and a maximum of six speeds. This move prompted Kreidler back into action for another shot at that elusive world championship title. However, over the preceding years, development had stagnated and the factory (via its Dutch importers, Van Veen) rejoined the fray with a 15bhp engine, which was still based around the 1965 rotary-valve, air-cooled unit.

Unfortunately for the Kreidler effort, it had reckoned without the Spanish Derbi team which had been slowly developing its single. It provided its leading rider, Angel Nieto, with a superb water-cooled, disc-valve machine to claim his first world title. This was followed up with a second in the following year.

Starting with a clean sheet of paper, Van Veen came up with a brand-new Kreidler Grand Prix racer for 1971, developed by the West German two-stroke wizard, Jorg Möller. This effort was financed by the vast sales being enjoyed by Kreidler, not only at home, but in the Netherlands - the 100,000th machine for sale in that country had been produced the same year.

Complete Kreidler water-cooled racing engine for privateers; in sectioned form.

The new GP racer not only featured a totally revised water-cooled engine, producing 17.5bhp, but also an entirely-new chassis with Italian Ceriani suspension and Fontana drum brakes, the latter being a double-sided device at the front.

So dramatic was this advance in development that the metallic-green flyer caught champions Angel Nieto and Derbi completely flat-footed.

Kreidler's leading rider in 1971 was the diminutive Dutchman, Jan de Vries, although occasional rides were given to the likes of Barry Sheene and Jarno Saarinen. With Derbi also drafting in Gilberto Parlotti, the 1971 50cc title hunt made excellent entertainment.

West German GP, Nürburgring, 30th April 1972. Ludwig Fabbender (Kreidler, 39), Angel Nieto (Derbi, 28) and Jan Bruins (Kreidler, 6) lead the pack into the first turn.

The 1973 works Van Veen engine developed 17.5bhp at 16,000rpm, enabling the machine to reach an astounding 125mph on the fastest circuits. The liquid-cooled unit now sported electronic ignition.

However, except for Sheene's win in the Yugoslav round, the championship contest was between only two men, Nieto and De Vries.

With five victories in Austria, West Germany, Belgium, Italy and Spain, compared to Nieto's three, De Vries finally put Kreidler's name on the World Championship trophy.

However, the Amsterdam-based Van Veen/ Kreidler team did not have it all its own way in the following year, for Derbi and Nieto responded to their defeat by coming up with an improved machine for 1972. Jan de Vries and the Spaniard were neck-and-neck all season, with the Dutch rider slightly ahead going into the final round - in Spain!

On home territory and spurred on by the fanatically partisan crowd, Nieto crossed the line at the front of the field. This result produced a dead-heat in the title race, for both riders had scored an identical number of points and each had won three races.

No title hunt had ever been this close before, so the FIM decided to take the five Grand Prix races, in which both riders had finished, and add up the total times. This gave Nieto the championship by only 21.32 seconds. The actual totals were: Nieto, 2 hours, 27 minutes, 26.29 seconds; de Vries, 2 hours, 27 minutes, 47.61 seconds.

Derbi announced its retirement from Grand Prix racing at the end of 1972, and the following year, Kreidler took the championship and four of the top five placings; Jan de Vries was World Champion with Kreidler for the second time in three seasons.

Back in 1969, the FIM had restricted the 50cc GP formula to one cylinder and a maximum of six-speeds. This suited Kreidler, with one of the 1971 engines shown here, sporting a 26mm Bing carb, rotary-disc induction and points ignition.

In 1974, Henk van Kessel took the title for the West German marque. To prove how total the Kreidler dominance had become, the top six riders were mounted on the Kornwestheim factory's machinery. In an attempt to get his championship back, Angel Nieto joined Kreidler for the 1975 season. He made the right choice, too, taking the title with victories at six of the eight rounds staged that year.

Nieto had chosen Kreidler for the simple reason that, at the time, it was the best machine by a huge margin. The ultra-professional Van Veen organisation had swept the opposition aside in a most convincing fashion.

It was because of this fact that the Spanish Motorcycle Federation (who effectively controlled the sport in that country) sanctioned Nieto to ride a foreign bike. The country was still under the rule of the dictator Franco, which meant that a Spanish rider could not usually race anything built outside the frontiers of Spain.

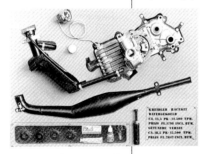

Amsterdam Show, 1974, and the Van Veen Kreidler race kit for sale to well-off privateers. The kit cost more than a complete Florett road bike!

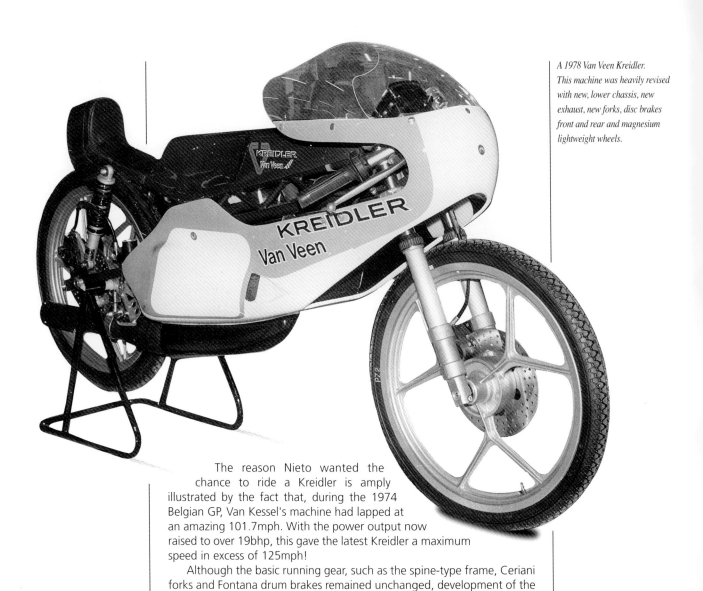

The reason Nieto wanted the chance to ride a Kreidler is amply illustrated by the fact that, during the 1974 Belgian GP, Van Kessel's machine had lapped at an amazing 101.7mph. With the power output now raised to over 19bhp, this gave the latest Kreidler a maximum speed in excess of 125mph!

Although the basic running gear, such as the spine-type frame, Ceriani forks and Fontana drum brakes remained unchanged, development of the water-cooled, rotary-disc-induction engine had been untiring, with the constant search not only for extra horsepower, but also improved engine torque. The latter was of vital importance following the six-speed maximum ruling.

After winning the 1975 title on the Kreidler, Nieto defected to his home camp in 1976, to ride a Bultaco (actually an Italian Piovaticci with Bultaco decals!).

The Spanish team had two aces - not only the undoubted brilliance of Nieto's riding, but the Piovaticci, which was a fully-developed GP contender. It had finished second in the 1975 title chase, ridden by Eugenio Lazzarini, before the team ran into financial difficulties and was snapped up by Bultaco, who wished to make a return to road racing.

Thus, Bultaco and Nieto took the 1976 world title, and retained it in 1977. However, Kreidler came back in 1978 with the former Piovaticci pilot, Eugenio Lazzarini.

Thereafter, Kreidler followed with a succession of GP victories and world championship titles until the demise of the 50cc class at the end of the 1984 season. In 1983 and 1984, the Austrian Stefan Dorflinger won on Krauser machines which, in fact, were Kreidlers under a different name, following the collapse of the Kornwestheim factory during 1982. These last bikes were tuned by Herbert Rittberger and developed 21bhp from the 41.5 x 36mm, six-transfer-port engine.

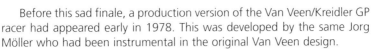

Before this sad finale, a production version of the Van Veen/Kreidler GP racer had appeared early in 1978. This was developed by the same Jorg Möller who had been instrumental in the original Van Veen design.

With a power output of 16.5bhp at 16,000rpm, the production racer was very similar to the mid-1970s works bike. It was a match for anything outside GP racing in the 50cc class.

Fitted with 18in cast-alloy wheels and front and rear hydraulically-operated disc brakes (of 210 and 190mm diameter respectively), the water-cooled, rotary-disc-valve machine sported the 40 x 39.7mm Kreidler bore and stroke measurements, which could be traced all the way back to the production roadsters of the 1950s. In reality, however, this was about all these machines had in common.

Steve Patrickson, ex-works Van Veen Kreidler, Elvington, North Yorkshire, early 1980s.

The single-ring Mahle piston and Nickasil bore had an operating clearance of micro-millimetres, and because of this, there were 15 piston sizes, each to suit a particular piston/cylinder measurement. As with the works machines of the period, the production racer employed Krober capacity discharge ignition, the trigger of which was mounted on a solid bronze outer disc housing. The 28mm Bing carburettor was normally ditched in favour of the superior 29mm Mikuni instrument, which could be obtained cheaply by boring out a standard production carburettor from one of the air-cooled RD250/400 Yamaha roadster twins.

During the 1983 West German GP at Hockenheim, privateers Gerhard Singer (Kreidler, 17) and Rainer Kunz (FKN, 27) have their own ding dong dice in the 50cc race.

When Stefan Dorflinger had piloted his Krauser/Kreidler to the 1983 50cc world crown, it had raised the factory's total to seven championships, a record that looks secure as the FIM has now abandoned the class. It is a fitting tribute to the marque which can truly claim to have been 'King of the tiddlers'.

Dorflinger during the 1981 Dutch TT - he crashed out on the last lap when leading.

Maico

9

1970-73 Maico RS125 single.

The history of Maico is very much one of the Maisch family and can be traced back to the year 1926 with the formation of Ulrich Maisch & Co., in Poltringen, near Stuttgart. However, it was to be another five years - in 1931 - before the first involvement with two-wheelers came about. Then the two young sons of the founder began bicycle manufacture in a small workshop at the rear of the plant, employing a combination of bought-in components and their own work.

Otto and Wilhelm Maisch.

The success of the bicycle enterprise led the brothers, Otto and Wilhelm Maisch, to consider manufacturing their own motorcycles. Not only did this lead to their first real bike, the 1935 MP120, an ultra-lightweight using a 118cc Ilo single-cylinder, two-stroke engine, but the adoption of the Maico trade name - a contraction of Maisch & Co. Until 1939, all Maicos employed Ilo power units, but on the very eve of World War 2, an autocycle appeared with a 50cc Sachs engine.

Additionally, the success of the Maico line had allowed the brothers not only to expand into new and larger premises at nearby Pfaffingen, but also to lay down plans for a new machine incorporating their own ideas. These included the very first engine assembly to be designed and built by Maico itself.

1970-72 Maico RS125 single.

However, with the outbreak of war, Maico found itself manufacturing not the new two-wheeler, but spare parts for the Luftwaffe (the German air force). Thus, the brothers' dream of producing their first all-Maico motorcycle was set back a whole decade. Production of the machine, the M150, did not begin until 1949. Even then, much of this came about by luck - unlike many of Germany's pre-war marques, Maico had escaped both the bombing and the results of being under the control of the Russians, the fate which had befallen DKW, for example.

During the 1950s, Maico steadily built up its business which, by the end of the decade, had become linked with luxury scooters and off-road sport - such as motocross and long-distance trials. Because of this, the company escaped the majority of problems which beset their larger, and more well known, counterparts within the German motorcycle industry.

Maico continued this niche-type marketing strategy into the 1960s with considerable success, but without any real involvement with either roadsters or road racers.

In 1963, however, all this was set to change, for Maico realised that it would have to respond to falling sales of its scooters by designing brand-new street motorcycles to meet a growing demand for high-performance ultra-lightweights. The answer was two machines, the MD50 and 125, both featuring a totally-new, rotary-valve, five-speed unit-construction engine. These were fast and modern, and they were to play an important role in launching the company back on to the tarmac - both on street and track.

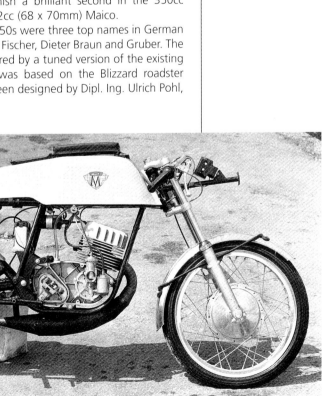

1969, 125cc Maico Production racer.

The next stage in the Maico racing story came in September 1966 when it was revealed that Maico would be taking part in European road-racing events the following year. They were to enter works machines for the 125, 250 and 350cc classes. Heading this programme was Dipl. Ing. Gunther Schier, who had joined Maico three months before as chief engineer in the construction department, mainly to get the racing machines under way and keep them going. One of Europe's top two-stroke men, Schier was full of enthusiasm for the project and was at the Nürburgring to see Toni Gruber finish a brilliant second in the 350cc German championship race on a 252cc (68 x 70mm) Maico.

Already down to ride 250s and 350s were three top names in German national racing at that time: Gunther Fischer, Dieter Braun and Gruber. The prototype 252cc machine was powered by a tuned version of the existing motocross engine which, in turn, was based on the Blizzard roadster design of the mid 1950s. This had been designed by Dipl. Ing. Ulrich Pohl, who had left to work for BMW.

Production 125 Maico RS, as it looked when it was first offered for sale during 1969. Specification included 21bhp, disc-valve induction and a six-speed gearbox.

A grid full of Maicos at a Dutch national event at Heeswyk, summer 1970. Number 60 is Piet Hogervorst.

During 1967, the Maicos were used with some degree of success in German racing, notably the overbored engine used in the 350cc class. The best results were obtained by future World Champion, Dieter Braun. However, the 125cc was the machine that showed the most promise. This employed an engine based on the.production roadster MD125 unit.

At the 1966 Cologne Show, the MD125 Sport had been launched. With a tuned engine, it gave 14bhp at 6,900rpm. It was this that was used as a basis for the pukka racing model. Not only did Maico themselves, but also the leading private tuner Anton Mohr, built prototype 125cc racers during the period 1967-8. Mohr's machine employed the roadster's bottom end and five-speed gearbox, but with a one-off alloy head and cylinder barrel, the latter with a rearwardfacing exhaust port. Other special components included the racing Dell'Orto carb, Oldani front brake and comprehensive, high-level, expansion-chamber exhaust system.

The factory prototypes were similar, but differed in details, such as brakes, carburettor, engine tuning and exhaust. They also had a conventional, front-facing exhaust port. There were also a low-level expansion chamber, Ceriani forks and Maico's own twin-leading-shoe, 180mm front stopper. The 123.67cc (54 x 54mm) engine shared the same square dimensions of the roadster, but running on a compression ratio of 15:1 gave a claimed 21bhp at 11,500rpm. As on the roadster, the 32mm Bing carburettor was bolted directly to the crankcase. The gearbox had six close ratios: 1st, 3.07; 2nd, 2.35; 3rd, 1.85; 4th, 1.59; 5th, 1.41; and 6th, 1.32. The dry weight, including streamlining, was a mere 68kg (150lb), and the maximum speed, 115mph.

First production version of the over-the-counter racer, the RS125, made its debut at the beginning of the 1969 season. Right from the off, it offered a highly competitive level of performance witnessed by a fine second place by the Swedish star, Kent Anderson, in the opening round of the 1969 125cc World Championship at the Spanish GP, held that year at the Jarama circuit. The same rider repeated this performance to finish second in the Dutch TT at Assen. Along with a fourth in Belgium, this gave the Swede - and Maico - fourth overall in the championship table.

Both Anderson and Toni Gruber had received 'works development' machines, rather than

This 1968 Amor Special, using a Maico roadster based engine tuned by Anton Mohr, may well have inspired Maico to produce the RS125 racer.

Maico RS125 1969

Engine:	Air-cooled, two-stroke single-cylinder with rotary-disc induction.
Capacity:	123.67cc.
Bore & stroke:	54 x 54mm.
Compression ratio:	15:1.
Carburation:	Bing 32mm.
Ignition:	Flywheel magneto.
Lubrication:	Petroil.
Gearbox:	Six-speeds.
Clutch:	Wet, multi-plate.
Frame:	Duplex, full cradle, steel construction.
Suspension:	Ceriani telescopic front forks; swinging twin rear shocks.
Brakes:	Front 180mm 2LS, rear 160mm SLS drums.
Tyres:	2.75 x 18 front and rear.
Dryweight:	68kg.
Max power:	21bhp @ 11,500rpm.
Max speed:	115mph.

English rider Chas Mortimer pilots the Giuseppe Visenzi-entered Maico RS125 during the Czech Grand Prix at Brno, July 1971.

standard production bikes, for the 1969 season. This move paid handsome dividends, with not only Anderson's performance in the classics, but Gruber's many excellent results at home. Even better was to follow. For 1970, Maico signed up another Swedish rider, Borge Jansson, as a replacement for Anderson, who had signed for Yamaha. Gruber provided the back-up again, but this time concentrating on the World Championship series. The first round was on home ground, over the twists and turns of the Nürburgring, where Gruber came in fourth. Then at the French GP at Le Mans, Jansson showed his potential by finishing an impressive second to Dieter Braun on an ex-works Suzuki twin. Gruber finished fourth in France, then came the Yugoslav GP at Opatija, where Jansson could finish no higher than fourth.

Next came the long and ultra-demanding Isle of Man TT, where Jansson again displayed his skill, once more finishing second to the combination of Braun and Suzuki. There followed a series of rather disappointing results before Jansson rode perhaps his best race of the year, to annex third place at the final round in Spain. He was one place ahead of the new 125cc World Champion, Dieter Braun, in a race won by local hero Angel Nieto (Derbi), while Barry Sheene (Suzuki 3) was second. Jansson's excellent rides that year had earned him third place in the championship, one better than Anderson's a year earlier.

The Maico factory, Pfaffingen.

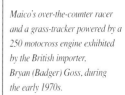

Maico's over-the-counter racer and a grass-tracker powered by a 250 motocross engine exhibited by the British importer, Bryan (Badger) Goss, during the early 1970s.

By now, sales of the standard over-the-counter RS125 were beginning to build up nicely, thanks in no small part to the performances gained at world level. To give this an even bigger spur, the factory gained the signature of the 1970 125cc World Champion, Dieter Braun, for the following season.

Maico engineers responded by carrying out further development work, which raised the power output of the works-supported machines to around 28bhp at 11,000rpm. The official team comprised Braun, Jansson and Gruber.

At the season's end, Jansson had ridden his Maico rotary-valve single to another third place in the championship series. Braun took his to fourth, while the privateer, Bender, scored a very creditable seventh. All three had scored runner-up positions: Jansson (Isle of Man, Czechoslovakia and Sweden); Braun (Finland); Bender (Belgium).

Development continued into 1972, and Maico was rewarded when Borge Jansson scored its first ever classic victory, taking the chequered flag in East Germany at the Sachsenring circuit. Jansson's average speed was 96.50mph. Not content with this, the Swedish rider won the next round at Brno, Czechoslovakia, too! This time he averaged 87.66mph. Jansson finished the year as the leading Maico rider yet again, with fourth position overall in the championship table.

By now, several privateers were beginning to score championship points, the best result being Bill Rae's excellent third place in the Isle of Man TT that year. What of Dieter Braun, you may ask! Well, he was becoming more and more involved with the 250 class. For 1972, a trio of his mechanics - Sepp Schlogl, Anton Mang and Alfous Zender built the highly-interesting and innovative SMZ (coined from the first letters of the three builders' surnames) narrow-angle v-twin. Both Schlogl and Mang were later to win fame - the former as a leading tuner, the latter as a multi world champion.

This interesting and historically important v-twin special was built by Josef Franz (Sepp) Schlogl, Anton Mang (later a world champion with Kawasaki) and Alfous Zender for Dieter Braun. The first prototype used some Maico components, including the cylinders. Later it was all their own work.

Three SMZs were constructed. The first used 125cc Maico cylinders and certain other components from the same source. However, the other two had special cylinders which had been designed by Schlogl and cast by Mahle. Each had five transfer ports and a single exhaust port. Other notable details included a Mahle crankshaft and pistons, and a six-speed Austrian Schafleitner gearbox. Disc-valve induction and water-cooling were also used, the power output of 64bhp at 12,000rpm being a highly competitive figure for the era. In fact, in terms of speed, it was actually faster than the Yamaha works development bikes ridden by the likes of Saarinen and Gould!

Dieter Braun in action on his RS125, West German Grand Prix, 30th April 1972.

Entered as a Maico, the SMZ's weakness was its poor handling. Furthermore, the fact that it was a truly private venture (no help was provided by Maico!) meant that it was at a huge disadvantage compared with its main competitor, Yamaha, and also the Italian Aermacchi marque that year, both of which enjoyed almost unlimited funds.

The best result gained by the SMZ in 1972 was a second behind the Japanese rider Hidi Kanaya at the Nürburgring in the 250cc West German GP. Although it had the speed, the team decided to opt for the 'safety' of its own water-cooled conversion for the newly-

Braun with the SMZ (Schlogl, Mang, Zender) special in 1972. This innovative predecessor of the current 250GP v-twins had twin contra-rotating cranks geared directly to the clutch, but with a much narrower cylinder angle of only 20 degrees (to save space).

released production TD3 Yamaha for 1973, and it was on this that Braun took the world title that year. Meanwhile, Mang took over the SMZ ride and, in doing so, took his first steps to world fame on his own account before leaving the SMZ saga, it should be said that the machine pointed the way to the future. Indeed, over a decade later, the mighty Honda team and its rider, Freddie Spencer, were to benefit from their own version of the narrow-angle v-twin concept.

Returning to Maico itself, the RS125 continued to be built and was campaigned by riders receiving works backing, such as Jansson. In addition, a large number of privateers used the rapid rotary-valve single to good effect. This continued well into the 1970s, by which time the quickest bikes were water-cooled. This conversion was usually achieved by machining the fins from the head and barrel, then fitting a cast-iron sleeve, various pipes and a radiator.

Bill Rae rounding Quarter Bridge during the very wet 1972, 125cc TT.

The factory was also involved in the 250cc class - not with the SMZ special, but a new 245cc (76 x 54mm), rotary-valve, six-speed single. This made its debut in 1974.

Originally conceived as a roadster, the 250 was soon used for both production and open-class racing events. In standard trim, it produced 27bhp at 7,800rpm - around 93mph. This, together with its superb handling, was enough to make it competitive in the sports machine class.

The same year also witnessed a full racing version developed by Rolf Minhoff - with the official backing of Maico through its chief designer, Dipl. Ing. Schier. Mounted in a much lower duplex chassis, the Minhoff-tuned engine pumped out a claimed 43bhp which, on the road, meant an optimum speed of around 136mph. However, although outstanding for a single-cylinder design, it was not in the same league as the then class-leading Yamaha TD3

Former BSA Bantam racing legend Fred Launchbury (6) pushes his Maico RS125 into life at the start of the 1974 Isle of Man TT.

twin. Even so, the machine gained a considerable amount of attention in the German motorcycling press, which provided Maico with much valuable publicity.

However, from then on, interest in road racing waned, the factory becoming ever more reliant upon its sales of military and off-road competition bikes. Even so, today it is still possible to see the occasional RS125 single giving loyal service in German club events - a lasting tribute to an essentially soundly engineered, but exceedingly simple design.

Münch

Münch

10

Formally associated with the Horex marque, Münch first sprang to worldwide fame for his Mammoth - a unique NSU car-engined Superbike before the term was invented.

Few men in motorcycling can match the chequered career of Friedl Münch. Ever since he was bitten by the two-wheeled bug as a six-year-old, when his father made him a small motorcycle at his car and motorcycle repair business near Frankfurt, way back in 1933, his enthusiasm simply kept on growing.

Münch's interest in engineering also blossomed, and after war service as a mechanic with the Luftwaffe, he raced a pre-war Horex single for two seasons before damaging his liver in an accident. Then he turned his attention to tuning and produced a competitive racer by converting a pushrod Horex Regina, with a rev limit of 5,500rpm, into a double-knocker that revved to 7,000rpm. After this came a spell in the Horex race shop during the 1950s, building 250 and 350cc singles and the dohc Grand Prix twins. He stayed on until the famous factory floundered during the late 1950s. His Horex experience was not wasted, however, and besides tuning a number of privately owned examples, he also sponsored the up-and-coming Klaus Enders on a Norton solo and a sidecar outfit, powered by a Horex Imperator twin with dual-choke Weber carburettor. However, the Horex was becoming obsolete, so eventually Enders took the chance of racing a BMW Rennsport outfit - his first step to becoming a multi sidecar world champion.

During the early 1960s, Münch turned his attention to the design and manufacture of his own racing drum brakes. These potent stoppers soon built up an enviable reputation and, with it, lucrative sales to the racing fraternity - both in Germany and abroad. Used on both solos and sidecars, these superbly crafted (and powerful!) brakes effectively set Münch on the road to becoming a motorcycle manufacturer in his own right.

The next phase was a four-cylinder, 498cc racing engine which was completed in early 1964. This dohc, across-the-frame, vertical unit was an extremely neat piece of work, and it proved that Münch could build more than just cycle components.

During the late summer of 1965, Friedl Münch was based in Friedburg, where he was approached by Frenchman Jean Murit. A former sidecar racer and record breaker with BMW machinery, Murit wanted a bike which was faster, stronger and more powerful than any standard production roadster then available from the established manufacturers.

Münch considered the options very carefully before selecting the air-cooled NSU Prinz 1000 car engine which had recently come on to the market - thus, the Mammoth was born. Arguably the world's first modern 'superbike' of the type so popular in the 1970s, around 500 would be built over the next two decades, the engine size eventually reaching an amazing 1,800cc! Almost as controversial were the various business partners which the Mammoth attracted over the same period. This was to prompt Münch to remember, 'All I ever wanted to do was build motorcycles, but all the people I got involved in business with ever wanted was to take advantage of that and try to get rich quick. I've been cheated, deceived, robbed and lied to but still today (1988) I'm a happy man because I can still hold my head up and know I never did any wrong to anyone. And most important of all, I'm still making bikes!'

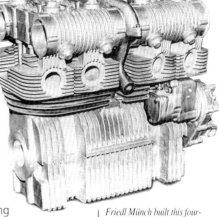

Friedl Münch built this four-cylinder dohc racing engine in 1963-64.

His first business partner was the veteran American motorcycle book publisher, Floyd Clymer. This meant that Münch was able to move from his cramped, stable-like premises to a brand new factory facility at Ossenheim, which opened in September 1967. Clymer, a former Indian works rider, had a dream not only of assisting Münch to build his Mammoth superbikes, but also relaunching the Indian marque. He had purchased the manufacturing rights to the American machine when the original factory went out of business in 1953. Normally a shrewd businessman, for once, Clymer acted on sentiment rather than sound commercial judgement. The result was that the reborn Münch-Indian v-twin was a dismal failure. However, Münch and Clymer continued their partnership, and at the Cologne Motorcycle Show, in September 1968, they unveiled some of their combined handiwork. This included an engine which they announced would be bidding for international racing success.

Münch (second from the right) with his co-workers as they prepare the first Mammoth for its initial run in late February 1966. The brakes were of Münch's own design and later graced many top privateer racers during the late 1960s such as Manx Norton and G50 Matchless machines.

The new powerplant was a 500cc, dohc, parallel-twin designed and built by Friedl Münch. The pair hoped that it would be battling in the European Grand Prix circus during the following season. Also on display was an sohc version, which was intended to bring success in AMA (American Motorcycle Association) events.

The GP parallel-twin, which was not based on Münch's 1964 racing four, had a bore and stroke of 71.5 x 62mm. Its double-knocker valve gear was driven by a chain that ran up the centre of the engine; there were four valves and a central spark plug for each cylinder. The crankcase was cast in magnesium, while the heads and barrels were of a new, high-strength, ultra-lightweight aluminium alloy. Designed in unit with the engine was a five-speed, close-ratio gearbox. Underneath the crankcase was a deeply-finned wet sump which contained six pints of lubricant, but the gearbox and engine oil were separate, unlike the single-overhead-cam production engine. Primary drive was by straight-cut gears, with a dry, six-plate clutch.

Münch experimented with several makes of carburettor, including Amal, Dell'Orto and Weber, with choke sizes ranging from 35 to 40mm. The show engine, however, was fitted with Amal GPs. Test results had revealed a power output of over 60bhp at 10,000rpm as the ultimate target. If the engine proved a success, it was planned to offer it for sale to selected top international-class competitors.

It was stated that the company was planning a thorough test programme throughout the winter months, and the complete machine was scheduled to be ready for race testing later in 1969. A twin-loop cradle frame had already been designed to house the GP engine, although Münch was also seeking assistance from established frame makers. These included the British Rickman brothers, well known for their Metisse chassis. Brand-new telescopic front forks, designed by Münch, had 148cc of damping oil and boasted a travel of 5.9in. The now familiar Münch front brake was to be used together with an Italian Fontana at the rear.

Like a modular series of roadsters, powered by the sohc engine ranging from 450 to 750cc, the double-knocker twin was destined never to see the race tracks. This state of affairs was not helped by Floyd Clymer's health, which deteriorated sharply, causing him to retire from the project at the end of May 1969. It was a well-founded rumour, at the time, that he had sold his entire interest in the Münch factory to an unidentified source, represented by the Chase Manhattan Bank of Frankfurt. Later, it transpired that this mystery backer was an American millionaire's son, George Bell, himself a Münch Mammoth owner. He bought the interest from Clymer's wife as the veteran publisher's health was leaving him. Clymer died in the spring of 1970.

Although, initially, Bell stated that he had intended increasing the production tempo and putting the company on a sound financial footing, it transpired that he saw the Münch enterprise very much as a means of acting the playboy in the world's road racing circus. Soon, he had Münch working on racing projects rather than production roadsters. The proof came in September with press headlines proclaiming 'Fath-Münch Tie-up!'

The story behind the headline was the joining of forces by two of Germany's greatest ever special builders - Helmut Fath (1960 and 1968 World Sidecar Champion and creator of the four-cylinder URS) and Friedl Münch (maker of the exclusive Mammoth superbike and his own four- and

twin-cylinder racing engines). The man behind this marriage of engineering brains was George Bell, who wanted the two to continue producing racing and record breaking machinery. Bell saw this as a quick route to success, with Münch building the record breaker, and Fath the Grand Prix racer. It should also be mentioned that Bell had already written off the Münch/Clymer dohc, parallel-twin project.

At the beginning of their collaboration with Bell and Münch, Fath and his partner, Dr. Peter Kuhn, would continue to operate from their existing premises. However, a brand-new factory, scheduled for completion in the following spring, was being constructed at Altenstadt, near the existing Münch works at Ossenheim. When this was completed, all Münch and Fath interests would be centralised there, and both men would co-operate on racing and roadster projects.

The bike completed during the winter of 1969-70 was a larger-capacity version of the NSU powered Mammoth, for an attack on the world one-hour speed record. This stood at 145mph and had been gained by Mike Hailwood and MV Agusta. Built in the short space of six weeks, the new bike was intended to provide valuable press coverage for the Münch roadsters. Moreover, as Bell was from Florida, where better to take this machine and to boost his ego than Daytona? So the 'Daytona Bomb' was born.

The Münch-URS race team as it was in April 1970. Left to right Helmet Fath, Karl Hoppe and Ferdinand Kaczor. Shortly afterwards, Fath quit after a dispute with Münch.

The engine from a 1,177cc 1200TTS Mammoth roadster was bored out to 1,370cc. It produced a massive 125bhp at 8,600rpm. Specially-cast alloy cylinders replaced the original's cast-iron components, but the drive to the camshaft was the same as on the standard engine - by duplex chain up the nearside of the power unit. The 13:1 pistons necessitated the use of rollers to start the brute. Carburation was taken care of by a cluster of four 35mm Dell'Orto SS1 instruments, each pair being fed from a remotely-fitted float chamber.

Lubrication was taken care of by a semi-dry-sump system, as the crankshaft was not submerged in oil. To cope with the extra stress, a larger-capacity system was employed, while the lubricant was stored in a separate magnesium sump bolted to the base of the engine. The flywheel was removed, leaving the five-bearing crank to be dynamically balanced after the primary drive pinion had been fitted. This was driven by specially-manufactured helical gears on the nearside of the engine, driving the standard Münch four-speed gearbox via a 12 plate, dry clutch. The last had been considerably enlarged from the standard unit to cope with the increase in output over the roadster.

An additional 10mm spark plug was provided for each cylinder. The original 14mm plugs were sparked by a Volkswagen car distributor, which sat at the front of the engine and was driven by a simplex chain with a tensioner pulley on the offside end of the crankshaft. The second set of plugs had their own distributor, mounted on the offside end of the camshaft with 38 degrees advance.

To cope with this vast amount of power, the frame was fitted with the Rickman heavyweight front fork assembly normally employed on Metisse motocross machines. At the time, this was the only assembly capable of withstanding the demands which would be made upon it, both in terms of weight and speed. To provide adequate stopping power, Münch's own 250mm Electron drum brakes were specified, with a four-leading-shoe arrangement at the front.

Following the end of the annual Cycle Week at Daytona, in March 1970, the team, comprising Friedl Münch, Helmut Fath and rider Ferdinand Kaczor, waited for a period of fine weather before proceeding with their initial runs in the last week of the month. When these began, the machine displayed its speed potential by rocketing around the Daytona speed bowl at no less than 178mph. But there were snags... major snags.

500cc Münch URS 1971 sidecar World Champion winner - rider Horst Owesle on right, passenger Peter Rutherford on left.

The 'Daytona Bomb' could not keep this up for more than three laps (around nine miles) before the rear tyre tread cried enough and great chunks began to fly off. Even changing tyres for other types did not ease the problem. The result was that there was nothing left to do, but return to Germany in an attempt to persuade the tyre manufacturers to back the project with tyres capable of standing up to the power output and weight of the 1,400cc giant. As for the bike itself, this stayed in Florida, awaiting the outcome of the action. However, it was destined never to make another attempt at the hour record. Instead, it languished in a Miami warehouse for the next 11 years, having been awarded, under a court order, to one of the project's American backers in lieu of payments owed.

Back in Germany, Münch, Kaczor and Fath returned to their respective tasks. For Fath, this meant readying the Münch-URS, four-cylinder GP bikes. Their debut, under the new colours, came at the non-championship Austrian GP, held over the Salzburg autobahn circuit in late April. Kaczor and the 47 year-old veteran Karl Hoppe made it a 1-2 for the new team, the fastest lap of the meeting going to Kaczor at 87.68mph. Two weeks later came the first round in the 500cc World Championship series. On home ground at Hockenheim, Hoppe finished a respectable fourth. However, more notably at the same event, tensions that had existed, almost from the initial founding by Bell of the Münch-Fath partnership, came to a head. During practice, Münch had insisted that Fath (who was still an active competitor) should race the latest low-line Münch-URS sidecar outfit.

Ferdinand Kaczor was one of the two-man Münch GP solo team which competed at Hockenheim in May 1970. He left the squad at the same time as Fath, only to be killed the first time out on Fath's 350 TR2B Yamaha.

URS Münch 750cc solo being prepared for Englishman Tony Jefferies to ride at Snetterton, Race of Aces, 29th August 1971.

However, Fath objected to this, wanting instead to use his own non-Münch machine. When Münch disagreed with him, Fath announced that he was quitting the team altogether. To complicate matters further, the team's number one rider, Kaczor, voiced his intention of going with Fath to race a 350 Yamaha and 500 BMW!

The Münch-Fath dispute had another twist, because when Fath originally agreed to join the team, Bell had, in effect, bought out the whole Fath racing equipe. This meant that even though Fath had not moved all his machinery to the Münch factory in Ossenheim, he was no longer the owner of the remaining hardware. The result was yet more ill feeling. 'I was cleared out,' stated an upset Helmut Fath afterwards, when he was left with an empty workshop. 'They came with a pantechnicon and cleared out every engine I had.'

Even though Fath and Kaczor had quit, Horst Owesle and Dr. Peter Kuhn, who had both worked with Fath before the Münch link-up, stayed with the Münch organisation. Although the new partnership did not have any real hope in the 500cc solo class once Fath had departed, Kuhn did develop a 750cc racing four and, with the help of Owesle, went on to garner some great victories on three wheels. Horst Owesle had been German National Junior Sidecar Champion in 1969 on a BMW. However, no one could have predicted that riding the latest development of the Münch (Fath) URS four-cylinder engine, and partnered by Englishman Peter Rutherford, he would become the 1971 Sidecar World Champion!

Owesle and Rutherford won three of the eight rounds - Holland, Finland and Ulster - finishing in front of a string of BMW Rennsport twins. After this exploit, both Owesle and Rutherford retired from racing, while Englishman Chris Vincent used the four-cylinder outfit during 1972 (finishing fourth in the title hunt).

Credit should also be given to Owesle for his technical expertise. Once Helmut Fath had left, it was he who put on not only leathers, but also overalls to become the team's techical wizard. The 1971 championship-winning engine was bench-tested at 86bhp, using four Japanese Keihin carburettors, higher lift camshafts and dry-sump lubrication.

The 500 and 750cc Münch solos never received the attention of the sidecar machinery, with the result that they languished unused and unloved, except for the occasional outing. The most notable of these were in Britain, where they were raced occasionally during 1971 by Tony Jefferies.

Racing was to prove the centre of the Bell-funded Münch company's problems. Despite warnings from Friedl Münch himself, Bell sank over half-a-million deutschmarks into the 1971 racing campaign alone, and although Owesle succeeded in taking the World Championship, the factory itself was in dire financial straits. With creditors pressing from all sides, George Bell quickly departed the scene and returned to America, leaving Münch to solve his own problems again.

This he did with the aid of a series of financial backers over the next few years, the story of which is outside the scope of this particular book. However, any dreams he may have harboured of future racing glory went with the departure of the highflying George Bell. From then on, Friedl Münch was to stick firmly with street-going motorcycles, leaving the glamour of the race circuit to others.

Münch technical wizard and 1971 Sidecar World Champion, Horst Owesle.

MZ

11

MZ 50 liquid-cooled single, 1969.

Before World War 2, the Saxony town of Zschopau was the home of the most advanced two-stroke motorcycles in the world. DKW (see Chapter 4) had earned the respect of other, predominantly four-stroke, manufacturers with its ultra-quick racing machinery in the years leading up to the outbreak of hostilities in September 1939.

When the conflict was over, the DKW factory was nothing but rubble, and Zschopau found itself in Germany's eastern zone, under the occupation of the Red Army. DKW, therefore, set up shop anew in Ingolstadt, in the western sector, resuming its pre-war activities as best it could.

Meanwhile, from the ashes of the old plant in Zschopau, arose a new addition to the ranks of the world's motorcycle manufacturers, MZ, or to give its full title, VEB Motorradwerk Zschopau.

Although to confuse the issue even more, until the mid 1950s, its products were marketed under the IFA (Industrieverband-Farhzuegebau) label.

The first racing MZ (entered as an IFA) appeared in 1950, four years after the first post-war roadster left the Zschopau production lines.

MZ factory 1907-1992.

The first IFA (MZ) racer appeared in 1950. Developed from its roadgoing brother, it featured piston-port induction, a three-speed gearbox and a massive magneto situated on the offside of the crankcase.

Like its street-going brother, the track bike was a rather unexciting 125cc single with piston-port induction and a three-speed gearbox, hardly a motorcycle to provide any hint of the much greater things to come.

Then, in 1951, a private German tuner, Daniel Zimmermann, modified his home-brewed IFA racer by means of a crankshaft-driven rotary disc valve. Thus was ushered in a new era of two-stroke design.

Zimmermann fitted the carburettor directly to the side of the crankcase, where it supplied mixture by means of a disc valve mounted in the crankcase wall. In addition, the cylinder barrel was modified so that the exhaust faced rearwards. Zimmermann also changed the engine's original bore and stroke measurements from 52 x 58mm to the now widely-used, square 54 x 54mm dimensions.

The East German riders, Krumpolz and Petruschke, rode Zimmermann-modified bikes to annex fourth and fifth places in the 1951 German Grand Prix. Although not counting towards that year's world championship results, nonetheless the event attracted a massive crowd of 400,000 spectators to the Solitude circuit, near Stuttgart.

The 125cc event garnered full works entries from DKW, NSU and the Austrian Puch concern, so fourth and fifth positions were an excellent performance. In fact, Krumpolz spent the majority of the race duelling for third place with the vastly experienced Ewald Kluge, who had won the 1938 Lightweight TT in the Isle of Man on one of the supercharged DKWs.

Zimmermann's modifications were so successful that MZ quickly took out patents, and subsequent development of the concept was taken over by the engineer Walter Kaaden, who joined the Zschopau factory at the end of 1952. Prior to this, Kaaden had built and ridden his own bikes, in the process gaining experience which was to prove invaluable.

1968-69 250cc water-cooled twin.

The Fast one from Zschopau
MZ ES 175
VEB Motorradwerk Zschopau

Alan Shepherd (14) and his replacement in the MZ team, fellow Lancastrian Derek Woodman; Italian Grand Prix at Monza, September 1964.

Kaaden set to work for his new employers, and his initial success can be judged from the fact that, at the beginning of the 1953 season, the 125 engine was giving only 9bhp at 7,800rpm, but at the end of the year it was pumping out 12bhp at over 8,000rpm - a healthy 25 per cent increase.

MZ Re 125, 1953-54. The first rear-facing exhaust tried by MZ.

Much of this extra power came from extensive changes to the transfer and exhaust ports, the compression ratio and the exhaust system. In fact, it was this last area that was to be perhaps Kaaden's most significant achievement. It was he who recognized the importance of a highly resonant exhaust system, combined with the extended port timing made possible by disc-valve induction, coupled with multiple transfer ports and a squish-type combustion chamber.

Horst Fugner taking his MZ to ninth position in the 1953 German GP at Schotten. Walter Kaaden had joined the Zschopau factory a few months before, at the end of 1952.

The MZ's only appearance in the West that year was at the German Grand Prix, held at Schotten. This was boycotted by several factories on the grounds of safety. However, in the 125cc category, this hardly applied, as MV, NSU and FB Mondial all had riders in action. The sole MZ was that of Krumpolz in ninth position, a lap down on the race winner, Italian Carlo Ubbiali's MV Agusta.

By 1955, Kaaden had developed the disc-valve single to a point where it was almost competitive with the very best of the twin-cam four-strokes. However, his efforts were largely blunted by the international community which, at that time, during the height of the 'cold war', treated East Germany as a leper. Therefore, MZ was not only denied the currency to enable it to improve its machines by way of Western components, but also its staff were denied the necessary visas for foreign travel.

Thus, MZ continued to participate in the two Germanys; its only Grand Prix appearance was at the one held in West Germany each year.

The 1955 event was staged over the famous Nürburgring, the pride of German racing. With its 14.165-mile lap, which rose and fell over nearly 1,000 ft, the setting was magnificent with its beautifully-wooded slopes next to the Eifel mountains. It was also the ultimate test of a rider's skill in continental Europe, with a confusing sequence of blind bends and undulations that could test even the most experienced pilot's skill.

Walter Kaaden - Father of the modern 2-stroke

Walter Kaaden was a true engineering genius. He was also a man of the old school - humble, honest and loyal - who was born on 1st September 1919, the year the DKW factory was founded. His father was chauffeur both to Dipl. Ing. Carl Hahn who oversaw DKW in the 1930s and to DKW founder Jorgen Skafte Rasmussen. When only eight years of age, the young Walter was able to accompany his father and Rasmussen to the opening of the famous Nürburgring circuit. Doubling as a racing circuit and industry test ground, it was vital to the development of motor vehicles in Germany.

Walter Kaaden entered the Technical Academy in Chemitz, some 15 miles from DKW's base at Zschopau. Chemitz was very much a centre of industry and commerce for the German state of Saxony and many other motorcycle marques including Wanderer, were based in this area beside DKW.

The Second World War broke out when Kaaden was twenty, and his engineering prowess saw him arrive at the infamous Peenemunde research centre, where he was to work under the likes of Wernher von Braum. At that time Germany was leading the world on rocket design and Kaaden is generally acknowledged to have built what was the prototype cruise missile - the 4S293, which today is on permanent exhibition at the Deutsches Museum, Munich.

MZ Re 250 engine, circa 1958. Air-cooled, with rearward facing exhausts, disc valve and remote float chambers for each carburettor.

The 125cc race was staged over five laps, a total of 70.83 miles. There were 11 finishers, all of whom were mounted on MV Agustas, except Petruschke and Krumpolz, who bought their MZs into fifth and sixth places.

Equipped with full streamlining, the East German 'strokers' were capable of around 95mph and produced 15bhp. They had just made the switch from three to four speeds, but were still at a distinct disadvantage on such a demanding circuit compared with the factory MVs, which had a fifth ratio.

In 1956, a youngster named Ernst Degner joined the team. He was to emerge as the Eastern sector's top rider over the next decade, but he also became involved in a highly controversial affair which rocked the racing world at the end of 1961; more of this later...

Kaaden (left) and Derek Woodman, circa 1965.

After Peenemunde was virtually destroyed by RAF bombers in August 1943, the research centre was relocated where work on the V2 rockets continued. Then in May 1945, Kaaden was interned by the Americans, before being handed over to the Russians. Zschopau meanwhile was in the part of Germany controlled by the Communist authorities and eventually in the early 1950s, Kaaden returned and soon entered the employ of DKW's successors, MZ (Motorradwerk Zschopau).

From 1953 Kaaden took charge of the MZ racing development (which meant he controlled all the factory's sporting activities). Kaaden then developed a series of engines where the carburettor was mounted to the side of the crankcase, where it supplied mixture by means of a disc valve mounted in the crankcase wall. He was also a pioneer in utilising the now widely-used square 54 x 54mm dimensions (on a 125cc single) with expansion chamber exhaust.

By 1961, the 125 single and 250cc twins were offering the equivalent of 200bhp per litre - an amazing figure for the time - and MZ looked like taking the 125cc world title. But it was not to be. Their chief rider, Ernst Degner defected to the West and went to work for Suzuki (who won their first ever world championship the following year).

Kaaden had been approached earlier, but had refused Suzuki's advance, putting his family and country before personal freedom or wealth. And from that time Kaaden's research has been reflected in all subsequent racing 2-strokes, not just those from Suzuki, but the rest of the industry. He died on 3rd March 1996, but his technology has outlived him and acts as a constant reminder of the man who is universally acclaimed as the 'Father of the modern 2-stroke'.

In torrential rain, MZ star Horst Fugner displayed the design's potential by finishing a brilliant fourth in the 1957 125cc German GP at Hockenheim. Full streamlining was banned at the end of that year. Power output was 18bhp.

1959, 125 MZ air-cooled single, disc valve.

For 1956, the German GP returned to the Solitude circuit. The nine-lap, 63.8-mile, 125cc race saw a galaxy of lightweight road-racing talent assembled on the grid. MV, FB Mondial, Ducati, KTM and the new Gilera twin massed the four-stroke ranks, while the two-stroke flag was flown by DKW, Montesa, Puch and MZ. Against such a formidable line-up, Degner's tenth, and the thirteenth and fourteenth placings of his team-mates, Fugner and Krumpolz, made a respectable showing. The latest MZs now sported six-speed gearboxes and improved power output over the 1955 bikes.

By 1957, the more informed observers had begun to realise that the small-capacity Zschopau two-strokes were making substantial progress. The season opened with the German GP in May, held over the ultra-fast 42-mile Hockenheim-Ring.

MZ had three entries: Ernst Degner, Horst Fugner and Werner Musiol. In a race won by Carlo Ubbiali (MV) at an average speed of 99.29mph, Fugner finished an excellent fourth, Degner sixth and Musiol eighth. This result spurred the MZ design team, led by Kaaden, to even greater efforts.

The result was that, at the end of 1957, MZ emerged from Germany's borders for the first time to compete in the Italian GP at Monza. The results of this expedition were nothing to get excited about, as only Degner finished, in seventh position and, a lap behind the winner Ubbiali (MV). However, it was a moral victory, for not only had MZ ventured out of the Fatherland, but Degner's was the first two-strole across the line. At this stage, the MZ 125 was delivering 16bhp at 8,300rpm.

Fugner having his machine fettled on the start line after a plug chop, prior to the 1958 Ulster GP. Note the machine's details including new-for-year alloy dolphin fairing, hi-level exhaust, Earles-type forks and twin leading shoe rear brake.

Back in the winter of 1953-4, first drawings had been carried out for a completely new MZ, a 250cc twin. The broad strategy was to experiment on the 125, then transfer the technology to the twin. (The 250 was actually two 125s with crankshafts spliced to a common primary drive). However, in practice, it was not quite as simple as this, with the result that it was not until 1958 that the larger bike was ready for Grand Prix action.

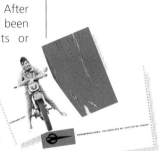

The setting was the Nürburgring, for only the second Grand Prix to be staged at this venue in the post-war period. First came the 125cc race. After all three Ducati Desmo riders had been forced out by either accidents or machine trouble in a single lap half-way through the race, it was left to the MZs of Degner, Fugner, Walter

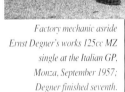

Factory mechanic astride Ernst Degner's works 125cc MZ single at the Italian GP, Monza, September 1957; Degner finished seventh.

Brehme and Musiol to take up the four remaining leaderboard positions behind the two MVs of Ubbiali and Provini. If this was not enough, Fugner gave the twin-cylinder MZ a fabulous debut by bringing it home second in the 250cc race, behind race winner Provini. Fugner's average speed for the six-lap, 85.04-mile race was 73.07mph (against Provini's speed of 73.94mph).

At the time of their appearance at the Nürburgring in the spring of 1958, Kaaden's engines were up to the impressive power output of 160bhp/litre, the 125 producing 20bhp and the 250, 36bhp. This also coincided with the factory deciding to take in as many of that year's championship events as possible. With stiff opposition from both MV Agusta and Ducati, the best overall performance came from the 125 single. However, the first ever MZ GP victory came from the 250 twin, ridden by Horst Fugner. It took the Swedish round, admittedly only after Provini was forced to retire.

The 1958, 125 MZ without its fairing. This shows rear facing exhaust and the massive dimensions of the hand-beaten alloy fuel tank. The 125 single now gave 20bhp; the 250 35bhp.

For 1959, MZ obtained the services of a foreign rider for the first time, the widely travelled Swiss star, Luigi Taveri. It was Taveri who came up with the idea of fitting the front forks from a Manx Norton.

The reason for the adoption of the Norton fork, on the 250 at first, was because with the power output growing, the handling was becoming increasingly poor. This trouble was eventually traced to the front suspension system, and the Norton fork was a great help. Braking on the 250 was another headache. This was due to the combination of speed (by now approaching 130mph) and the lack of engine braking effect from the two-stroke, twin-cylinder engine. Kaaden's answer to this problem was to design a set of truly excellent drum brakes, the single-sided, single-leading-shoe front one being fitted with a type of centrifugal fan to circulate cooling air through the drum. The rear unit was a single-sided, twin-leading-shoe type.

But how was MZ to acquire stocks of the Norton Roadholder racing fork? The answer came from a meeting between the legendary English tuner, Francis Beart, and Kaaden at the 1959 TT. It transpired that Beart had a number of new Norton forks at his Guildford tuning establishment. These had been taken from complete machines whose engines he had fitted in Formula 3 cars (Norton would only sell complete bikes!). Beart agreed to a trade, forks for brakes, so MZ's lack of Western currency was solved. This deal was brokered by Shell Mex/BP trade baron, Lew Ellis.

Kaaden signed his first foreign rider at the beginning of 1959, the Swiss star, Luigi Taveri, who had formerly raced factory MVs and Ducatis.

138

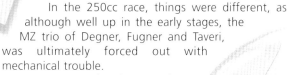

Another breakthrough during the same year was Kaaden's adoption of a third transfer port (bridged like its two companions to prevent the single Dykestype piston ring fouling). Perhaps equally important, however, the side effect of this improved cylinder filling and extra power was the much superior lubrication of what was rapidly becoming a source of unreliability, the caged Ina needle-roller small-end bearing. Another change was the substitution of the alloy dolphin fairing for a much cheaper and easier to construct fibreglass version.

Through 1959, the MZs became ever quicker and more effective as viable top-class Grand Prix machines. The season had started well when Taveri had finished second in the 125cc TT, with Fugner supplying excellent support in fourth place. When one considers that Taveri was sandwiched between Tarquinio Provini and Mike Hailwood, this was truly a great result.

In the 250cc race, things were different, as although well up in the early stages, the MZ trio of Degner, Fugner and Taveri, was ultimately forced out with mechanical trouble.

Next stop on the championship trail came at Hockenheim, where Degner came home sixth in the 125 race, and Fugner fourth in the 250. At the Dutch TT, MZ had Derek Minter on a 125 (the Kentish rider rode a Morini in the 250 race). Minter was fifth behind team-mate Fugner. In the higher class, Fugner and Degner occupied fifth and sixth positions respectively.

Ernst Degner astride his 250 MZ disc valve twin before the start of the 1959 Ulster GP. The Norton forks came from a deal involving forks for brakes between British tuner Francis Beart and Walter Kaaden. This barter solved MZ's lack of Western currency.

The 1959 250cc Ulster Grand Prix was won by the meteoric Rhodesian Gary Hocking, on an MZ.

Just before the Swedish GP at Kristianstad, Kaaden acquired the services of the talented Rhodesian Gary Hocking, who had made something of a name for himself with some excellent performances on a pair of single-cylinder Nortons that year. Hocking repaid Kaaden's faith on his debut by winning the rain-lashed 250cc race by nearly a minute. This was no empty victory, either, as behind the MZ were some of the world's finest riders, men such as Ubbiali, Duke, Hailwood and Dale.

The next GP was in Ulster, where Hocking rode both the 125 single and 250 twin. In the smaller capacity class, he (and Degner) had to concede to Mike Hailwood, while the British rider scored his first ever GP victory (aboard his single-cylinder desmo Ducati). In the 250cc race, however, Hocking turned the tables, beating Hailwood, who was now Mondial-mounted. Again, Degner was third.

After these outstanding results, Count Agusta stepped in and promptly signed up Hocking to contest the final classic, the Italian at Monza. To counter this, MZ obtained the services of Minter (again) and Tommy Robb. Meanwhile, Taveri returned to ride one of the 250 twins. (He had quit MZ to ride for Ducati after the German GP earlier in the year.)

In the 125 race, Degner and Ubbiali fought it out tooth and nail, victory finally going to the German pairing. The same close finish transpired in the 250cc event, but this time, the Italian won by a matter of inches. After such an excellent end to the 1959 season, much was expected of the MZ team in the following year.

MZ 125cc single 1960

Engine:	Air-cooled, single-cylinder two-stroke with rotary-disc induction; rearward facing exhaust port.
Capacity:	123.6cc.
Bore & stroke:	54 x 54mm.
Compression ratio:	15:1
Carburation:	Amal TT carburettor with remote float chamber.
Ignition:	Magneto.
Lubrication:	Petroil.
Gearbox:	Six-speeds.
Clutch:	Dry, multi-plate.
Frame:	Double cradle, tubular steel.
Suspension:	Front leading link with shock absorbers; rear swinging arm, twin shocks.
Brakes:	190mm drums front and rear.
Tyres:	2.75 x 18 front and rear.
Dryweight:	68kg.
Max power:	23bhp @ 10,700rpm.
Max speed:	115mph.

Unfortunately, events did not go according to plan. For a start, after trying to sign various Western riders - Mike Hailwood and Alan Shepherd included - Walter Kaaden eventually settled upon his number one, home-grown star, Ernst Degner, and the Englishman, Dave Chadwick. This final choice was surprising, as, when the news broke in February 1960, Chadwick was still recovering from a serious arm injury sustained in the previous year's TT.

The German sports director said that the main aim of the MZ factory was to win the 125 and 250cc classes and that Degner and Chadwick would contest all the classic races. He also revealed that MZ intended to enter the 350cc title chase, with an overbored 250. However, these plans received a terrible setback when Dave Chadwick was killed whilst racing a Norton at Mettet, in Belgium, in mid-May.

John Hempleman accelerates his MZ single into the Glenclutchery Road, 125cc TT, 13th June 1960.

In March, news had come of a new company in Italy, headed by Leopoldo Tartarini, which intended marketing MZ-powered roadsters. To launch the new venture, Tartarini arranged with the East German factory to send some works racers to Italy. In addition, the former Ducati star, Alberto Gandossi, joined MZ. He was to head the Ital-MZ team in Italian events. It also meant that Gandossi would ride in the World Championship series.

The first classic which catered for 125 and 250cc machines was the Isle of Man TT in early June. Following Chadwick's death, MZ signed up several other 'foreign' riders: the New Zealander John Hempleman and the English trio of Bob Anderson, Dickie Dale and Eddie Crooks.

Degner and Hempleman (the latter is seen here in the TT) scored an impressive 1-2 for MZ in the 1960 125cc Belgian Grand Prix, with the New Zealander also setting the fastest lap at 101.35mph - some going for a 125 single.

For the 1960 Isle of Man TT, Kaaden signed Englishman Bob Anderson (seen here) and Eddie Crooks; plus New Zealander John Hempleman.

During the winter months, the development team had been hard at work, the 250 twin-cylinder model receiving most attention. Although basically the same as the 1959 version, it sported a stiffer frame of larger-diameter tubing, while the Norton forks, introduced on a couple of bikes half-way through the previous season, were standardised on all of the 250cc models. Power output had been stepped up from just over 40bhp at 10,500rpm to 45bhp at 10,000rpm. Top speed was in the region of 140mph.

With the fastest four-stroke twins (MV and Ducati) pumping out slightly less bhp and being significantly heavier at the same time, the latest MZ looked a potential championship winner. Unfortunately, its reliability was to prove abysmal that year, with only four finishes in the top six at the GPs - Hempleman (fourth) and Degner (sixth) in Holland, Dale (fourth) in Germany, and finally, a third place by Degner at the last round at Monza.

Compared to the twin, the 125 single was much more successful. By 1960, its 123.6cc, six-speed engine was producing a very healthy 23bhp at 10,700rpm, while maximum speed was up to 115mph.

Hempleman and Anderson set the ball rolling by coming home fourth and fifth respectively in the Isle of Man. Then Gandossi placed an excellent third at the Dutch TT. However, it was at the ultra-fast Belgian GP where MZ really proved what a potent bike it had. Degner and Hempleman showed the rest of the field the way home, the latter also setting the fastest lap at 101.91mph.

Bob Anderson, 125 MZ, 1960 TT.

Alan Shepherd working on one of his factory-supplied MZ racers during the early 1960s. He rode for the factory during 1961, 1962, 1963 and 1964.

Degner followed this up with a couple of third positions in the two remaining classics in Ulster and Italy, to finish third in the championships. This was MZ's best position to date.

Meanwhile, development of the new 300cc MZ had shown that enlarging the two air-cooled cylinders had resulted in serious overheating, leading to piston problems.

In December 1960 came the first hint that the up-and-coming Lancashire rider, Alan Shepherd, might be signing for MZ. Confirmation came in late February when a contract was signed. Strangely, Shepherd freely admitted to have never ridden a 125cc machine, saying, 'I suppose I must be rather unique in that I've signed a works contract to race a class of machine that I've never ridden before.'

Speaking about the 350cc-class MZ, which had been the problem child of the East German team during the previous year, Shepherd said, 'I believe it's still not ready, but when it is, I expect I'll race it, although it's not mentioned in my present contract.'

However, the run of ill-fortune with its foreign pilots continued, Shepherd being hospitalised following a heavy fall at Imola in late April. A week later, the team, now minus Shepherd, made the journey to Montjuich Park, Barcelona, for the Spanish GP. This was the first round of the 1961 championship series.

John Hempleman, 125 MZ, 1960 TT.

Start of the 250cc class at the German Halle-Saale circuit, 23rd April 1961. This race was won by MZ factory rider Werner Musiol on the latest version of the Re250, at an average speed of just over 77mph. 104, 102 and 105 are all MZs - Musiol is number 104.

The 1961 MZs had many modifications. Most notable was the deletion of the rearward-facing exhaust pipe from the rear of each cylinder. Instead, MZ had adopted the more orthodox system, the exhaust pipe coming out centrally from the front of the cylinder and then curving down and under the crankcase.

Walter Kaaden said the reason for this was to give him more latitude when it came to determining exhaust-pipe length - critical in two-stroke racing engines and governed, at that time, by FIM regulations, which stated that exhaust pipes must terminate before the rear of the machine. The latest machines were also fitted with magneto ignition in place of the coil set-up used in 1960, and new frames. On the 250, each cylinder had its own magneto with two sets of contact-breaker points.

Most of the success garnered in 1961 was gained by the revamped 125, which had its best ever year. The single now produced 25bhp at 10,800rpm which, on optimum gearing, gave a road speed approaching 120mph. This level of performance meant that in the 125cc class, MZ was the bike to beat.

Degner set off on the classic campaign trail by finishing second in the Spanish GP. Then he won the Grand Prix of West Germany at an average of just under 100mph, followed by team-mates Shepherd (now recovered from his Imola injuries), Brehme and Fischer.

The 1961 125cc single with a factory mechanic having removed the cylinder head to check the burn condition of the piston. At this time, both 125 and 250cc engines were air-cooled.

Honda-mounted Tom Phillis just managed to pip Degner for victory in the French GP. Then came the Isle of Man. Here, even the gifted Kaaden could do little to prevent the poor showing, due to the inherently temperamental nature of his highly strung 'strokers' and the uniquely searching character of the long and ultra-demanding 37³/4 mile mountain circuit. The result was that not a single MZ lasted the distance in either the 125 or 250cc races.

1961 MZ single - first 125 to reach 25bhp. This gave a road speed approaching 120mph.

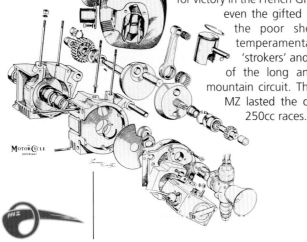

MotorCycle
COPYRIGHT

Back on the shorter Continental GP circuits, the MZ stamina returned and Degner put up some excellent performances. These were headed by victories in East Germany (Sachsenring) and Italy (Monza).

With two rounds left - Sweden and the Argentine - Degner led the 125cc World Championship. In late September came the Swedish event at Kristianstad, situated in the south of the country. The day dawned with not a cloud in the sky. Before the first race got under way, it had become swelteringly hot, without a breath of air. The four-mile rectangular circuit shimmered in a heat haze. It seemed that nothing, except possibly molten tar, could prevent records being broken.

Right from the first flag-fall, for the 125cc race, Degner was in business. He was leaving all the other competitors behind within a mile. His screeching MZ had never sounded better. Then, suddenly, after some two-and-a-half laps and 200 yards from the next man, his bike screamed to a halt with a seized engine. However, as his challenger for the world title, Honda's Tom Phillis, had managed to finish no higher than sixth place, Degner still led the championship race.

The drama was not over yet. The morning following the Swedish GP, MZ's racing chief, Walter Kaaden, was asking 'Where's Ernst Degner?' The truth was that Degner had defected assisted by members of the Japanese Suzuki management - and had travelled from Kristianstad to Denmark, and thence to West Germany. There, he joined his wife and two children who had been smuggled out of East Germany.

Compared with the previous year, the 1961 Re250 had many changes. Most notable of these was the deletion of the rearward-facing exhausts. Instead, Kaaden had chosen to adopt the more orthodox layout with the pipes taken centrally from the front of the cylinders.

MZ rider Ernst Degner (2) leads Honda mounted Tom Phillis (26) on the first lap of the 125cc Dutch TT in June 1961. Number 22 is Mike Hailwood (Honda) who went on to win the race.

Another of the locally-grown MZ riders was Hans Fischer, seen here on a 125 single in 1961.

MZ dominated both lightweight classes of the non-championship Austrian Grand Prix in May 1962. In the 250cc event Walter Musiol (seen here in the 125cc race), not only won but also set a new class lap record in 2min 36.6sec, an average speed of 72.85mph.

This incident caused a political storm, which was to have severe repercussions for MZ, both on and off the track. Not only was it robbed of the World Championship, but Degner's defection meant that MZ's technology was known to Suzuki. Just how significant this was can be gauged by the fact that, until Degner joined the Japanese company, its efforts at producing racing motorcycles were anything but successful. In fact, I would go as far as to say that the Suzuki effort had been awful, their machinery being hopelessly slow and exceedingly unreliable into the bargain.

Degner's exit also virtually ended MZ's success in the 125cc class, and it was to turn more and more to the 250cc twin in the future. Although in 1962, the Zschopau factory did build a couple of 50cc singles to contest the new world series introduced for the tiddlers that year. Their only appearance in a classic race, however, was at the Sachsenring in August. One machine was water-cooled and the other air-cooled. In the hands of Walter Brehme and Dieter Krumpolz, they finished in eighth and ninth places, but they were not competitive against the West German Kreidler or the Japanese works machines and were never seen again.

After years of work with air-cooled engines, MZ introduced a semi-liquid-cooled version of its 250 twin in early 1962. This had water jackets around the barrels only to disperse excess heat between the cylinders; the heads remained air-cooled. Another change was to pressure lubrication of the main bearings, from the gearbox supply. Development work on a fully water-cooled version was already in hand, and by June 1962, such a machine was ridden in practice, but not raced, at Schleiz. It used twin radiators.

A year later and MZ made a successful return to the Austrian event, when MZ's new signing, the Hungarian champion Lazlo Szabo, stormed to an impressive double, winning the 125 and 250cc races in superb style.

The Möhringer "Bitza"

Siegfried Möhringer with his home-built MZ 125cc 'Bitza'. Aboard this machine Möhringer won the 1967 West German Junior Road Race title. The bike featured a horizontal cylinder, water-cooling for the cylinder barrel (head remained air-cooled) and cycle parts came from a works 125 MZ. He beat several factory-backed bikes.

For 1968 the famous West German mail-order company Josef Neckermann Versand KGA of Frankfurt-Main became MZ importers and promptly signed up Möhringer. Neckermann was also the Jawa importer and Möhringer raced the 250 Jawa in 1968, together with his existing MZ Special.

Neckermann sponsored a number of riders on the East German two-strokes in long distance trials. They also arranged for the entire DDR MZ-mounted, 1967 ISDT Trophy team to attend the Elephant Rally at the Nürburgring in January 1968.

Siegfried Möhringer raced this home-brewed MZ special to win the 1967 West German Junior Road Race title.

For the East German GP, in mid August, MZ not only had the services of Alan Shepherd, but also the 1961 250cc World Champion, Mike Hailwood. Ranged against these, in the 250 race, was the entire Honda works team, headed by Jim Redman. In front of 200,000 wildly-excited spectators, Shepherd became the early leader. However, after he was forced out with a broken crankshaft, Hailwood proved that his performance was no fluke by being locked in combat with Redman throughout a sensational race.

In the end, however, even though Hailwood shattered the lap record at 100.78mph, Redman eventually took the chequered flag by just two tenths of a second.

The performance of the two-stroke twin was on a par with, and sometimes better than, the Japanese four. For example, although the Honda was faster around the bend prior to the finishing straight, the MZ more than made up the distance on the straight itself.

The 1963 season dawned with the news that Shepherd had signed for the Italian MV Agusta team. This left MZ without the services of a top-line Western rider. Walter Kaaden had tried to sign triple British Champion Derek Minter as a replacement, but this idea collapsed when Minter agreed to ride for the Scuderia Gilera team managed by Geoff Duke.

However, these problems did not stop MZ from getting off in fine style at their first appearance of the 1963 season in Western Europe. MZs swept all before them at the non-championship Austrian GP over the 3.12-mile, semi-autobahn circuit near Salzburg on 1st May.

Both the 125 and 250cc races were won by a newcomer to the team, Hungary's Lazlo Szabo. Riding a 250 twin, Mike Hailwood pushed the lap record to over 75mph before retiring.

Walter Kaaden (looking at camera), Alan Shepherd (standing over bike) and an MZ mechanic with Shepherd's TT mounts, Isle of Man TT 1964. This was one of the four occasions that year when MZ personnel were able to obtain travel visas.

With problems of obtaining visas for its East German riders and mechanics, MZ was frustrated once again in its attempt to mount a full Grand Prix challenge. Eventually, it was only able to compete in the two Germanys, Finland and Italy. The first of these events, the West German GP over the ultra-fast 4.8-mile Hockenheim circuit, at the end of May, saw Szabo take an excellent third place in the 125cc race, while Shepherd, who had fallen out of favour with MV, was back in the MZ camp and scored sixth. In the 250cc race, the twin-cylinder models were down the field in sixth (Szabo) and seventh (Shepherd). On 22nd June, three East German MZ works riders were injured during a multiple pile-up at Opatija, Yugoslavia. This left Hans Fischer with a broken wrist and Wolfgang Moses with a fractured skull, whilst Horst Enderlein sustained a broken leg.

Without doubt, however, the biggest MZ news story of 1963 was Mike Hailwood's sensational win in the 250cc class of the East German GP at Sachsenring in August.

Motor Cycling summed it up, 'Two hundred thousand East Germans rose to their feet shouting, cheering and waving flags as Mike Hailwood scored the most popular win of his fabulously successful career at the Sachsenring on Sunday. Piloting a locally built MZ two-stroke twin in the East German Grand Prix, Mike had spreadeagled the opposition to win the 250cc class at a record speed of 98.30mph.'

To add to the delight, MZs also filled second (Shepherd) and fourth (Szabo) places on the leaderboard.

The reason behind much of this success was the work carried out by Kaaden and his team during the winter of 1962-3, which had lifted the power output to 48bhp at 10,800rpm. The maximum speed had risen to 155mph (timed at the Belgian GP in 1962). A single, light-alloy radiator and finning on the water jackets were used. However, the fins were for strength, not cooling. A new crankshaft had also been introduced following Shepherd's retirement during the 1962 East German GP. Incidentally, this was the first time a 250 MZ had succumbed to bottom-end failure. More usually, the retirement had been caused by piston seizures.

As already related, the early experimental engine had had sheet-metal jackets simply welded around an existing cylinder after the fins had been ground away, while the cylinder head remained air-cooled. For 1963, the change was made to water-cooling both the cylinder and head, using entirely new components. Water circulation was provided by the thermo-syphon method with no water pump. When the engine was running,

Walter Kaaden with Mike Hailwood at the East German Grand Prix, August 1962.

In early MZ experiments with liquid cooling, water jackets around cylinders were used with conventional air-cooled heads. However, the engine which carried Mike Hailwood to a sensational 250cc victory at Sachsenring - the home of the East German Grand Prix on 18th August 1963 - featured water-cooling for both cylinders and heads.

Shepherd's 1964 Grand Prix winning engine. Rearward facing exhaust, Amal carbs, magneto ignition and water-cooling.

heated water inside the cooling jacket would rise and flow up through a large-diameter hose to the top of the radiator, where it would displace cooler water that would flow downward, through another hose, and into the cylinder jacket.

MZ had also reverted to rearward-facing exhausts. It had been found that with the exhaust ports at the front, any slight gain from having an increased exhaust-pipe length to play with was more than offset by the drop in power output and decreased reliability.

Another reason for positioning the exhaust port at the rear of the cylinder had been to improve piston sealing (with a forward-rotating engine, rod angularity during the power stroke pushes the piston against the rear cylinder wall), as there had been a noticeable power loss with the relocated exhaust port. Most damning of all, however, was that the forward-port engines proved even more prone to piston seizures! This was probably caused by the reduced sealing effectiveness allowing some of the flame to blow down past the piston on the exhaust port side. This caused overheating of the piston and, additionally, burned away the lubricant on that side of the cylinder. Finally, the power output was raised from the 1962 figure of 46bhp to 48bhp, while fuel consumption at racing speeds was in the region of 22mpg.

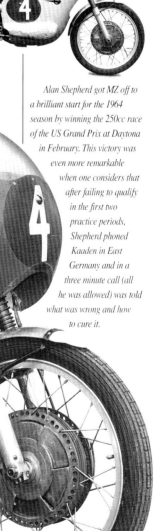

Alan Shepherd got MZ off to a brilliant start for the 1964 season by winning the 250cc race of the US Grand Prix at Daytona in February. This victory was even more remarkable when one considers that after failing to qualify in the first two practice periods, Shepherd phoned Kaaden in East Germany and in a three minute call (all he was allowed) was told what was wrong and how to cure it.

Alan Shepherd was considered by Kaaden himself as his best rider, with the possible exception of Mike Hailwood. When one realises that Shepherd was very much a 'lone wolf' - rider and mechanic - his achievement of finishing third in the 1964 250cc world championship series, against the combined might of Honda, Suzuki and Yamaha was a superb achievement.

One other major problem still remained unsolved - the political one. There is no doubt that this, combined with the shoestring budget within which MZ race development had to work, was a great and unseen handicap. Even with these problems, MZ attempted to step up its World Championship challenge in 1964. Thus, it was decided to provide as much backing as possible to its number-one runner, Alan Shepherd. In practice, this meant that the Englishman was left very much to his own devices, as it was still not possible for factory mechanics to be with him at the vast majority of meetings.

When one realizes that Shepherd was very much a 'one man band' - rider and spannerman - his achievement of finishing third overall in the 1964 250cc World Championship, against the combined might of Honda, Suzuki and Yamaha, was impressive to say the least.

Shepherd and MZ got off to a flying start at the United States Grand Prix at Daytona. This came after very poor performance in the first two practice sessions. A three-minute telephone call to Walter Kaaden in East-Germany advised Shepherd how to reset the MZ engine to run on the lower octane fuel supplied by the Americans. He followed this by finishing second in the Isle of Man, third in Belgium, fourth in Ulster and fifth in Italy.

For the TT, a new, lower Featherbed-type frame was built. In addition, a new double front brake appeared. Power was upped to 53bhp at the lower engine speed of 10,400rpm.

After Shepherd left to join Honda, Derek Woodman became the sole foreign rider for MZ in 1965. He repaid their faith by finishing third in the 125cc championship table. Woodman is seen here at the TT that year; he was fourth, averaging 92.19mph.

Walter Kaaden in reflective mood with the new disc-valve twin at the 1970 TT; the machine's first ever competitive outing.

It was Dieter Krumpholz's day at the 1965 Austrian GP, with victory in the 250cc event and runner up in the 125. He is seen here in the latter race leading team-mate Heinz Rosner. The latest 125cc MZ was water-cooled and had an eight-speed gearbox.

1969 125cc TT, with MZ team leader Heinz Rosner sidelined with a broken collarbone, his machine was loaned to the up-and-coming youngster John Ringwood with instructions from MZ race chief Walter Kaaden to finish rather than attempt anything dramatic. Even so at the end of the first lap Ringwood lay second behind champion elect Dave Simmonds (Kawasaki). But the next lap, at Sulby crossroads, the MZ man was out with engine trouble, tough luck indeed.

Then, detail development over the following winter raised the output still further by 1bhp, while peak revs rose to 10,900rpm. At the same time, a 350cc-class machine was at last made available, but with a capacity of only 251cc (Hailwood debuted the new bike with a superb second in the Japanese GP). However, most work went into making the machines handle better and a weight-reduction exercise.

For a start, the 1965 twins were 100mm (4in.) narrower, with new frames and 18in wheels at both ends. A slimmer fairing was also constructed. Other modifications aimed at improving reliability were the use of British Lucas transistorised ignition, which replaced the ancient IKA magneto; a one-piece crankshaft, which was not only stronger, but with less flex meant that ignition timing was more accurate; and, finally, inter-connected cylinders with common breathing to improve the carburation.

By now, the 125cc single was becoming obsolete, following the arrival of the very latest crop of Japanese multis in the ultra-lightweight class.

During the 1964 Italian GP, at Monza, Alan Shepherd had signed to ride for Honda in the following year. His MZ swan-song was at Scarborough in mid-September, when he achieved a double on works MZs in the 125 and 250cc races. The following month, fellow Lancastrian Derek Woodman was signed as a replacement.

Led by Gunther Bartusch and Laslo Szabo, a gaggle of 125 MZs negotiate Hohenstein-Ernstthal during the 1968 East German Grand Prix, over the famous 5.35 mile Sachsenring road circuit. MZs finished in 19 of the 21 places! Unfortunately, the two remaining places were occupied by Phil Read and Bill Ivy, on four-cylinder Yamahas who finished 1st and 2nd respectively.

Following Degner's defection in 1961, the next East German rider to develop into world class material was Heinz Rosner; seen here on an Re125 in the summer of 1964, early in his MZ career.

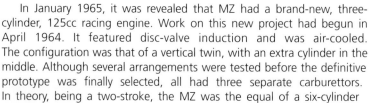

In January 1965, it was revealed that MZ had a brand-new, three-cylinder, 125cc racing engine. Work on this new project had begun in April 1964. It featured disc-valve induction and was air-cooled. The configuration was that of a vertical twin, with an extra cylinder in the middle. Although several arrangements were tested before the definitive prototype was finally selected, all had three separate carburettors. In theory, being a two-stroke, the MZ was the equal of a six-cylinder four-stroke of the same capacity. Unfortunately, the triple never made it to a Grand Prix - ignition troubles and an ultra-tight power band finally sealed its fate. Instead, MZ carried on with its ageing 125 single and 250 twin, with the odd outing in the 350cc class on an overbored 250.

Although he did not score any GP victories, Woodman gave sterling service to MZ for three seasons (1965, 1966 and 1967). The highlight was a third position in the 1965 125cc World Championship.

After Woodman left, it was the East German Heinz Rosner who took the reins. Then, in the early 1970s, the Italian Silvio Grassetti rode for a while, in the process, scoring a couple of GP victories.

However, the chance for real glory had passed MZ by, for the massive Japanese racing effort of the mid-late 1960s had simply been too great for a company with only limited resources, even if it had an engineer of truly rare quality in the shape of Walter Kaaden.

At least both man and factory can take comfort from the indisputable fact that it was they, and not the mighty Japanese, who pioneered the modern, high-performance, two-stroke engine.

Heinz Rosner (14) leads the 250cc race of the 1968 Belgian Grand Prix from Phil Read's works four-cylinder Yamaha. By this time, he had become MZ team leader, following Woodman's departure at the end of the 1967 season.

Skorpion 660 racer, ridden by Mike Edwards to runner-up spot in the 1994 British Championships.

Skorpion RS and Sport Cup

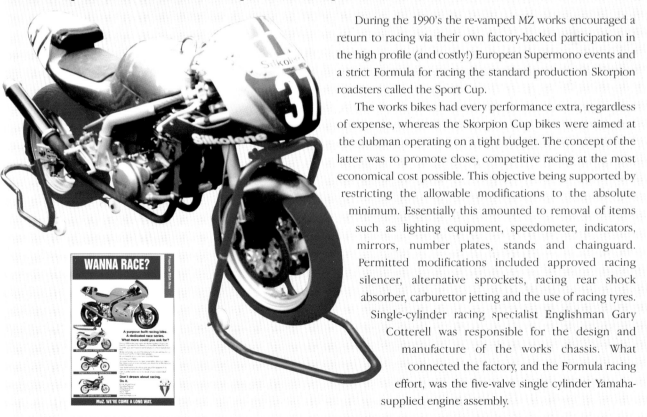

During the 1990's the re-vamped MZ works encouraged a return to racing via their own factory-backed participation in the high profile (and costly!) European Supermono events and a strict Formula for racing the standard production Skorpion roadsters called the Sport Cup.

The works bikes had every performance extra, regardless of expense, whereas the Skorpion Cup bikes were aimed at the clubman operating on a tight budget. The concept of the latter was to promote close, competitive racing at the most economical cost possible. This objective being supported by restricting the allowable modifications to the absolute minimum. Essentially this amounted to removal of items such as lighting equipment, speedometer, indicators, mirrors, number plates, stands and chainguard. Permitted modifications included approved racing silencer, alternative sprockets, racing rear shock absorber, carburettor jetting and the use of racing tyres.

Single-cylinder racing specialist Englishman Gary Cotterell was responsible for the design and manufacture of the works chassis. What connected the factory, and the Formula racing effort, was the five-valve single cylinder Yamaha-supplied engine assembly.

One new MZ which did reach the track, albeit briefly, was an unusual 125cc twin. This debuted during practice for the Isle of Man TT in June 1970. Never previously race tested, it was brought straight from the test-bed of the East German factory to the Isle of Man. Because of differing atmospheric conditions encountered for such a long and hilly course, the Mountain circuit was considered by race boss Walter Kaaden as 'the ultimate test in the world for a two-stroke'.

On the Tuesday evening practice session the twin was given its first run-up and, in wet and miserable conditions Gunter Bartusch, another newcomer to the TT, was second fastest in the class at 77.92mph.

The power unit of the in-line twin was virtually two separate water-cooled 62cc engines together, with the primary drive on the nearside and the clutch exposed outside the primary gear case. The induction disc valves were on the offside. Ignition was by twin magnetos mounted on the left.

At the time Kaaden revealed 'Power output is about three to four horses up on our best single, but the effective power band is much narrower. I would be a lot happier to have nine or ten gears instead of the six forced upon us by the FIM regulations.'

The in-line twin recorded 119.6mph through the 176-yard electronic speed trap, manned by former sprinter Arthur Breese at the Highlander. This compared with Dave Simmond's Kawasaki (124.01mph) and Dieter Braun's Suzuki (120.4mph).

Bartusch elected to give the new in-line twin its first race in the 125cc TT. He came home third behind Braun and the Swede Borge Jansson (Maico) at an average speed of 85.93mph. But after the race Bartusch said he would have preferred to have raced the old MZ single instead of the new twin. 'The single is easier to ride and the speed difference is not very much. The wider power spread makes the single more suitable for the TT course.' Bartusch also revealed that he would probably have finished as runner up if a petrol spillage had not prevented him from seeing through the windscreen! Bartusch also finished third in the 1970 250cc TT, averaging 92.43mph.

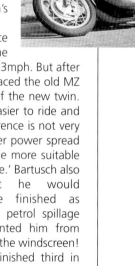

MuZ the new era

After the fall of the Berlin Wall and the subsequent takeover of the state-owned industries by a trust, known as Deutsche Treuhand, in September 1990, MZ rapidly went downhill. Sales of its production roadsters fell dramatically and in December 1991 the trust put MZ into liquidation. Between the autumn of 1990 and the formation of a brand new company, Motorrad und Zweirddwerk (Muz Gmbh) on 1st July 1992, the number of employees fell from 3,000 to 80!

The new organisation was headed by three partners; Josef Brune, Petr-Karel Korous and Dr. Hans Graalmann. The first thing the new management team did was to instigate a drastic reduction of the production times. This was helped by a move to smaller, more modern premises at Hohndorf, some 4 kilometres from MZ's old Zschopau headquarters. Also for the first time in its history MZ contracted outside suppliers for engines - first from Rotax and then Yamaha. In addition it engaged design consultants from Britain, Richard Seymour and Dick Powell.

There was also a return to racing with one of the 659cc five-valve Yamaha XTZ660 engines in a specially constructed chassis. Known as Skorpion this was built to do battle with machines such as the Ducati Supermono, Rumi-Honda, BYRD Yamaha, Bimota GB1, Fuchs-Suzuki and a whole host of other machinery using Husqvarna and Rotax power units.

The new four-stroke MZ proved a most competitive bike, not only winning the national single-cylinder championship on more than one occasion, but also doing well in the European Supermono series, whilst in Britain Mike Edwards rode a factory-backed Skorpion to runner up spot in the 1994 British Championships.

Then in early August 1996 came the dramatic news that MuZ was bankrupt and in the hands of the receiver. It was revealed that MuZ had debts totalling up to £30 million. In addition, Petr-Karel Korous was in talks with Malaysian bike builders and distributors, Hong Leong.

Then in early September it was announced that Hong Leong, headed by Ron Lim, had purchased the German company for an undisclosed sum and was injecting £8 million into developing MZ over the next three years to create a family of four-stroke engines for a new model. Lim also stated that Korous would be staying on as chief executive, alongside himself, and that the Skorpion single would be improved and remain in production.

'We plan to turn MZ into one of Europe's leading motorcycle producers', commented Lim. Since then MZ has made a sensational return to Grand Prix racing. Qualifying in pole position for the 500cc class of the Cataluna GP on Saturday 19th June 1999. The following day the rider, Dutchman Jurgen Van De Goorburgh, finished 8th in the race. The engine was developed by Swiss Auto from a unit first used by sidecar ace Rolf Biland, who is also the entrant of the new MuZ effort. The team is funded by MuZ and Albert Webber. Perhaps the most amazing thing of all is that Swiss Auto is a tiny concern with only twenty staff who, for at least one day, have humbled the might of Honda, Suzuki and Yamaha.

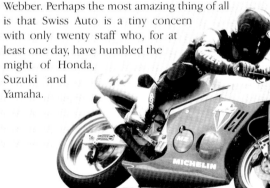

Mike Edwards, Donington Park, 1st May 1994.

A year on, MZ returned to the TT with Gunter Bartusch and last minute addition Peter Williams. The former came 9th in the Junior (350cc) race after being clocked at 143.2mph (second fastest) through the speed trap. In the 250cc race Williams hounded winner Phil Read (Yamaha), but was forced into retirement at the end of lap two. The in-line twin was again raced by Bartusch in the 125cc event, but this time clutch problems meant an early retirement. This was the last year MZ submitted a works entry at the TT.

The Italian rider Silvio Grassetti, MZ (10) leading the Yamaha trio of Jarno Saarinen (48), Barry Randle (24) and Jack Findlay (3) in the 350cc Italian GP 12th September 1971.

Classic bike collector, Warwick Blackwell with his two ex-works MZ Re250s at Donington Park, 27th July 1986. Quite how he came by these bikes is a story in itself.

Reiner Hattig/Alison De Angelis 1935 494cc ohc NSU single sidecar outfit. Festival of Sidecar, Mallory Park, October 1998.

The NSU story began in 1873, when a couple of engineers, Heinrich Stroll and Christian Schmitt, set up a modest business, specialising in the manufacture and repair of knitting machines, at the small town of Riedlingen, on an island in the channel of the River Danube. This enterprise was so successful that by the following year the company moved once more. It was Schmitt who established his new business - still based firmly around the manufacture of knitting machines - at the town of Neckarsulm, where the rivers Neckar and Sulm met.

1939 499cc (63 x 80mm) supercharged dohc twin.

Although Christian Schmitt died four years later, at the early age of 39, his brother-in-law, Gottlob Banzhaf, took the reins and soon fulfilled one of his predecessor's dreams, that of manufacturing bicycles. The first year these were produced was 1889, and by 1892, the company's main source of revenue was from the new product. That year also saw the first pedal cranks produced - a successful line that was to continue almost unbroken through two world wars and various financial upheavals, until as late as 1960.

Banzhaf was nothing if not innovative, and he was not a man to stand still very long. Soon, the manufacture of knitting machines was phased out, to be replaced by the exciting prospects of how best to utilise the invention of the internal combustion engine for powered two-wheelers.

1914 NSU 1.5bhp ohv single.

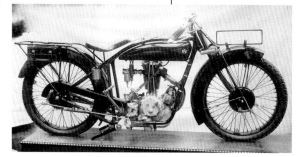

Walter Moore-designed NSU ohc single, circa 1935.

By 1900 these experiments had reached a satisfactory stage, and the company (now called NSU - Neckarsulm Strickmachen Union) had produced its first prototype, production commencing in 1901. Although it was a sturdy affair, the design was to modern eyes crude in the extreme. A Swiss-made ZL (Zedal) clip-on engine was mounted at an incline in the centre of the frame. Engine power was transmitted through a direct belt drive, and a conventional bicycle pedal crank and chain was retained to allow the machine to be 'pedalled' if the engine was not functioning.

Almost from the beginning, NSU recognised the importance of motorcycle sport as a proving ground for its technology and a marketing tool for its products. As early as 1905 it offered a purpose built competition motorcycle, the 50mph, 402cc *Rennmaschine* (racing machine). In the same year NSU opened a sales office in London. Sales exceeded even the most optimistic forecasts. British riders purchased almost a quarter of Germany's total motorcycle exports in 1906.

There is no doubt the NSU marque's success in the British market in the early 1900s was a major reason why the German company took part in the very first Isle of Man TT races in 1907. Martin Geiger, NSU's manager in Britain, rode his Neckarsulm machine to come home fifth in the single-cylinder class.

Heinz Herz (son of Wilhelm Herz) with 1939 499cc NSU supercharged dohc twin, Centennial TT, Assen, May 1998.

1953 Reynolds framed Rennmax twin, now owned by John Kidson.

There were other sporting interests too, from a very early stage in the company history. In 1908, realising the importance of record-breaking in capturing the public imagination, NSU rider Liese achieved a two-way speed of 68mph. It was claimed as a world record - even though no official records were maintained at the time. The following year, Lingenfielders clocked 77.5mph just outside Los Angeles to claim another record. His success propelled NSU into the lucrative North American market. These early attempts demonstrated that NSU could see the importance of being able to lay claim to the 'world's fastest' title. It was to become even more significant in the light of the later, post-World War 2 events.

The first NSU motorcycle appeared in 1901, powered by a Swiss-made Zedal engine. Soon the company switched to engines of its own design, including a range of v-twins with engine sizes ranging from 496 to 996cc, mounted in steel tubular frames.

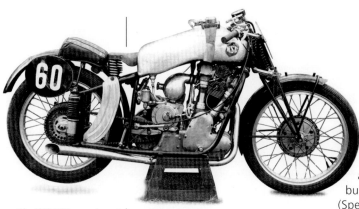

The 1938 NSU supercharged
344.82cc (56 x 70.5mm), dohc,
parallel twin racer.

These early speed records were thanks in no small part to a series of v-twins ranging in size from 496 to 996cc, mounted in steel tubular frames. This larger capacity allowed NSU the chance to build a *Spezial Rennmaschine* (Special Racing Machine) with which it could beat the best the world had at that time, at least in the speed stakes.

The next major phase in sporting development came in 1929 when NSU 'bought in' the expertise of Norton's leading designer Walter Moore. Moore claimed the Norton racing singles design as his own on the grounds that it had been done in his own time. As a result, Moore's new 1930 NSU Rennmaschine's 494 and 592cc engines, although using a four-speed gearbox, looked so much like a 1928 works Norton that they were laughingly dubbed 'Norton Spares Used'. Even so, they were good enough to remain in the NSU line-up until 1935.

In 1938 came the technically advanced 348cc (56 x 70.5mm) supercharged dohc parallel-twin (also raced in 248cc form that year) ridden by Heiner Fleischmann, Karl Bodmer, 'Crasher' White and Wilhelm Herz. But Walter Moore left the company at the beginning of the War. It was not until he had been succeeded as chief designer in 1947 by Albert Roder that NSU had the management leadership to return to racing.

Roder first produced an unblown version of the pre-war supercharged 350 parallel twin racer. Its double overhead cams were arranged in 'Y' formation. He had also been instrumental in the development of the production lightweight, the Fox 4, and a year later a racing version, the Sportfox appeared. The power unit was basically a tuned roadster engine which gave 7.5bhp at 7,000rpm, and was mounted in a stripped-down standard chassis. The factory had originally intended making thirty of these under-100cc racers for loan to promising youngsters, in order to encourage fresh blood to gain racing experience and fulfil its potential. A laudable aim, but commercial reality intervened and the machines were offered for public sale after

*In 1938 NSU had its best year
so far, when nearly 63,000
motorcycles were produced.
It was also the year which
heralded the technically
advanced, supercharged
344.82cc (56 x 70.5mm), dohc,
parallel-twin racer.*

The Anglo-German Rennmachine

Designed by the Englishman, and ex Norton chief designer Walter Moore, the NSU 501SS Supersport and 601SS Supersport were NSU's racing entries during the early to mid 1930s.

Often referred to as the 'German Nortons', both designs drew heavily from Moore's time at Bracebridge Street, Birmingham. He was after all the designer of the original 490cc ohc CS1 Norton single.

Both the 501 and 601 were built between 1930 and 1935 and featured a single overhead camshaft driven by shaft and bevels, exposed hairpin valve springs, dry sump lubrication, Bosch magneto, Fischer Amal carburettor and four-speed, foot-operated gearbox.

The 501 had a capacity of 494cc (80 x 99mm) and produced 30bhp at 6,000rpm. Its larger brother, the 601, displaced 592cc (87.5 x 99mm) and put out 38bhp at the same rpm.

The fearsome 499cc (63 x 80mm) version of the pre-war supercharged 350. It pushed out 98bhp. Such machines were used until 1951 when Germany rejoined the FIM.

enormous interest had been shown at the Frankfurt Show in March 1950. It was probably this event which was to set in motion NSU's huge Grand Prix effort, with the 125 singles and 250 twins, over the next few years.

NSU's early post-war racing programme was centred firmly around the pre-war 348cc parallel twin - now code-named RK1 - in both the original supercharged and unblown forms. These were joined in 1949 by a 499cc (63 x 80mm) version, also called RK1, which gave 85bhp at 8,000rpm with a supercharger fitted. As Germany was then excluded from the FIM, it continued to develop supercharged machines even though the FIM had banned them from competition in 1946.

By 1950, with 98bhp on tap, the supercharged 500 twin was a highly potent machine for its time, even though it weighed 484lbs and was unstreamlined. Ridden by Heiner Fleischmann one sped through the electronic timing eye at 143.75mph during a race at Hockenheim in May 1950. But Fleischmann, and the other NSU stars Wilhelm Herz and Walter Zeller, were brave men to pilot these machines, when one considers that their phenomenal power output was matched with far from perfect handling and braking. For example, at the front were pre-war girder forks and at the rear, an early form of plunger controlled damping. It could not have been easy to control all that power.

But with Germany rejoining the FIM by the beginning of 1951, the days of the dohc parallel-twin as an effective machine in the blue riband 500cc category were effectively over.

Although both machines featured a rigid full-loop tubular steel frame, a degree of springing was provided by way of central spring, girder front forks plus a single sprung saddle.

A double overhead camshaft version (also built in 348cc form) debuted in the middle of the decade, in many ways mirroring developments taking place at Moore's previous employer.

NSU's top rider at that time was another Englishman, Tommy Bullus, who had joined the NSU squad in 1930.

Probably thanks to Moore's influence there were several NSU entries in the Isle of Man TT.

After moving over to the initial design and development of the dohc supercharged parallel twin layout, Moore returned home to Britain on the eve of war in 1939.

NSU's sidecar pairing of Hermann Bohm (left) and passenger Fuchs in 1949. The lady is Inge Lowenstein, who was then Miss Germany. This dohc 500cc parallel-twin was a much improved version of the pre-war design.

Reynolds framed Rennmax twin, circa 1953.

Heiner Fleischmann with the 1951 four-cylinder R54, 500cc Grand Prix racer, making its debut appearance in the Spring of that year.

On the 29th April 1951 came the first public appearance of a brand new racing machine, no less than an across-the-frame four! The exciting newcomer was displayed at the annual Eilenriede-Rennen, a national championship race meeting near Hanover.

The story of the 500-four racer project really began in July 1949, when NSU's new chief designer, Albert Roder, completed an Alpine publicity tour aboard the newly introduced 98cc ohc Fox roadster. In Switzerland he made a point of staying in Berne in order to watch the Swiss Grand Prix at the Bremgarten circuit. For the first time since the war, Roder had the opportunity to study non-German racing machinery at close quarters. Without question the machine which most held his attention was the four-cylinder Gilera, and on his return to Neckarsulm, Roder devoted himself intensively to producing a similar machine. Within the incredibly short period of four months, he formulated a complete design and produced a set of drawings for his potential world beater.

With German racers still using compressors, he drafted two versions - a supercharged machine with the chance of producing 125bhp at 10,000rpm, and an atmospheric induction model capable of around 60bhp at the same engine revolutions. Both versions shared the same 54 x 54mm bore and stroke dimensions, which gave an exact capacity of 494.68cc. Fortunately, both design options were favourably received by the company's senior management. It was unanimously agreed by the Board that to gain world prestige through racing was excellent publicity for the sale of standard production machines. Furthermore, because of Germany's impending entry back into the FIM fold, authority was given to produce and develop the unblown version.

By the end of 1950, the European motorcycle racing community was abuzz with rumours that NSU had produced a really novel machine, incorporating much new thinking and technical innovation. The machine, now given the code name R54, was finally unveiled at the Eilenriede-Rennen race meeting. The prototype displayed a great turn of speed, but was put out of the running in the race on the fifth lap by a broken petrol pipe. However, its performance attracted considerable press coverage and was reported in *Motor Cycle*, 17th May 1951, 'to show great promise'. It also proved that the Neckarsulm company was not afraid of venturing into completely new territory.

NSU 500cc dohc across-the-frame four.

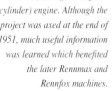

Externally the engine appeared, at first sight, to be a fairly conventional across-the-frame four-cylinder, with dohc. The two camshafts were driven by a train of gears from a crankshaft mounted pinion to the four-speed gearbox and oil pump. This pinion also powered two twin-spark Bosch magnetos which were situated immediately behind the cylinders above the gearbox. The heavily finned crankcase casting was in two halves, split horizontally, and carrying a heavily finned separate sump. There were four separate alloy cylinders with horizontal finning, and four massively finned aluminium alloy cylinder heads. These had different finning around the exhaust ports, into which four slender exhaust pipes were retained by screwed-in finned clamps. The exhaust pipes themselves terminated in short shallow, chrome-plated reverse cone megaphones. Carburation was via four clip fitting 20mm Amal remote needle instruments, with synchronised throttle slide operation from an inlet cambox-mounted linkage. Two independent, rubber-mounted float chambers were housed between each pair of carburettors.

The outside of the engine might have appeared conventional, but inside it was a completely different story. The massive nickel-chrome steel crankshaft assembly was fully machined and highly polished all over, a truly magnificent piece of engineering in its own right. It was built up using Hirth couplings, brought together by differentially threaded bolts. A Hirth coupling consists of a series of radial serrations machined on two mating faces formed at 90 degrees to the shaft axis. A different pitch is used for the internal thread in each of the mating parts so that tightening the double-ended bolt engages the threads and clamps them securely together. This unique method of construction results in an extremely rigid assembly, and permits accurate assembly of the various components and also allows roller bearing big-ends to be used with one-piece connecting rods.

The Albert Roder-designed R54, 494.68cc (55 x 54mm) four-cylinder racer made its debut in April 1951; it was inspired by Roder's trip to the 1949 Swiss Grand Prix where he witnessed the Gilera fours in action.

The valve gear was unique amongst motorcycles. First used in the Max roadster in 1952, the Ultramax system drove the valve gear by long connecting rods housed in a tunnel, cast integrally on the nearside of the cylinder. At their ends, these rods carried eye-encircling, counter-balanced eccentric discs connected to the half-time pinion and the overhead camshaft.

Ultramax System

Albert Roder became NSU's chief designer in 1947, and under his leadership (together with Dr. Walter Froede), the Neckarsulm company enjoyed unparalleled success. Besides Roder's various racing-only models, his two most important designs were the Max motorcycle and Quickly moped (NSU sold an amazing 1.1million of the latter between 1953 and 1965).

The very unorthodox 247cc Max, with a bore and stroke of 69 x 66mm, debuted in September 1952. Its frame-and-fork design had the pressed-steel chassis and leading-link front forks of NSU's Fox and Lux models, but the Max's overhead cam engine was entirely new and featured a type of valve gear unique among motorcycle engines. Known as the Ultramax System, the drive to the overhead valve gear was powered by long connecting rods housed in a tunnel, cast integrally on the nearside of the cylinder. At their ends, these rods carried eye-encircling, counter-balanced, eccentric discs connected to the half-time pinion and the

In the NSU design the crank had two bobweights per cylinder. Eight main bearings were used to support the crankshaft, of which six were mounted in special housings independent of the crankcase castings. From these housings were mounted six pairs of long slender studs which were used to retain the upper half of the crankcase, the cylinder barrels and cylinder heads. This unconventional method of construction resulted in an immensely strong bottom end and the elimination of crankshaft 'whip' at the high revolutions. The bottom half of the crankcase casting was bolted to the upper half by a series of studs and was totally unstressed.

NSU took great care to ensure adequate lubrication, even to the extent that the SAE 20 vegetable racing oil was pre-heated to about 90 degrees celsius by NSU technicians before the engine was started. The oil pump was of a complex design and extremely well made. It was situated within the heavily finned sump and was driven by the gear pinion, in the centre of the crankshaft, at one quarter engine speed. Oil was fed constantly to the big-end bearings by four 2.2mm diameter nozzles squirting directly on to bearing surfaces. Lubrication to other parts of the engine unit was controlled by ten 1.2mm phased jets, while the supply to the overhead cam gear was via external pipework running alongside the camshaft drive housing. From the camboxes, oil was gravity fed to the cylinder head and drained down through external pipework back to the crankcase and sump.

The dry multi-plate clutch had fabric friction inserts and lay in a ventilated housing on the left of the machine. Drive was transmitted through a conventional four-speed close ratio gearbox to the main drive sprocket on the right. Final transmission was by chain.

Front end of the R54. The forks are noteworthy for their curved legs, rubber suspension units and individual cast-aluminium trailing links.

overhead camshaft. As the engine revolved, the eccentrics imparted a reciprocating motion which was transferred to the valve gear. Roder also used hairpin valve springs and enclosed the entire mechanism.

Production of the Max hit its stride in 1953, when NSU built 24,403 bikes. In 1955, the company introduced a racing version for sale to customers, the Sportmax, and on a factory-backed example Hermann Peter Müller scooped the 250cc world title. In subsequent years many world famous names campaigned the Sportmax, including such legendary riders as John Surtees and Mike Hailwood.

1955 also saw the Special Max roadster hit the streets; whilst in 1956 the definitive Max roadster - the Supermax - went on sale. The final Supermax rolled off the production lines in 1963, and NSU stopped making two-wheelers in 1965. In 1969, they merged with the Volkswagen Group, becoming Germany's largest automobile complex. In just over a decade, NSU had sold over a hundred thousand Max-based models, including the Sportmax racer, and the Max series is acknowledged to be one of the finest quality motorcycles ever to have reached series production.

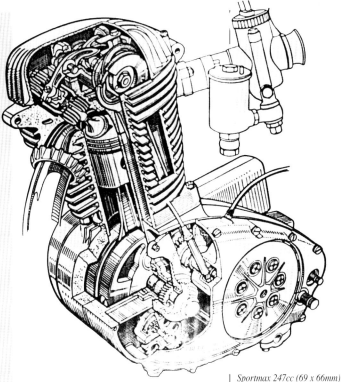

Sportmax 247cc (69 x 66mm) engine cutaway to reveal valve gear, piston, crankshaft and ancillaries.

The engine/gearbox unit was housed in a duplex tubular cradle frame of all-welded construction, in which the widely-splayed front downtubes connected with the crankcase assembly via a separate linkage. Rear suspension was controlled through a triangulated swinging fork pivoting on the frame at a point beneath the nose of the saddle. Rebound damping was controlled by adjustable friction dampers mounted on each side of the frame.

A rubber-in-torsion rear suspension may have been quite revolutionary, but the front suspension was also ahead of its time. It had two curved legs extending forwards and above the front wheel spindle. These were rigidly held together by heavy top and bottom lugs at the steering head. At the foot of each fork member was a steel pressing containing a rubber suspension unit and individually cast aluminium trailing links. The trailing links retained a short operating arm which engaged with the rubber suspension unit. Rebound damping was controlled by a large, wing-nut operated friction damper, situated at the trailing link pivot.

Braking was by built-up full width hubs constructed in light alloy, containing twin leading shoes at the front and single leading shoes at the rear.

The dry weight was considerably more than the contemporary Gilera and MV Agusta four. The machine became heavier still when fuel was added to the hand-beaten 27-litre alloy fuel tank.

The R54 was entered in numerous German events during the 1951 season and ridden by NSU development riders Herz and Fleischmann. In addition, an R54 engine assembly, mounted on a girder fork, plunger sprung frame was used in sidecar events by the German national champions, Hermann Böhm and Karl Fuchs.

In spite of intense development the design only achieved moderate success. At its inception engine output was 15bhp, which was promising enough, but it was hobbled by many mechanical problems. No doubt, given time, these could have been solved, but an edict by NSU management shelved the machine before this could happen.

The policy decision was based on the fact that although NSU was producing a range of roadsters in 1951 from 98 to 500cc, the company's long term aim was to rationalise the range to four engine sizes: 125, 200 250 and 300cc - plus a complementary range of mopeds and scooters. If NSU was to concentrate sales on smaller capacity machines, it made sense to strive for racing success in the ultra-lightweight and lightweight (125 and 250cc) classes. And so, from the ashes of the short lived 500-four project there sprang up a series of single- and twin-cylinder NSU lightweight racing machines.

The lessons learned in the development of their larger brother were quickly and effectively put to use in the new challenge for honours.

June 1951 saw the first appearance of a brand new 125cc racer. The R11 Rennfox was one of the first machines which benefited from technology gained from the abortive four-cylinder project. Like the 500, it used square 54 x 54mm bore and stroke dimensions, which gave a capacity of 123.67cc. Power output of the dohc single was 12bhp at 10,500rpm, with a forged three-ring piston that worked at 9.8:1 compression ratio, and Amal RN9 26mm carb. The engine was an extremely neat piece of work with full unit construction, and a huge cambox. A mass of gears on the right of the unit had power transmitted to it by bevel shaft. There was also another gear assembly with a conventional pressed-up crankshaft and one piece con-rod with roller bearing big-end. Integral with the crankcase was a massive oil chamber for the wet sump lubrication system. External plumbing for the pump was stainless steel braided hoses. A large oil filler cap protruded from the engine alongside the forward-mounted magneto drive pinion. The cylinder head and barrel were inclined 12 degrees from vertical.

The engine unit was mounted on a pressed steel chassis, based on the road-going Fox, with leading-link front forks of a different design to the 500-four. These were controlled by an external damper, while at the rear was a form of monoshock rear suspension without rebound damping. Brakes were aluminium alloy, full-width drums front and rear, which carried flanges secured by rivets for the alloy wheel rims. The machine's appearance was dominated by an exhaust system. Its long, shallow-taper megaphone ran back on the right, almost as far as the extreme rear of the machine, while a neatly crafted 14-litre alloy tank proclaiming 'Fox NSU' really set the little bike off. Weight was 198lb and top speed was 93.75mph.

An interesting sideline to the sporting programme in 1951 was the Renn-Lambretta racing scooter. However, very little of this machine bore much more than a passing resemblance to the then-current range of production NSU-Lambretta scooters. Its tuned engine produced 9bhp at 8,000rpm and had a top speed of almost 80mph. A special frame was used, plus larger 3 x 12inch wheels, conventional motorcycle-type fuel tank and a front mudguard-cum-fairing. The two latter components were made in hand-beaten alloy.

A notable rider of the Renn-Lambretta was the Italian Romolo Ferri. He later raced works Gilera and Ducati machines. Ferri was one of a threesome, with Ambrosini and Rizzi, who had been entered by Innocenti

The R11 Rennfox as it began
the 1952 season.

for a speed record attempt on 5th October 1950, at Monthléry in France. On a supercharged 125 Lambretta streamliner, they shattered the world's 125cc records for the 1,000km, 6-hours and 12-hours, with speeds of 82.34, 82.59 and 82.34mph respectively. During 1951 the same machine captured the 50km at 100mph, 100miles at 98.5mph, and the 1-hour at 98.2mph.

This revised Rennfox appeared at the Nürburgring in early August 1952. This view clearly shows the engine, suspension and brakes.

But the most magnificent of this whole series of records was a solo attempt by Ferri. On the 8th August 1951, he took NSU's blown stroker (claimed to develop 13.5bhp at 9,000rpm) out onto the Munich-Ingoldstadt autobahn. He then recorded the outstanding speeds of 124.8 and 125.442mph over the flying kilometre and mile distances.

Towards the end of that year, talk in Grand Prix pit lanes began to hint that NSU had built a 250cc twin racer and that 1952 would see the factory extend its racing activities.

For 1952, the 125 Rennfox was reported as 'considerably improved'. But by studying the 1952 model, it was evident that it was essentially an enhanced 1951 bike, rather than a new design. Major visible changes included the dry clutch and front suspension, with new-style leading links and internal hydraulic spring/damper units, plus revised brakes with the operating lever on the left. Other engine changes encompassed a shallower sump and vertically-mounted oil pump, with delivery via a cast-in feed to flexible hoses on top of the right-hand casting and, a four-stud fixing blanking plate covered the magneto drive pinion. Less evident was the engine tuning, with power now up to 14bhp at 11,000rpm. During the 1952 season, there were more suspension developments. The rear fork was now controlled by twin external spring, hydraulically-damped suspension units.

Motor Cycling, 10th April 1952, reported that NSU had recently advertised throughout Germany for riders willing to compete for a place in the factory team. In the first week alone there were 274 applications. At the same time, although the 250 twin project was spoken of, it was still reported to be on the secret list.

The debut of the new team was at Germany's first major event of the year, the international *Rhine Cup* at Hockenheim on 11th May. In the 125 race, four NSU machines were entered and ridden by Romolo Ferri, Wilhelm Hofmann, Hubert Luttenberger and Walter Reichert. With a great show of reliability the four riders came home third, fourth, fifth and sixth respectively. However, the Rennfox at this time clearly could not match the speed of the FB Mondials ridden by race winner Ubbiali and second place Müller. Ubbiali made fastest lap at 85.69mph.

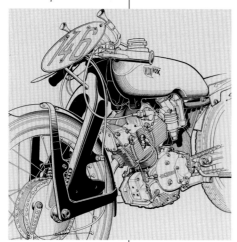

Rennfox 125cc. The 'snorkel' devices above the front number plate are breathers for the duel petrol and oil tanks.

1952/53 125cc

The 125 Rennfox and the 250 Rennmax both owed much of their technology to the R54, 500 four-cylinder model which had debuted during the 1951 season. All three were the work of NSU chief engineer, Albert Roder, and his boss, Dr. Walter Froede.

During the early 1950s, NSU created one of the largest (and most productive) racing divisions in the world. It was housed in an entirely new building divorced from the main production facilities and employed ten designers and engineers plus around 40 mechanics. This was responsible for the factory-entered racing machines and was to assist private entrants, running over-the-counter racers (including the popular Sportmax), with their problems.

In common with the R54 four and the original R22 Rennmax twin, the Rennfox employed 'square' 54 x 54mm bore and stroke dimensions. Later, as with the Rennmax, the Rennfox went over to a short stroke.

Although the 1952/53 engines were basically the same, the cylinder head on the 1953 engine was altered internally to allow more space for the rocker gear.

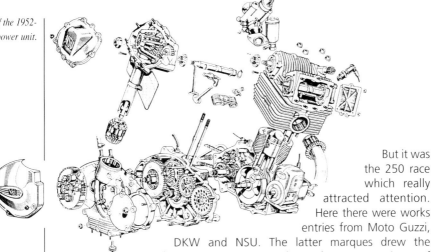
An exploded view of the 1952-type R11 Rennfox power unit.

Rennfox

The crankcase and gearbox were composed of three main castings, the middle one of which formed the timing-side half crankcase as well as housing the spur-gear primary drive to the multi-plate clutch.

Drive to the twin overhead camshafts was by means of a vertical shaft and bevel gears. Mounted on the timing side of the engine, the vertical coupling was driven by a bevel gear attached to the spur pinion, interposed between the crankshaft and clutch pinions. The top bevel box also housed the spur pinion gears driving the camshafts; it extended the entire length of the cylinder head - the cam pinions incorporating a vernier-type adjustment for timing purposes.

The valves were not operated by conventional tappets direct from the cam lobes, but via short-radius rockers bearing on each hardened valve stem. Valve springs were of the hairpin variety, enclosed within the cam box.

The magneto, mounted forward of the inclined cylinder, was a Bosch instrument - whereas the Rennmax twin employed battery-coil ignition.

But it was the 250 race which really attracted attention. Here there were works entries from Moto Guzzi, DKW and NSU. The latter marques drew the following comment in the 15th May 1952 issue of *Motor Cycling*; 'Among the several interesting designs entered for last Sunday's international Hockenheim meeting in Germany were two which may materially help to put that country back into a position of serious rivalry to British and Italian factories'.

How right this was to prove, especially in relation to NSU. For the three machines entered were the first

of what was to prove the definitive NSU racing motorcycle, the 250 R22 Rennmax dohc parallel-twin.

Unlike the 125 Rennfox, the twin was the work of Dr. Walter Froede. Contrary to popular belief, this initial Rennmax was not based on a projected road-going twin-cylinder model, but was completely purpose-built. The 1952 Rennmax shared the square 54 x 54mm dimensions of both the 125 single and 500-four, giving a capacity of 247.34cc. Initially the power was 25bhp at 9,000rpm, improving to 29bhp at 9,800rpm by the season's end.

125cc Rennfox being put through its paces by Roberto Columbo.

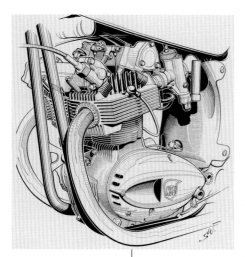
Official NSU illustration of the early-type Rennmax showing the engine...

The engine was again full unit-construction with primary drive by enclosed chain, to a four-speed close ratio gear cluster. It featured a pressed-up crankshaft assembly supported by three roller bearings. Early failure of light alloy big-end cages at high engine speeds was overcome by the use of an improved alloy and by anodising the friction surfaces. There was an Alfin cylinder barrel, with an aluminium alloy head. The twin overhead camshafts were driven on the offside of the engine by separate 'Y' bevel shafts, in the same manner as the earlier 350/500 parallel-twins. A feature of the early 250 was the use of torsion bar valve springs, but after initial problems, these were changed to hairpin springs, which remained thereafter on all the later Rennmax models.

Two single float chamber 24mm (later 25mm) Amal RN carburettors were fitted, inclined at 30 degrees downdraught. As on the smaller machine, both megaphones were of the long shallow taper type. Ignition was by battery and coil but with no generator. Two 6-volt 7amp/hour batteries, wired in parallel, were housed in a light alloy pressing beneath the seat. The use of coil ignition on the twin was not due to any desire to save the small amount of power absorbed by a magneto, but was dictated by repeated magneto problems encountered in the early stages of development with the 125 Rennfox. A distributor, housing the points and condenser, was mounted in the timing chest and driven by a skew gear from the lower bevel for the inlet camshaft drive coupling.

A full cradle, twin downtube, tubular frame was employed with twin shock swinging arm suspension and telescopic front forks. It was the only NSU racer to use them. An aluminium alloy fuel tank and full width, single leading shoe brake hubs built into 18inch alloy wheel rims, were indicative of the bike's character. Dry weight was 253lb. On some of these early Rennmax machines a large hand beaten alloy tail shell was employed, but on many other machines the rear end was left naked.

...and the front fork and brake assembly.

Neckarsulm's competitions department concentrated throughout 1952 on development work and preparation in anticipation of the 1953 World Championship for 125 and 250 classes. In the classics, the factory's best result in 1952 was from new boy, Werner Haas. In his first big race for the marque at the German Grand Prix at Solitude, he displayed the hallmarks of a future world champion by winning the 125 race. Haas had taken on and beaten the Mondial of Carlo Ubbiali and the MV Agusta of World Champion-elect Cecil Sandford. Haas had served his racing apprenticeship on a home-built Puch split single. Coincidentally, this man, who was born in Augsburg in 1927, had chosen an NSU 501 OSL as his first motorcycle.

Other positions gained by NSU riders in the 125 class that year, were a fifth at Solitude, by Luttenberger, and a sixth by the same rider at the final Grand Prix at Monza. It was also at Monza that the 250 showed its form in the World Series. Haas finished in second place, behind race winner Lorenzetti's factory Guzzi. Roberto Columbo on another Rennmax came home fifth, a taste of things to come.

In December, Englishman Bill Lomas signed to race 125 and 250 NSUs for the 1953 season. His fellow countryman, Cecil Sandford, although originally considered for a place in the team, finally elected to ride Italian MV machinery in the 125 and 500cc classes. The official factory race team for 1953 announced at the end of January was Lomas, Daiker, Haas and Luttenberger.

Evidence of NSU's meticulous approach is demonstrated by Lomas and Haas being sent to the Isle of Man ten weeks before the 1953 TT began. At the majority of meetings, machines were warmed by a system in which heated air was directed at the engines through large diameter flexible pipes from a hot air pump. The oil was also pre-heated. Ducati used a similar system for its 1958-60 works bikes.

Power unit of the 250 Rennmax twin, circa 1952.

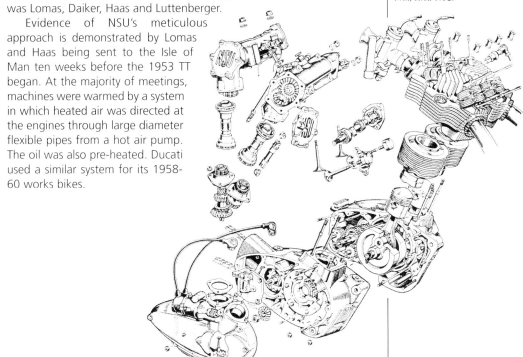

*Prototype 250 Rennmax twin
during a test programme,
summer 1952. Rider is
Otto Daiker.*

The primary purpose of the Isle of Man trip, in retrospect, was to enable the experienced TT rider Lomas to   pass his valuable course knowledge on to his fellow team member. Haas arrived with no outline in his mind about the course. But after Lomas' instructions, and only two days covering the ground, he could recite from memory all the bends from the start to the Glen Helen section. A drill was devised by the two men that divided the circuit into eight sections and a day was spent on each, memorising all the details of this exceedingly tricky 37³/4 mile circuit. Incidentally, Haas' first impression was that the TT was 'less difficult than the Nürburgring'. Both teacher and pupil for these sessions used standard Max roadsters.

The first international race meeting of 1953 was the popular annual Belgium event, around the 13.6 kilometre Floreffe course. This usually acted as a reliable pointer to form for the forthcoming Grand Prix season.

In the 250 race, Fergus Anderson came to the line with his new four-valve twin carb Guzzi single. In practice it was Anderson who was fastest. His nearest rival was Bill Lomas (the only NSU entered), enjoying his first competitive outing on Neckarsulm raceware. From the start, Anderson opened a large gap between himself and the NSU rider. And it looked as if Lomas had resigned himself to runner-up spot when, on lap five, the Rennmax came past the start/finish line in first position with a very long lead. News soon filtered through that the Guzzi had retired with a blown-up motor. Lomas sped on to win and the German national anthem and *God Save the Queen* rang out across Floreffe's sun-dappled woodlands.

In appearance the latest Rennmax was considerably different from its 1952 predecessor. A brand new pressed steel chassis, leading link front forks, wrap around 'bikini' aluminium fairing and fuel tank were just some of the more apparent advances. The compression ratio was

*This nearside view of the 1952
type Rennmax engine showing
the tacho drive from the exhaust
cam, hairpin valve springs and
air scoop in the outer cover to
direct air to the clutch.*

By mid 1953 the Rennfox engine had been subject to the major redesign shown here - virtually a new unit. This is the first engine of the new series.

increased to 9.8:1, larger 25.4mm Amal RN9 carbs were used, and hotter cam profiles resulted in power output being bumped up to 32bhp at 10,000rpm. Much of this tuning was a result of closed-season testing.

A fortnight after Floreffe, at Hockenheim, Lomas again led the 250 race before retiring. Haas then completed an NSU double, for he had earlier won the 125 event on a 1953 specification Rennfox which had been completely revised for the new season.

The new machines' engines were smaller externally and of different appearance to the original type. The vertical coupling (bevel shaft) to the ohc was on the left hand side of the cylinder instead of the right, as on the earlier model. And the old Rennfox's 'square' style engine finning had been replaced by a new round-look head and barrel, with the new dimensions of 58 x 47.3mm. Another notable change was that coil ignition was selected on the 250s, and the contact breaker was driven by a worm gear from the camshaft coupling. The frame on these machines was a composite of pressed-steel and tubular steel. It was completed by hydraulically-damped front and rear suspension. The Hockenheim version of the 1953 Rennfox had a single overhead cam, but later machines used a dohc version after an extensive development programme. Engine cooling arrangements, brakes, suspension and streamlining were also modified as the season unwound.

German GP at Schotten, 19th July 1953. NSU works rider Otto Daiker in action during the 125cc event.

Following Hockenheim came the Isle of Man TT, NSU entered Lomas and Haas for both the 125 and 250cc events. The 250 was billed as a duel between NSU and the Moto Guzzi trio of Fergus Anderson, Enrico Lorenzetti and Bruno Ruffo. In the smaller class, MV Agusta was the challenger. Les Graham, Cecil Sandford and Carlo Ubbiali presented formidable opposition to Neckarsulm.

One of the 1953-type Rennmax twins.

Things warmed up early. A practice spill put out Ruffo with a broken arm. Haas came off during a 125 practice ride, but was uninjured. Then in the final session the pride of the NSU stable, Lomas, first put himself on the leader board in the 250cc class with a standing start lap and then did the same in the 125cc category. But on his third lap, things went wrong and he crashed at Sulby Bridge. Although at the time he was reported uninjured, when race day for the Lightweight (250cc) TT on 10th June dawned, the Derbyshire rider was a non-starter. It later transpired that he had damaged a hand and it had to be set in plaster. This setback not only kept him out of racing for some time, but ended his association with NSU. The unfortunate Lomas was later to class himself as, 'NSU's favourite, unluckiest rider'. In both races, Haas had to be content with finishing second - in the 250 behind Anderson and in the 125 behind Graham.

The dohc 125 engine had first been seen during practice for the TT. These new machines were first raced at the Dutch TT, at Assen. Here Irishman Reg Armstrong supplemented the team in the larger class, while Dickie Dale took out another 125.

The 250 race came first. Though Fergus Anderson had not been unduly pressed by Werner Haas in the Isle of Man, the brilliant young German's performance on the difficult and unfamiliar Manx circuit had suggested that the latest Rennmax would be extremely formidable on the majority of European tracks. So it was to prove.

As the traffic light starting signals blinked from red and amber to green, Haas streaked into the lead on his high-pitched, screaming Neckarsulm twin. His heeling round the De Haar curves, which are close to the start, was a superb sight. In addition to setting the fastest lap at 92.36mph, the German rider won. But only just, as the wily Scottish Guzzi team leader steadily pulled back so that towards the finish, Haas and Anderson were neck-and-neck.

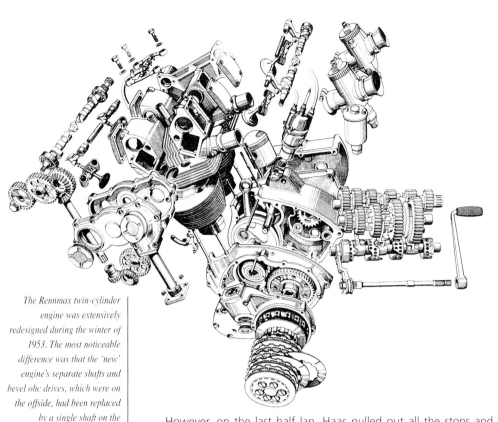

The Rennmax twin-cylinder engine was extensively redesigned during the winter of 1953. The most noticeable difference was that the 'new' engine's separate shafts and bevel ohc drives, which were on the offside, had been replaced by a single shaft on the other side, at the rear of the cylinder ...

However, on the last half lap, Haas pulled out all the stops and the Guzzi had to accept second spot. New boy Armstrong finished a creditable third on his debut ride.

This set the scene for the rest of the season. Haas won the World title with victories in Germany, Ulster, Switzerland and the Netherlands. His second place in the Italian Grand Prix at Monza sealed the title for the man who was the first German to carry off a World Championship. Just to prove that this was not a fluke, Haas and NSU also took the 125 title. Following his second place in the Isle of Man, Haas went on to score first in Holland, second in Germany, first in Ulster and finally another win in Italy.

Armstrong came second in the 250 World Championships with wins in Ulster and Switzerland, and a fourth in Italy, to add to his third in the Dutch TT. Originally the Assen race had been a 'one-off' ride as a stand-in for the injured Lomas. But Armstrong's excellent showing, and Lomas being injured for much longer than expected, meant he was made a full member of the NSU team.

But it was very much Haas' year. Not only was he double World Champion, but also double German Champion. In December Haas was voted Germany's 'Sportsman of the Year' for 1953. Among those at the NSU factory when Haas was presented with a new Mercedes car by the management, was Tommy Bullus, the Englishman who rode for NSU before the war.

... In turn, this drove the inlet cam and was driven from the immediate gear of the primary train. Spur gears transmitted the drive from the inlet cam to the exhaust camshaft.

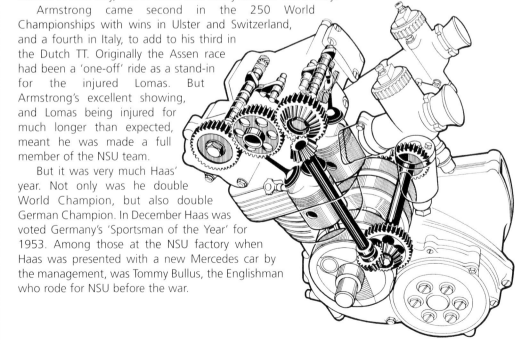

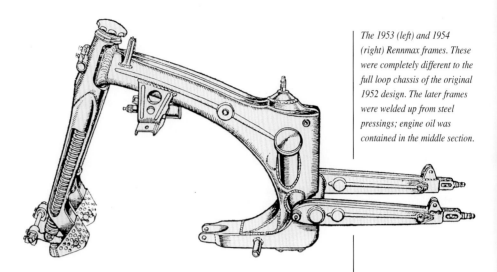

The 1953 (left) and 1954 (right) Rennmax frames. These were completely different to the full loop chassis of the original 1952 design. The later frames were welded up from steel pressings; engine oil was contained in the middle section.

March 1954 brought news that the entire works racing team for the coming Grand Prix season, except Reg Armstrong, was on the Isle of Man for course instruction. Werner Haas acted as the professor of the bends. The team was Hans Baltisburger (at one time a team mate of Walter Zeller at BMW before joining NSU in 1954), Hermann Müller and Austrian, Ruppert Hollous. All flew into Ronaldsway airport with race manager Ernst-Gustaf Germer. Their course learning machinery arrived the same day by sea. The bikes were Max roadsters, except for the team leader's whose mount was a Geländemax trials mount. The double World Champion was allowed to indulge in a spot of off-road riding when time allowed.

The 1954 international road racing season got under way with what was proclaimed as the *Grand Prix Dress Rehearsal*. This was the 21st Circuit de Floreffe, near Namur, Belgium on 2nd May. It lived up to its name, with the Norton, Guzzi, MV and NSU factories all using it as a testing ground for the models to be raced during the classics that summer. The wisdom of so doing was proved by the number of teething problems revealed. Furthermore, the gusty conditions in racing and practice gave each team a realistic idea of how their exaggerated streamlining would perform on the mountain sections of the Isle of Man TT.

NSU riders left to right; Werner Haas, Hans Baltisburger and Hermann P. Müller. The latter two mainly raced works-supported Sportmax singles.

For NSU it was the public unveiling of the latest version of the Rennmax which had received a major redesign during the winter. In spite of appearing larger, the 1954 Rennmax was 8.5lb lighter than the 1953 version, weighing in at 258lb. The most noticeable difference between the new twin-cylinder engine and its predecessor was that the former's separate shafts and bevel overhead cam drives, which were on the right of the engine, had been replaced by a single shaft on the other side at the rear of the cylinder. In turn this drove the inlet camshaft and was driven from the intermediate gear of the primary train. Spur gears transmitted the drive from the inlet camshaft to the exhaust camshaft. In addition the tacho-drive was taken from the exhaust cam.

The new power unit was appreciably shorter in height than the earlier model. This showed up in the bore and stroke measurements which were now oversquare at 55.9 x 50.8mm. The engine was also narrower due to the elimination of the bevel drives from the right hand side of the crankcase. The new camshaft drive allowed a shallower casting. Battery and coil ignition was retained. Power output

1953 Rennmax dohc 250 twin.

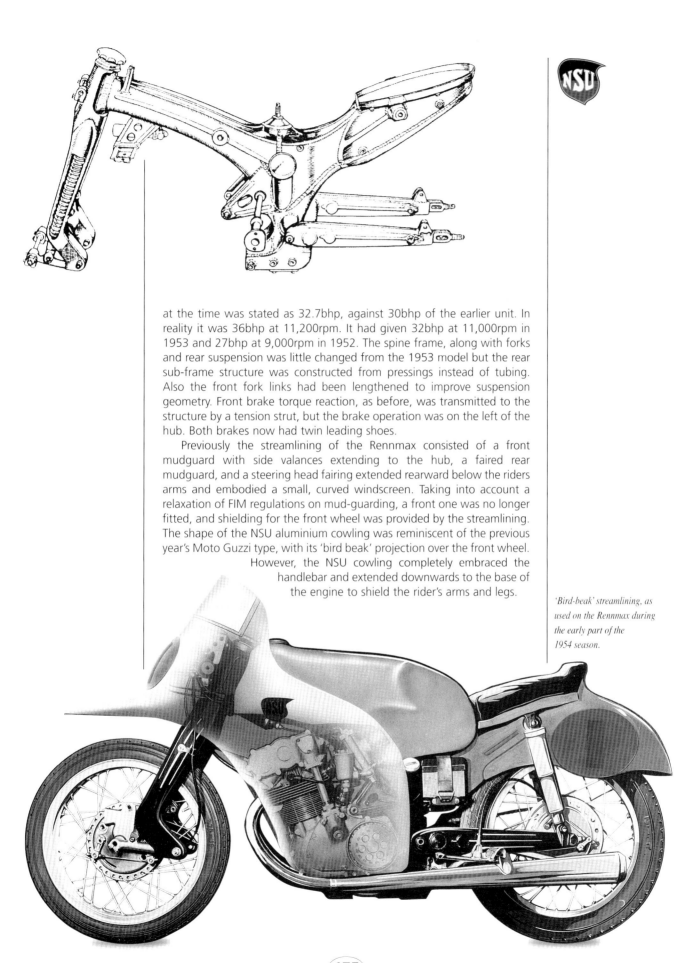

at the time was stated as 32.7bhp, against 30bhp of the earlier unit. In reality it was 36bhp at 11,200rpm. It had given 32bhp at 11,000rpm in 1953 and 27bhp at 9,000rpm in 1952. The spine frame, along with forks and rear suspension was little changed from the 1953 model but the rear sub-frame structure was constructed from pressings instead of tubing. Also the front fork links had been lengthened to improve suspension geometry. Front brake torque reaction, as before, was transmitted to the structure by a tension strut, but the brake operation was on the left of the hub. Both brakes now had twin leading shoes.

Previously the streamlining of the Rennmax consisted of a front mudguard with side valances extending to the hub, a faired rear mudguard, and a steering head fairing extended rearward below the riders arms and embodied a small, curved windscreen. Taking into account a relaxation of FIM regulations on mud-guarding, a front one was no longer fitted, and shielding for the front wheel was provided by the streamlining. The shape of the NSU aluminium cowling was reminiscent of the previous year's Moto Guzzi type, with its 'bird beak' projection over the front wheel. However, the NSU cowling completely embraced the handlebar and extended downwards to the base of the engine to shield the rider's arms and legs.

'Bird-beak' streamlining, as used on the Rennmax during the early part of the 1954 season.

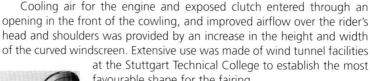

The 1954 Rennmax without its fairing.

Cooling air for the engine and exposed clutch entered through an opening in the front of the cowling, and improved airflow over the rider's head and shoulders was provided by an increase in the height and width of the curved windscreen. Extensive use was made of wind tunnel facilities at the Stuttgart Technical College to establish the most favourable shape for the fairing.

Some likened the resultant profile to a dolphin's snout. NSU mechanics accordingly dubbed it the 'dolphin', and later, in 1958, when the FIM had banned full fairings, *dolphin* was the term used to describe the new type of permissible fairing.

Rennmaxes were ridden at Floreffe by Baltisburger, Müller and Hollous. The former two had the latest 1954 specification engines, whilst Hollous used a 1953 type. In addition, Baltisburger and Hollous' machines had alloy 'bird beak' fairings and Müller a totally unstreamlined bike.

The race developed into a duel between Ken Kavanagh (Guzzi) and Hollous, who despite using an older model knocked two seconds off the class lap record and, when rain began to fall towards the end of the race, drew away from Kavanagh to win by 100 yards. A faulty distributor was blamed for Müller being forced in for two pit stops, and it was noticeable that the new engine on Baltisburger's machine appeared to be running unevenly.

The 'circus' training session then went to Hockenheim, where a week later, on 9th May, the problems with the new 250s seemed to have been resolved with World Champion Haas winning ahead of Müller. Haas also put in the fastest lap at 107.37mph. This race followed the 125 event where the team took the first four places on their speedy Rennfox singles. Haas again took the chequered flag.

A quartet of works Rennmax models in the warm up area at the French Grand Prix in May 1954. This superb period photograph captures the spirit of the Continental circus as it was in the mid-1950s. Not a motorhome in sight!

May 1954 Hockenhiem shot, showing 'bird beak' streamlining used by NSU for their 125 Rennfox model.

Though the basic dohc 125cc engine design remained unchanged, engine power had been boosted to 18bhp at 11,500rpm. As before, a six-speed gearbox was employed because of the need to keep the engine operating within its effective power band. But now, as a result of new streamlining and increased power, top speed was 5mph quicker. Twin leading shoe brakes were fitted on both wheels, but even so the weight was reduced from 184lb to 177lb. This advantage, however, was off-set by the burden of the full streamlining.

The 1954 Rennfox's frame was revised and carried similar streamlining to the latest Rennmax. Firstly, there was a 'bird beak' dolphin design with a large hand-beaten alloy fuel tank and tail fairing. Mid-season, this was replaced by an ugly full dustbin with 'droop snout', followed by more shapely 'blue whale' streamlining. Finally NSU settled upon blue whale streamlining on the definitive design used for the Sportmax models in 1955.

In the last 'warm up', a week before the first of the classics - the French Grand Prix - the NSU team appeared on 23rd May, at the 17th International Eifelrennen at the Nürburgring. That man Haas set the all-time (at that date) outright lap record during his winning ride in the 250 race on his Rennmax. He sped round the tortuous track in just 10min, 52.4sec - a speed of 78.12mph. To understand what an achievement this was, the fastest lap put up in the 500 race, by winner Ray Amm on a Norton, was a mere 77.44mph. The record still stands...

The prototype 250 Sportmax ohc single at Hockenheim in May 1954. The rider was Walter Reihart.

Tommy Robb (second left) about to test a pair of Terry Hill's NSUs, circa 1958. Left is a Sportmax, right, one of two specially converted Quickly 'racerised' mopeds.

Ruppert Hollous won the 125 event, and these two NSU results were to prove an accurate forecast to the forthcoming World Championships. Battle commenced at the French Grand prix on Sunday 30th May. This was staged for the first time at the exceptionally fast 5.18mile Rheims circuit. There was no 125 class in France and because of the event's nearness to the TT, only NSU and Gilera were there in any force. The factory riders set such a pace in their respective classes, that most of the privateers were completely outstripped.

In the 250 race, both Haas and Müller notched speeds well in excess of Pierre Monneret's winning speed in the 350 class. The Frenchman rode a triple knocker works AJS. Yet the two NSU riders, together with Hollous and Baltisburger, all had 1953 power units. The new engines were reserved for the more strenuous and more important Isle of Man honours. The Rennmax machines appeared with a new style of streamlining which totally enclosed the front wheel.

From Douglas, Isle of Man, *Motor Cycling* reported in the issue of 10th June, 'Herr Germer, the NSU boss, has set up shop 50 yards away from the Italians and was kindness itself when we called there this afternoon. Arist Crawley was given a petrol tin to sit on; models - all in the 250 class - were shifted around to suit Eric Coultham's camera, exposure meter and the brilliance of the afternoon sun. What beautiful, watch-like pieces of mechanism these semi-streamlined '250s' are. And if this lightweight class is likely to be won by careful staff-work, the quiet efficiency of the Neckarsulm factory camp practically has the Trophy in the bag even at this stage'.

And so it was. Run in brilliant weather on Monday 14th June, the Lightweight TT proved to be as much of a triumph for NSU Werke as had been the 250 class of the French Grand Prix at Rheims. With five machines entered, four took the first four places and the other came home sixth. Werner Haas not only led the race from start to finish, but created a new lap record on each of his three laps. He finally covered the 37.73 mile circuit at 91.22mph and brought his race record up to 90.88mph. Ruppert Hollous just beat Reg Armstrong into second place, with Hermann Müller a close fourth. Hans Baltisburger was sixth.

The 125 TT was rather different. After a closely fought battle which lasted for 107.9 miles over the 10.79 mile Clypse circuit, on 16th June, the 22 year old Austrian Ruppert Hollous, took a well-deserved victory from Italy's Carlo Ubbiali and Britain's Cecil Sandford on MV Agustas. Hollous, who put in the fastest lap at 71.53mph, took 1hr, 33mins, 32.5secs to cover the 10 laps, averaging 69.57mph, and finished only 4 seconds ahead of Ubbiali, who had contested every yard of the distance with him. The only other NSU finisher was Baltisburger in fourth place. Haas retired after twice falling off on roads soaked by the overnight rain which had ceased, fortunately, before racing commenced. Müller retired on the second lap after suffering misfiring problems from the start.

Extremely adverse weather a week after the TT, with rain and gale force winds and the non-appearance of several riders of Italian machines, combined to spoil some of the glitter surrounding the third round in the World Championship series, the Ulster GP, the second to be held over the 7 mile, 732 yard Dunrod circuit, near Belfast.

Dutch TT race winner Werner Haas, on a 250 Rennmax, 10th July 1954.

A trio of dustbin-faired Rennmaxes at the Swiss Grand Prix in August 1954. Left to right 16: Ruppert Hollous (race winner), 12: H.P. Müller (3rd) and the 1954 250cc World Champion, Werner Haas (crashed). A few weeks later whilst practising for the Italian Grand Prix, Hollous crashed and was fatally injured.

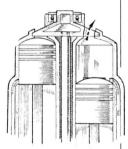

One of the many ingenious ideas created by the NSU technical team, led by engineers Froede and Roder, was this patented rotary valve design. The axis of the valve was inclined to the axis of the pair of cylinders at 15° to 45°. The design was equally suitable to four-stroke or two stroke engines having two, or any multiple of two, cylinders.

The 250 race on Thursday 24th June, had five NSU riders on the grid. The TT quartet was joined by Ireland's own Reg Armstrong. Baltisburger led from Haas and Hollous, with Müller a steady fourth. Armstrong fell back early on, and was later to retire with ignition trouble. By the seventh lap, Haas and Hollous had caught the leader, but towards the end of the 11-lap, 96.4 mile race, Hollous suffered the same ignition failure which had put Armstrong out. Haas nudged in front of Baltisburger to take victory by a few yards.

In the 125 event, run two days later on Saturday 26th June, Hollous repeated his Isle of Man victory, followed by Müller, Baltisburger and Haas. There were three works MVs and Johnny Grace on a Spanish Montesa. Only MV team leader Ubbiali caused problems, but after setting the fastest lap, he crashed after running into trouble at Wheeler's Corner. Here a sudden gust of wind caught his fully faired MV and sent him into a bank. His race was over.

At the Dutch TT at Assen, on Saturday 10th July, the 250 race came first and soon became monotonous. Haas and Hollous, about half a mile apart, held their lead and only the possibility of a fight for third place between Baltisburger and Australian Guzzi rider Ken Kavanagh, kept the crowd's interest alive. But by the end, with his Guzzi failing, Kavanagh had to settle for fourth in front of Müller. With this win Haas made certain of retaining the Championship title for a second year. The 125 race again saw Hollous take victory from Müller, Ubbiali (MV), Baltisburger and Haas. Trying to keep up with the flying NSUs, MV riders Sandford and Copeta were both forced to retire with wrecked engines.

Solitude, Germany, Sunday 25th July 1954 - the Grand Prix of the Fatherland - was held beneath a sweltering sun over a 7.1 mile serpentine circuit, among beautifully wooded hills overlooking Stuttgart. Race and lap records were pulverised in all classes before a massive crowd of half-a-

Riders eye view of the 1954 Rennfox 125, showing the combined fuel/oil tank fabricated from hand-beaten aluminium. Fuel is in the front, oil in the rear section.

million spectators. The first of NSU's new sleekly streamlined 125s appeared on the grid at this meeting. Evolution of the Blauwal (Blue Whale) had begun. The 125 race started the proceedings and it turned out an exact repeat of the Dutch result - Hollous, Haas, Ubbiali and then Müller. Continuing his triumphant progress, Hollous pushed the lap record up to 79.92mph during the 71.12-mile race. His victory assured him and NSU of the 125 World Championship.

Next came the 250 race. Moto Guzzi withdrew the four factory entries, even though the riders wanted to race. It was an admission that Moto Guzzi could not hold the NSU steamroller. Ironically, NSU's strength was reduced by the absence of Baltisburger. He was in hospital following a practice crash.

At the end of the 1954 season NSU announced its withdrawal from Grand Prix racing. This photograph shows many of the factory sponsored motorcycles, including the Grand Prix racers and Baumm's sleek record breakers.

Helmut Hallmeier, on a two-stroke Adler twin, surprised everyone by making a lightning start to lead the pack into the first corner. However, his glory was short-lived and it was no surprise when Haas headed team mate Hollous over the line at the end of lap one. Müller was chased for third spot by the Adler rider, and although the NSU was noticeably quicker, Müller was later forced to pit with a loose streamlining shell. This allowed Hallmeier and the Adler to finish third behind winner Haas, and Hollous. Müller eventually rejoined the race and pulled back up to eleventh. The fastest lap was set by Hollous at 85.95mph - a new record.

With the 250cc classes in the German and French Grand Prix won at higher speeds than the 350cc events, the obvious thought of pundits was that NSU should bore out a 250 and enter it in 350cc class racing. This took no account of the shortage of good riders with which the Neckarsulm factory would be faced in the following year. The position was made more acute by the company policy to employ only the smallest and lightest jockeys. Not only did Hollous die in practice at the Italian GP at Monza, September 1954, and Baltisburger was seriously injured from his practice crash at the German Grand Prix, but Müller - then turned 45 - was reported to be retiring. The same was said of Haas who was just in the process of entering business, as the proud owner of a new service station on the autobahn near his home town of Augsburg.

Speculation by von Heydekampf of NSU became reality on 22nd October 1954, when

1955 250 Sportmax

Engine:	Air-cooled sohc single-cylinder, with Ultramax system (drive to valve gear by long connecting rods).
Capacity:	247cc.
Bore & stroke:	69 x 66mm
Compression ratio:	9.8:1.
Carburation:	Amal GP $^{13}/_{16}$".
Ignition:	Battery/coil.
Lubrication:	Wet sump.
Gearbox:	Four-speeds.
Primary drive:	Gears
Final Drive:	Chain, $^{1}/_{2}$ x $^{3}/_{16}$".
Frame:	Pressed steel, backbone type.
Suspension:	Front, leading link forks. Rear, swinging arm with hydraulic shock absorbers.
Brakes:	Front drum 210mm. Rear drum 210mm.
Tyres:	Front 2.75 x 18in Rear 3.00 x 18in
Dry weight:	112kg (246lb).
Fuel tank:	22 litres (4.84 gals).
Max power:	28bhp @ 9,000rpm (rear wheel).
Max speed:	125mph (201kph).
Model code:	251 OSB.

it was officially announced that NSU would not be contesting the 1955 series of road racing World Championship meetings with a works team. In part compensation for the void left by the decision not to race the Rennfox or Rennmax, NSU announced that distribution of the 247cc single-cylinder Sportmax production racing machine, was to begin in early 1955. This generously gave privateers ample time before the racing season got under way.

The prototype of what was to emerge as the Sportmax was first seen at the end of the 1953 season, during the Spanish Grand Prix at Montjuich Park, Barcelona. Thereafter, development continued both on the track and in the test shop. The first machines made their appearance on 9th May 1954 at Hockenheim. Here, one finished in sixth place against international opposition. But it was on 22nd August that year that the NSU single really showed its character, when Georg Braun finished second behind Hollous at the Swiss Grand Prix and in front of Müller. Both Hollous and Müller were on Rennmax twins. In addition, other Sportmaxes came home eighth and eleventh.

At the Italian Grand Prix, 12th September, Sportmax machines were privately entered by Kurt Knopf and Georg Braun. They duelled with Englishman Arthur Wheeler on his home streamlined and prepared 'privateer' Guzzi single. Wheeler eventually won, Knopf was third and Braun retired.

All these early development machines were essentially similar to the 'production' models, but used a smaller diameter front brake and had other minor differences. Karl Kleinbach was responsible for the development of the Sportmax, but there has always been some confusion as to just how many genuine Sportmax models were actually produced by the factory. NSU publicity officer Arthur Westrup stated seventeen, whilst other well informed sources go as high as thirty-four. In addition, a number of other machines were built later from spare parts, when the race shop was sold to the Herz family in the late 1950s.

Then again many people converted the various Max, Special Max and Super Max roadsters into so called Sportmax replicas. Some were very crude. The roadster frames and forks, not to say anything of the brakes, give these spurious copies away.

Max converted roadster (207), Cadwell Park, 1959. A popular conversion at the time for those who couldn't afford the real thing.

Fully faired Sportmax of the type used by Müller in 1955. Streamlined shell, seat base and fuel tank are all constructed from hand-beaten aluminium.

The genuine Sportmax or Type 251 RS (250, one-cylinder Rennsport) had a capacity of 247cc (69 x 66mm) and a compression ration of 9.8:1, giving 28bhp at 9,000rpm (maximum safe revs 9,500rpm). The piston was a forged three-ring Mahle and an Amal Grand Prix $^{13}/_{16}$ carb was used. The distinctive 22-litre tank was hand beaten alloy and the dry weight was 246lb. Front tyre was 2.75 x 18in and the rear 3 x 18in. Top speed was 124mph and a wide variety of sprockets was available for alternative gearing. Compared with the prototype which had 180mm diameter front brakes, the production machines sported massive 210mm units.

The Sportmax proved even more successful than NSU could have ever dreamed. During the 1955 classic racing calendar, Hermann Peter (Happy) Müller astounded the very people who said at the end of 1954 that he was about to retire. On a semi-works Sportmax he scooped the 250 world title.

In achieving this feat, the 46 year-old veteran was third in the opening round in the Isle of Man, won at Nürbugring on home ground, fourth at the Dutch TT, sixth in Ulster and fourth in the final round at Monza. However, more than anything, his Championship will be remembered by the controversy it created. Müller had the same points at season's end as Englishman Bill Lomas, but Müller was awarded the title following the latter's down grading at Assen. Here, Lomas, who had been first across the finishing line, had been demoted to second place by the international jury for having filled up with petrol without stopping the engine.

Bitter controversy raged following this decision, but Müller won the title and promptly retired from a racing career which spanned more than two decades. He competed not only on two wheels, but also raced cars with great distinction. Immediately before the war he raced the fearsome rear-engined Auto-Union Grand Prix cars.

Several other prominent stars campaigned the Sportmax in 1955, these included Hans Baltisburger, Georg Braun, John Surtees and Pierre Monneret. Baltisburger, recovered from his 1954 German Grand Prix practice crash, concentrated on the German championship. Although he won the national title he had to be content with second spot in the final Grand Prix of the season, but he was ahead of Ulsterman Sammy Miller (Sportmax), World Champion Müller and Bill Lomas. He lost only to Carlo Ubbiali on his factory MV.

Sammy Miller had earlier been second on his Sportmax back home in the Ulster Grand Prix. It was a race dominated by Surtees on yet another of the fleet Neckarsulm singles. Surtees was invincible that year on the Sportmax in British short circuit events. In fact this was just the start of a run of successes for the Sportmax. Its record of placings in the top six was unequalled by any other production 250 racer during the decade. Even into the 1960s, a well-ridden and well-prepared Sportmax could offer a serious challenge. Ultimately, of course, it was outclassed by the two-strokes like the water-cooled Bultacos and early Yamahas in the middle of the decade.

The 1955 250cc World Champion, Hermann Peter (Happy) Müller. Happy was his nickname!

For 1956, the first round of the classic road racing season was the Isle of Man TT races in June. There were four Sportmax entries - Hans Baltisburger, Sammy Miller, Horst Kassner and Australian Eric Hinton, who was a non-starter, but the other three more than made up for this.

With the race run over the Clypse circuit, the Lightweight TT was held on Wednesday 6th June. The opening laps suffered atrocious conditions; heavy rain with a strong biting wind. Retirements were numerous. At first, Mondial-mounted Cecil Sandford led, followed by the NSU trio, but Miller soon took the lead when the Mondial's battery leads came adrift. At the end of lap five Miller still led, followed by the MV pair of Ubbiali and Colombo, with Kassner in fourth, but on lap six, Miller's Sportmax cried enough and the Irishman was out with a seized engine. On the ninth and final lap, Kassner and Baltisburger reached Signpost Corner side-by-side, and it was Baltisburger who crossed the line in third place, 50 yards to the good and having put up the fastest lap of the race at 69.35mph.

Another factory-backed Sportmax of the type used by Müller; rider unknown.

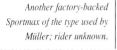

A pair of Sportmax models battling it out at Old Hall Corner, Oulton Park in 1961.

In the rest of the season's 250 Grands Prix, Sportmaxes achieved several good positions. In the Dutch TT at Assen, Kassner was fifth, while in the Belgian Grand Prix at Spa, the leaderboard read third Kassner, fourth Koster (Holland), fifth Simons (Holland) sixth Bagle (France). The German Grand Prix at Solitude saw fourth go to Baltisburger, fifth Brown (Australia), sixth Heck (Germany). Sammy Miller was sixth in the Italian Grand Prix at Monza.

Sadly on 26th August 1956, Hans Baltisburger, at the age of 33, was killed while competing on his Sportmax during the Czechoslovakian Grand Prix at Brno. It was not even a championship event.

The end of 1956 saw another tragedy for the racing world with the death on 13th November of Werner Haas - perhaps Germany's finest ever road racer - when the private aircraft he was piloting crashed shortly after take-off at Neuburg/Danube airport. Haas was then 29 years old.

Compared to previous seasons, NSU machinery (in other words the Sportmax) did not gain too many top six placings in the classics during 1957.

At the German Grand Prix at Hockenheim the former Adler rider Hallmeier, now Sportmax mounted,

Ulster Grand Prix, 1995. The two Terry Hill machines in restored condition. Hill purchased these Sportmax models back in 1955. Left to right; Noel Orr, David Andrews, Terry Hill and Mrs Hill.

Jim Lilley's story

I first came across NSU in 1953 at the Dunrod Circuit, when the works Renmax models appeared in Grand Prix racing, and I have followed them ever since. They were one of the most successful GP series built.

Dubliner Reg Armstrong was NSU's main foreign factory rider. When he left their employment, NSU presented him with his own Rennmax. It was sold to Glen Henderson, then to Ernie Johnson in the North of England and is now owned by John Kidson. The original alloy fairing is owned by Irishman, Owen O'Reilly.

One of the greatest races in Ireland was between a trio of Sportmax machines in May 1958 at the annual North West 200 meeting. After the first three laps Tommy Robb, on Terry Hill's Sportmax, led by five seconds. Mike Hailwood, on the ex-John Surtees NSU, then Sammy Miller on Reg Armstrong's machine were close behind. At Black Hill, Robb hit a patch of oil and came off. He pulled off his broken windshield, straightened his bent footrest and pushed his machine to the top of the hill to restart. Having lost well over two minutes Robb, on his damaged machine, managed to break the lap record on every remaining lap and came in third, only eighteen seconds behind the winner, Miller, with Hailwood taking second place.

Another memorable line-up featured such legends as Carlo Ubbiali, Luigi Taveri, Bill Lomas and Cecil Sandford; all riding Italian works models at the 1955 Ulster Grand Prix. Amazingly, John Surtees and Miller on the Hill machine, both privately entered, took first and second place.

The Hill machines, ridden by Miller, Robb, Andrews and Orr, dominated Ireland's road races in the 1950s. In the 1956 TT, Miller led the race right through and was set to win, when

he suffered a mechanical failure on the sixth lap. The Hill family were known for their engineering expertise, especially in engine tuning for the flying boat at Short Brothers aviation company, Belfast. Terry Hill himself was well known in his own right, competing all over the Continent in the late 1930s, especially the International Six Day Trials. Blair Maine, a World War 1 Victoria Cross winner from Newtownards, accompanied the young Terry on his first overseas competition.

Much credit for the performance of the Hill bikes must go to Terry's mechanic, the great Albert Clarke. An unassuming, quiet man, Clarke is surely one of the shrewdest mechanical engineers Ireland has produced. Now retired, Albert still assists in the preparation of machines for classic parades, and riders both past and present are indebted to him for his invaluable advice and friendly tips. Probably his finest hour came in 1956 when the NSU Quickly, which he had built for Terry to race in the 50cc class in Ireland, won the Temple 100. Hill's second machine, ridden by Jim Morrow, was equally competitive, even though Clarke built it from spare parts.

Miller travelled with Terry to the Continent, and when he was lying a clear second at Monza (1955) an ignition wire burnt almost through, but he managed to nurse the machine to a creditable third, ahead of all the works teams.

When Hill and Surtees first acquired their bikes, delivered to NSU Great Britain in London, 1955, they both raced them without streamlining (as seen in photographs of that time). Hill had the idea of using a fibreglass fairing. He sent Albert Clarke to Peel Fairings in the Isle of Man, where he decided on a came home sixth behind MV Mondial and Guzzi machinery, and finished third in the 350 race on a 305 Sportmax. Next, at the Isle of Man TT, the Swiss sidecar ace Florian Camathias, who also rode 125/250 solos at the time, brought his Sportmax home ninth. The only other NSU finisher was Irishman David Andrews in eleventh place. Australian Bob Brown had been ninth during the race but had fallen before the finish.

NSU only figured in the first six at one more Grand Prix. This was in Ulster, where future star Tommy Robb first showed his mettle by finishing third behind the Mondial of winner Cecil Sandford; Dave Chadwick on a factory MV Agusta was second. Sandford was World Champion that year.

Tommy Robb, David Andrews and Sammy Miller were able to race with the Sportmax because of the sponsorship of Terry Hill, the Northern Ireland agent for NSU. Hill owned five Sportmax models at the time, and also constructed a 50cc racer from a standard Quickly N model.

Elsewhere, without factory opposition, the Sportmax reigned supreme. John Surtees was outstanding with his NSU when his factory MV contract would allow. Other successful Sportmax riders in 1957 included Horst Kassner, German 250 Championship winner, and Helmut Hallmeier who took the 350 title on a 305 Sportmax.

Fred Stevens with his George Leigh entered Sportmax at the International Scarborough road races, September 1962. By then the German machine was beginning to be outpaced by more modern rivals such as Aermacchi and Bultaco.

1958 Isle of Man Lightweight TT (Clypse circuit). David Andrews 247cc Sportmax entered by Terry Hill; the Irishman came home in 10th spot averaging 69.17mph. Note Norton front brake referred to in text.

dustbin fairing which, compared to the works alloy type, lightened the machines and proved very successful. At that time many racers were converting to the Peel company's Dolphin fairings.

Artie Bell, former Norton factory rider, took a personal interest in Terry's machines and travelled to most meetings including the Isle of Man and The North West, to offer expertise and encouragement to the riders.

One great performance was from David Andrews, riding the number one machine with full dustbin fairing. Not only did he win the 250cc class, but also finished ahead of the five-hundreds, smashing the lap record by over 10mph. Another great victory was Tommy Robb's at Oulton Park. A numb, wet Robb crossed the finishing line in such atrocious conditions that he didn't even realise he'd beaten the field. Robb and Miller recorded many victories on the British short circuit at that time and there was thrilling rivalry between Hill's bikes and those of Scotland's Glen Henderson witnessed on our Irish circuits. As well as the two machines delivered to London for Hill and Surtees, a third was supplied to former NSU works rider, Reg Armstrong. This bike was ridden by Dickie Carter who won many races in Ireland at that time.

With Artie Bell, Terry Hill decided to replace the standard NSU Sportmax front brake assembly, which was prone to overheating and warping, pulling the front wheel out of alignment, by using Manx Norton front hub and brake. Whilst the Norton brake was hard, it did become more flexible during the race. Most competitors, having seen the benefit of this improvement, followed suit.

Artie Bell was especially connected with the floating carburettor bowl system. While still riding for Norton in 1948,

he noticed that on circuits with lots of corners, frothing occured and caused misfires and slow acceleration out of the bends. He solved this by removing the carburettor float bowl from its fixing and attaching it to rubber tubing which allowed it to float freely and reduce the effect of the frothing.

"Thrust Combing" was another NSU innovation, which in later years increased the power of the Sportmax. Three small slots at the end of the exhaust system created a backflow and increased power by two or three mph.

Hill's first purchase of an NSU Sportmax was from Dr. Gerd Stieler Von Heydekampf and a long relationship developed between the two men, and through Terry Hill's great relationship with the NSU factory, a vast body of knowledge and expertise has been available over the years.

One of the original employees of NSU Great Britain, Michael Bracken is alive and well at time of writing, now living on the Isle of Man. Another was the brother of the former English test cricketer, Jim Engineer.

The "Flying Doctor", Jack Murgatroyd, himself a successful Sportmax competitor in the late 1950s, took over at NSU (GB) in 1960. By then NSU was running down its motorcycle division in favour of cars, but Jack was still responsible for the service and spares department. He travelled the country servicing engines and particularly race machines.

Richard Quick, (Mr Quick to his friends), a London motor dealer who moved to Southern Ireland in the sixties, bought up all Sportmax bikes and spares he could find, and to this day remains a major source of spares.

During the winter of 1957-58, Stanley Michael Bailey Hailwood - Mike Hailwood - the 18 year-old Englishman from Nettleton, Oxfordshire, put together a string of successes on a racing tour of South Africa in his first season. Hailwood campaigned with the ex-John Surtees NSU Sportmax. There were two other Sportmaxes in the Hailwood camp.

Former World Champion Geoff Duke made an accurate forecast in *Motor Cycling*, 1st May 1958; 'If the results in South Africa are anything to go by, the name Mike Hailwood should appear on many leaderboards'. Upon his return to Britain in late April 1958, Hailwood soon got off to a flying start for the British short circuit season. He had a pair of wins at Crystal Palace in the 200 race (on an MV) and the 250 with one of his NSU's.

Hailwood was not only a naturally gifted rider, but unlike many others, his father, Stan Hailwood, was in a position to provide almost unlimited sponsorship for the Ecurie Sportive team. Throughout Britain during the summer of 1958, Mike Hailwood and his NSU's were described in headlines as 'Untouchable' and 'Giant Killer'. His victories and lap records included Brands Hatch, Crystal Palace, Mallory Park, Aintree, Snetterton, Scarborough and Aberdare. At the end of the season, the youngster had claimed no fewer than three of the four ACU solo Road Race Stars (the British Championships), the 125, 250 and 350cc classes.

He shone no less brightly on the international scene too, starting with a memorable finish in second place behind race winner Sammy Miller, in the 250 class of the North West 200 in Northern Ireland, on Saturday 17th May.

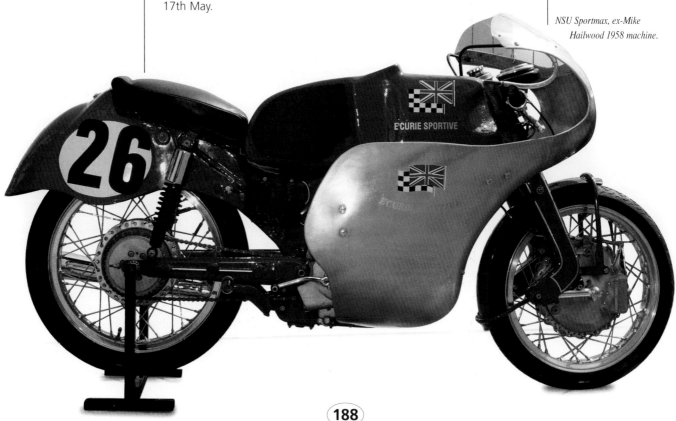

NSU Sportmax, ex-Mike Hailwood 1958 machine.

Australian Bob Brown (9) leads Mike Hailwood (18). Both are mounted on Sportmax models. This 1958 TT battle finished with Hailwood 3rd and Brown 4th. It was the Hailwood's first visit to the Isle of Man.

Then came Hailwood's first Isle of Man TT. In his first race on the Clypse Circuit, in the Lightweight TT on 4th June, he had a long duel with the experienced Australian rider Bob Brown, on another Sportmax. It ended with the teenager Mike Hailwood passing his rival to take third place. In this event there were ten NSUs including those of Hailwood and Brown. The others were Eric Hinton (7th), Tommy Robb (8th), Fron Purslow (9th), David Andrews (10th) and Glenn Henderson (12th). Alan Povey retired on lap two and Alan Harth and Peden retired on lap one. New Zealander Neil McCutcheon was a non-starter.

First in the international calendar was the non-championship Austrian Grand Prix on 1st May, where Italy's Carlo Ubbiali took his MV to victory. Sammy Miller was second on a works CZ four-stroke. Sportmax machines took the next four places with Hallmeier, Autengruber, Scheider, and Thalhammer respectively. This meeting was followed by the International Rhein Pukal Rennen, at Hockenheim on Sunday 11th May. It was won by hard-riding Horst Kassner on a Sportmax, ahead of a pair of Adler two-stroke twins.

First of the Continental European classics was the Dutch TT at Assen, on Saturday 29th June. Hailwood, on his first visit to the circuit, was first Sportmax rider home coming fourth behind the works MVs and an Adler twin. Kassner was sixth, and Thalhammer eighth, followed by several other NSU competitors.

Shrewsbury rider/dealer Fron Purslow taking his Sportmax to victory in the British Championships at Thruxton in August 1958.

A week later in Belgium there was no 250 class, so it was at the Nürburgring for the German Grand Prix that battle resumed on Sunday 20th July. A brief dice between MV riders Ubbiali and Provini enlivened the first few laps of the 250 event, but ended when Ubbiali fell without injury on the third circuit, after rain had made the track surface unpredictable. NSU hopes suffered a setback when first Hailwood went out in the first lap with a binding front brake then Dickie Dale, on another Sportmax, retired with a seized engine on the last-but-one lap after a battle for third spot with Dieter Falk (Adler) and Horst Kassner. At the end it was Falk who finished third, behind race winner Tarquinio Provini (MV) and Horst Fugner from East Germany on an MZ twin. NSU riders were placed: fourth Kassner, fifth Heiss, sixth Reichert, seventh Schneider, eighth Klager, and Holthaus tenth.

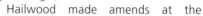

Fred Stevens, NSU Sportmax Scarborough, 1962.

Hailwood made amends at the Swedish Grand Prix at the 4.51-mile Hedemora circuit. Here, 50,000 spectators witnessed some memorable racing on Saturday and Sunday 26-27th July. Sunday's 18-lap 250cc race seemed an MV certainty. In reality, things panned out somewhat differently. Ubbiali was forced out on lap 12 with gearbox trouble. He was followed shortly after by Provini who, nearly a minute ahead of the pack, pulled in to retire after a few frantic moments of pit work. It was diagnosed that he had a cracked gearbox casing. This left MZ-mounted Fugner to win from Hailwood, with British rider Geoff Monty third on his home constructed GMS special.

The Ulster Grand Prix at Dundrod on Saturday 9th August provided a sensation. With MV and MZ works teams present it was local lad Tommy Robb aboard Terry Hill's Sportmax which had the crowds all around the 7 mile 732 yard circuit cheering when they realised that Robb was not just with the leaders, but was actually overtaking them. Robb fought off a determined challenge from the MZ riders Ernst Degner and Fugner - and MV-mounted Chadwick - to take second behind race winner Provini.

Both Hill's Sportmax machines had just been modified by fitting Manx Norton front brake hubs, and the front suspension was altered to accept modified Girling units. Hill said that the changes had resulted 'in greatly improved braking'.

Arthur Wheeler (23) leads the Austrian Josef Autengruber in the 1959 Lightweight (250cc)TT. Both rode NSUs.

At the final Grand Prix, the Italian at Monza in September, Autengruber was fifth and was the only NSU rider in the top six. Even so, having missed both the Belgian and Italian events and retired in the German, Mike Hailwood still managed to finish the season fourth in the 250 World Championships.

Not content to 'put his feet up' during the winter he then went on another South African Safari during the 'close season'. During the 1958 season Hailwood won a total of 16 races with his Sportmax and was awarded a vast number of trophies, of which perhaps the most prominent was the Pinhard Trophy for the most notable contribution to motorcycling by anyone under 21. Later, in 1959, he transferred to an ex-works Mondial, then Desmo Ducati twins which had been specially constructed for him, before becoming a full works rider with MV Agusta and Honda amongst others. However, Hailwood owed much of his apprenticeship to the NSU single.

Another notable racing personality campaigned one of the Neckarsulm machines in 1959. This was ex-World Champion Geoff Duke, who through Reg Armstrong (now retired) had the use of the only ex-works Rennmax twin to 'escape' from Germany. Originally, so the story goes, both Armstrong and Duke had expected a 1954 six-speed example. They were to be sorely disappointed. The machine that arrived was one of the earlier four-speed 1953 models with the 'Y' drive to the dohc on the right of power unit. Before being raced it was converted early in 1959 to something of a special, using a Reynolds frame and front fork assembly, Manx Norton front wheel and Lyta alloy fuel tank.

In what was to be his last season, the association between Duke and the Reynolds/Rennmax was never happy. Even at the Austrian Grand Prix at Salzburg 1st May, the machine was fractious, and insisted it would fire only on one cylinder. At the Isle of Man TT, in practice on the Clypse circuit using (so Duke claimed), 'a mere 9,000rpm instead of the NSU's permitted 10,400', the engine suddenly slowed. A rapid withdrawal of the clutch was imperative.

When stripped, it was found that the gudgeon pin on the right hand cylinder had broken. Fragments of metal had then found their way into the oil pump, and starved of lubrication the gears sheared. With spares of this nature unavailable, Duke had no alternative but to advise his sponsor, Armstrong, that he would be a non-starter in the Lightweight TT.

After the TT, Duke accepted the offer of a works ride on a Benelli single and so the NSU went back to Reg Armstrong. It was then sold to Glen Henderson from Ayr in Scotland. After this in 1963, it passed on again, this time to North Shields rider Ernie Johnson. Finally, in early 1969 it was sold to its present owner John Kidson - well known for his exploits in the Isle of Man during the 1960s on Moto Guzzi singles.

Many Max, Special Max and Super Max roadsters were converted into Sportmax replicas. Here is one such machine belonging to L.A. James at Silverstone in 1960. His mechanic, Val Blower, is in the background with the same rider's 350 Norton.

From four wheels to three

During its final days as a motorcycle manufacturer in 1965, NSU released a new car, the Prinz 1,000. This was built in two versions, the standard 1,000 and the 1,000TT. Both used a 996cc (69 x 66.6mm) air-cooled four-cylinder sohc engine, and even though it was designed purely for four-wheel use, it was subsequently to be used with considerable success in sidecar racing, and also as the motive power for the Münch Mammoth luxury sports/tourer (see chapter 11).

In standard form the Prinz engine produced 40-43bhp at 5,500rpm. In the TT version it originally gave 55, later bumped up to 65bhp. With additional tuning this figure could be made to increase significantly further.

The mid-late 1960s was an era when the big (usually restricted to 1,000cc) sidecar class in national racing throughout Europe (the Grand Prix being limited to a maximum capacity of 500cc), suddenly began to examine the possible use of small automobile engines as a means of extracting more performance at an affordable cost.

In Britain, for example, car engines such as the NSU Prinz and Hillman Imp were soon found to be ideal for chair use. Both units were relatively compact, generally reliable and spares were readily obtainable. They also proved a match for all but the very best of the conventional motorcycle engined brigade.

In Britain there was also an unlimited sidecar class. This meant that the larger NSU 1,200 engine could be used. This displaced 1,177cc (75 x 66.6mm).

Record Breaking

In the early 1950s, the NSU factory was the largest and most important of some 100 companies that were producing a vast range of products for a post-war Germany hungry for practical, cheap transport. For a short mid-decade period, if one counts the sales of the Quickly moped, NSU was the largest manufacturer in the motorcycle world. Against this background, the old established Neckarsulm concern was not only to mount a formidable challenge for Grand Prix honours, but amass a truly amazing number of world speed records.

The company's speed records era started at the end of the 1940s with the appearance of a 500cc version of the pre-war supercharged twin. Such machines were still allowed in German national events at that time, even though they had been banned from international competition by the FIM in 1946. NSU soon realized that it had a potential record breaker on its hands when, in May 1950, works rider Heiner Fleischmann had been timed at 143.75mph at Hockenheim on the big-bore twin. When one realizes that, in supercharged form, this engine gave almost 100bhp, it is perhaps easier to understand. (This was double what a normally aspirated works 500 Norton was giving at the time!)

To confirm this potential, Wilhelm Herz broke the world speed record (then held by BMW) with a speed of 180.17mph, using one of the blown 500 parallel-win engines mounted in a streamlined alloy shell. The venue was the Munich-Ingolstadt autobahn on 12th April 1951.

The 'Flying Hammock' getting underway during a test session in Germany, 1956.

Gustav Baumm's NSU 'Flying Hammock'.

Wilhelm Herz (with crash helmet) and NSU race shop mechanic Mack, inspect the supercharged 500 twin-cylinder machine prior to the successful world speed record attempt, April 1951.

This feat was followed later the same day by Hermann Bohm, on the same machine equipped with a third 'outrigger' wheel, who set a new sidecar record at 154mph. Even though he had achieved over 180mph, at the time, Herz said that had a more suitable course been available, then an even higher speed would have been obtainable. The reason was that the part of the autobahn which the team were able to use was not long enough, rather than having an unsuitable surface. The problem centred around the effect two bridges across the autobahn had on the steering of the streamlined machine. So great was the sideways thrust at these points even on a calm day - that the distance had to be reduced. An unusual facet of the record attempt was that narrow ribbed 19in tyres were used on both wheels. Besides the 499cc engine, a 348cc supercharged unit was also fitted into the chassis to obtain a new world record in this category for the flying kilometre at 172.5mph. On this run, the engine was over-revved, with the result that valve float caused indentations in the piston crowns to a depth of nearly 2mm!

Wilhelm Herz about to set off with his blown NSU twin on the Munich-Ingolstadt autobahn, 12th April 1951.

The next piece of news concerning NSU and record breaking came shortly after dawn on Tuesday 21st April, 1954, when a bearded commercial artist, named Gustav Adolf Baumm, gained worldwide recognition by breaking a total of 11 small-capacity world speed records with NSU powered streamliners designed by himself and built in the Neckarsulm company's race shop. The most unusual aspect of the Baumm design was that the rider himself lay horizontally with his feet forward. As *Motor Cycling* reported in their 29th April 1954 issue, this 'could scarcely have been ideal for the gusty conditions which prevailed.' Various records, at speeds between 79.4 and 111.2mph were broken in the 50, 75 and 100cc classes.

Hermann Bohm, left (750cc sidecar) and Wilhelm Herz (500cc solo) world record-breakers in 1951.

For the smaller classes, the engine used was based upon the 49cc Quickly moped unit, but tuned to produce 3.4bhp at 7,000rpm. The larger unit was from a 98cc Sportfox, which provided 7.5bhp at the same revolutions. Both ran on alcohol fuel, but the main reason for the increased speed was the effectiveness of the fish-like alloy streamlining.

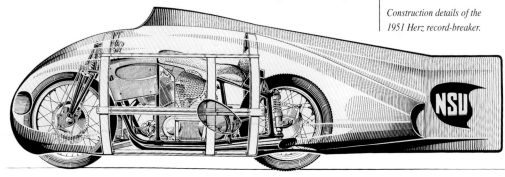

Construction details of the 1951 Herz record-breaker.

The miniature projectiles had disc-type 16in wheels, while the suspension, front and rear, was by rubber bands on the Quickly-powered machine, and pneumatic damping on the larger bike. On each machine, both wheels were fitted with brakes. Steering was effected by two levers, one on each side of the reclining rider, and the various controls were fixed to the appropriate levers.

The record venue chosen, once again, was a section of the Munich-Ingolstadt autobahn, near Munich itself. The weather, it was claimed, ensured that speeds obtained with the smaller engine were lower than had been expected.

Bohm with the 'sidecar' record breaker. Essentially, it was the same machine employed for solo runs, but fitted with an outrigger wheel.

However, very much overshadowing these events was the rumour that an attempt would shortly be made to raise the world's maximum to some 200mph - using the Baumm shell and one of the latest works Rennmax racing twin-cylinder engines.

Originally, Baumm had conceived the idea for his 'flying hammock' record breaker in 1950, when employed as a draughtsman at the NSU factory. At first, his concept was accepted by only one man, the head of the racing department, Dipl. Ing. Froede. After designing the Rennmax, Froede had transferred its development to Ewald Praxl, allowing Baumm's design to be fabricated under the direct supervision of Froede himself. Froede realised the potential of Baumm's concept, not only as a record breaker, but also as the layout for a racing machine of the future and even for every-day touring work.

Readers should realise that Froede not only had the responsibility of overseeing Baumm's project, but was also directly involved with several other important engineering projects at NSU, including fuel injection, rotary valves, rotary engines (later to emerge as the Wankel), and hydraulic transmission systems. He was a brilliant engineer, but also a very busy one.

By the end of 1954, following the 'lukewarm' official reception of the Baumm concept, the whole of NSU's senior management had decided to back it fully. No doubt, this was helped by the decision, at least for the time being, to retire from Grand Prix racing. To replace the prestige which they felt they would lose through their GP withdrawal, a policy was agreed to attempt to gain speed records not already held by the company. There was a simple policy statement: 'Maximum speed with minimum engine capacity.'

Wilhelm Hertz (third from left)
NSU record breaker, 1951.

It was apparent that longer distances would be needed if a rider was to accelerate to higher speeds when using low-power outputs, so it was agreed that it would be necessary to travel outside the German borders for the majority of future attempts. The site chosen was the salt flats in Utah, on the western side of the USA. As early as December 1954, 2.00 x 16 tyres were being laboratory tested up to 240mph. Throughout the winter of 1954-5, Baumm, Froede and other NSU engineers toiled away on the new breed of record breaker, and the following spring it was announced that certain world speed categories would be attempted during the period 27th April to 5th May 1955. For these, however, the Munich-Ingolstadt autobahn would be used rather than the salt flats.

Unfortunately, bad weather prevented the record attempt until Tuesday 10th May, when NSU established a total of 22 world records in the 50, 75, 125, 175, 250 and 350 categories with 50 and 125cc machines. The records were set by Gustav Baumm, using a pair of streamliners of the same type as those employed in his previous record spree. One machine was fitted with the tuned Quickly-based engine described previously, the other with one of the 1954 123cc Rennfox works racing engines. Six of the previous records were already held by Baumm, and all the others, save two, were in Italian hands (Ceccato, Lambretta and Moto Guzzi). One of the exceptions was the 75cc five-mile record, which

Baumm feet forward machine.

had been established by the Englishman, Hall, in 1929 on a Rocket-JAP. No 50cc figure had previously been created for five miles. Each of Baumm's NSU's attacked the flying start kilometre, mile, five-kilometre and five-mile distances. The 50cc machine recorded mean speeds of 93.2, 93.8, 90.4 and 91.3mph for the respective distances, setting up records in both 50 and 75cc classes; the margin over the earlier speeds varied from 56.5mph, in the case of Hall's record, to 9.3mph for the 75cc kilometre record. Perhaps even more remarkable was the performance of the 125 streamliner in covering the distances at respective mean speeds of 134.8, 135.4, 129.8 and 131mph. The speed brought NSU the appropriate records in the 125, 175 and 250cc categories, as well as the 350cc five-kilometre and five-mile records. The smallest gain was approximately 2.5mph on the previous 250cc kilometre speed, whereas Baumm's old five mile 125 speed was bettered by nearly 24mph.

Originally Baumm had conceived the idea for his 'flying hammock' record-breaker in 1950, when employed as a draughtsman at the NSU factory.

Later, at a dinner party for delegates to the FIM congress in Dusseldorf, given by the NSU management on Thursday 12th May, Baumm was guest of honour. One of his record machines was also on show, together with the two engines used in the successful attempt.

There were distinct differences between the two streamliners used. The smaller-engined machine was higher and shorter than the larger-engined model; the latter had a less-rounded top to its shell. There were good reasons for these differences, for although Baumm was officially described as an artist, in fact, he was a highly-skilled designer in his own right, who had been employed on aircraft development during the war. So carefully had Baumm worked out the contours of his 'feet-first' machines, that even with a gusty 12mph side-wind blowing, the steering during the record attempts 'was unaffected'. Baumm suggested that the flatter shell of the 125 might be thought to have been aimed at keeping the front wheel on the road. However, he revealed that experience had shown that as the speed rose, so more weight was transferred to the front wheel, to such an extent that very powerful springs had to be incorporated in the front suspension of the larger model. On the day of the successful attempts, the wind had been blowing so hard that Baumm claimed to have lost around 500rpm from the maximum figures for both engines in preliminary testing.

The unsupercharged dohc Rennfox engine employed fuel injection. Originally, there had been plans to run it on alcohol, but the performance characteristics of these units, when using premium grade petrol, were so exactly determined and documented that NSU technicians decided to rely upon the known, rather than introduce an element of experimentation. When asked about the safe limit at which his streamliner could be navigated,

By the end of 1954, following a distinctly 'lukewarm' reception to his project, Baumm received the offer of full support from NSU senior management. This drawing shows the general layout of the design.

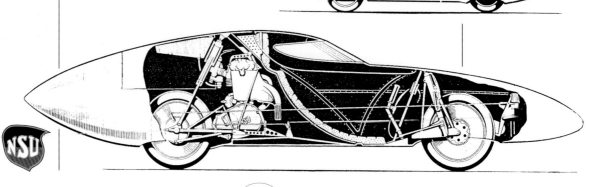

Baumm estimated 'about 150mph', but revealed that a similar design, built for higher speeds, might be able to approach 300mph if propelled by a 500cc engine. A little-known fact was that Baumm was then in the process of designing a four-wheeled passenger vehicle embodying some of the aerodynamic features of this record breaker. However, this was a private venture without the support of NSU.

The front section was very similar to an aircraft. Note how the canopy lifted upwards, whilst small panels folded down to allow the rider's (pilot's?) feet to make contact with the ground when the machine came to a halt.

Sadly, a mere 11 days after the Dusseldorf dinner, on Monday 23rd May, — Baumm was killed when testing a prototype of the streamliner with which it was planned that NSU would make a comeback in the 1956 125 and 250 Grands Prix. Baumm was track testing this machine at the Nürburgring in mixed company, including Porsche cars, when he lost control and ran off the circuit into some trees. He suffered a fractured skull and died from his injuries. So ended the dreams of the bearded 36-year-old Bavarian. Moreover, many of NSU's future plans were to take a totally different course.

Baumm was not only developing the machine that was to be the basis for NSU's racing comeback, but also a series of production versions that were to have precise handling, improved speed and dramatically better fuel consumption for any given capacity. The company received bad press over the Baumm accident and, as it turned out, this was to influence its very future. The whole project was shelved, and thereafter, NSU concentrated on other things, notably a return to car production.

Gustav Baumm with one of his astounding feet-forward world record-breakers. He proved the validity of his highly original approach, only to lose his life whilst testing a racing version at the Nürburgring, on the 23rd May 1955, a few days after a celebration to mark his achievements in setting a number of new world records.

All that remains of the Baumm era today is one of his machines, owned by the Herz family, in the new Hockenheim-ring Museum. This machine is actually the later one used by Müller in his endurance/fuel consumption trials at the 'Ring' in May 1956. This was one of the shelved racers, shorter than the record machine, longer than the proposed roadster. It is rumoured that a shell from one of the record breakers exists too.

Following record sales in 1955 (NSU produced more powered two-wheelers that year than anyone else in the world), came the first news at the beginning of July, that 1956 was not continuing this trend, and NSU announced that 640 workers were to be dismissed over the following two months owing to sales being lower than expected. At the same time, reports filtered through that more record attempts were in the wind, testing being carried out on the same section of the autobahn again.

Hermann Müller was there with 'Baumm II', a revised version of Gustav Baumm's original Rennfox-powered streamliner, while Wilhelm Herz had the 'Delphin III', the latest version of the 1951 record breaker. This had a completely-redesigned form of streamlining, with enclosed cabin, nose

Hermann Müller about to get under way for a run in one of the Baumm-inspired NSU streamliners, 1956.

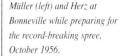

window, taller tail fin and various other changes which, like those on the smaller machine, had been developed in the Stuttgart Technical College wind tunnel. The result was a cut in the drag co-efficient from 0.29, in its original form, to 0.19. With its 110bhp supercharged engine, NSU claimed that the rehashed twin could better 125mph in first gear.

Another version of the Baumm-type machine had a Rennmax 250 racing twin GP engine unit installed, fulfilling the dream of the late Gustav Baumm who, together with Dr. Froede, had planned this very machine.

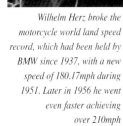

Wilhelm Herz broke the motorcycle world land speed record, which had been held by BMW since 1937, with a new speed of 180.17mph during 1951. Later in 1956 he went even faster achieving over 210mph

The purpose of the testing was a massive effort to wrest the maximum number of world records, and to this effect, no expense was spared. The venue was to be the Bonneville Salt Flats, Utah, in the USA. Accompanying the tri-coloured machines (they were red on top, white in the middle and blue-grey below to make them easily visible against the salt) was a party of 30, including timing experts from the Longines factory. The riders were to be Herz and Müller, while Werner Haas went as a reserve rider.

On 29th July, a day before the full record-breaking feast was due to start, Herz and Müller made some experimental runs, which were not claimed as records. Herz, with the 350 supercharged twin, bettered 180mph for both the kilometre and mile, and clocked over 182mph on the five kilometre and five-mile runs, while Müller, with a 125, was close to 140mph in both the kilometre and mile dashes.

Herz also took a turn on the unblown 250 Baumm Special. Reported to have been travelling at a speed in excess of 200mph, he was struck by a blast of wind from the side which overturned the machine. Amazingly, he escaped with no more than bruises, but the damage to the shell was enough to retire it from any further use. The Rennmax engine was then transferred to a more conventional streamliner for further record attempts.

Müller (left) and Herz at Bonneville while preparing for the record-breaking spree, October 1956.

The cockpit of Wilhelm Herz's Delphin III, on which he achieved a new motorcycle speed record at 210.64mph.

After rain made the surface of the lake tricky, the programme was delayed until Wednesday 1st August. Knowing that the capabilities of the 350 had not been reached, Herz again ran this machine, while Müller was to make a repeat performance on the 125. On the return run for the first round trip of the day, Herz was again plagued with problems, this time hitting a patch of wet salt which veered him far enough off the course to wipe out a timing-light stand. Fortunately, he was still able to return to the pits under the machine's own power. Damage to the nose needed repairing and, in any case, the still damp surface prevented any further attempts by Müller for the rest of the day.

The next day, 2nd August, Herz set the following flying-start 350cc records: kilometre, 188.5mph; mile, 189.5mph; five-kilometre, 183mph. On the same day, Müller took out the 125 Baumm-type machine to claim the following flying-start records (all of which stood to the late Gustav Baumm): kilometre, 150mph; mile, 150.78mph; five kilometre, 148.5mph; five mile, 149mph.

On Saturday 4th August, came the big one, a new world's fastest motorcycle speed was achieved when Herz, the 46-year-old from Ludwigshaven, rocketed his flying, enclosed, supercharged, 500 parallel-twin over the Bonneville Salt Flats to an amazing two-way average of 210.64mph.

This represented a 25mph increase over the existing record set by Russell Wright in New Zealand, on 2nd July 1955, with an unblown, 998cc Vincent v-twin. It was also 18mph faster than the unofficial 192mph record established by American Johnny Allen with a 649cc Triumph-engined, cigar-shaped streamliner on 25th September 1955. Also that day, following Herz's successful run, four 100cc flying-start records were set by Müller, using a 'Baumm II' machine powered by a stroked and sleeved down racing Rennfox unit (99.7cc, 56 x 40.5mm, 15.5bhp at 11,000rpm): kilometre, 137.86mph; mile, 137.86mph; five-kilometre, 136.62mph; five-mile, 137.24mph.

Strong winds then caused more record attempts to be cancelled for a couple of days. When these were resumed, Müller broke the standing ten-mile, two-way average with a speed of 151mph in the 125 streamliner. On the brown, 49cc, two-stroke unit, he averaged 119mph over the flying mile, and with the 250 Rennmax engine in the 'Delphin III', Herz averaged 152mph over the same distance.

When the dust had settled, NSU was to claim a total of 54 new records. Besides the obvious outright speed record, the most noteworthy was the bettering of the ten-kilometre and ten-mile 350cc-class records by the 'Baumm III' streamliner powered by a 125 Rennfox engine. Since the existing figures had been set in the previous October by Dickie Dale with a 350 Guzzi works racer, the NSU performance deserved high praise.

NSU factory personnel preparing Herz's Delphin III record-breaker on Bonneville Salt Flats.

With the marathon American record session over, the team returned to Germany; the last chapter of NSU's glorious post-war speed effort had ended. Then the machines were sent on a world-wide tour to gain the maximum amount of publicity.

At the time, this was badly needed, as the press were carrying headlines like, 'German Industry Slowing'. There were reports that from September 1st, NSU had started a 36-hour week because of slack trade. Following so quickly after the large dismissal of workers in July, this was a clear warning that all was not sweetness and light in Neckarsulm.

Although, unlike the majority, NSU survived the mass of closures throughout 1956-8, the German motorcycle industry was destined never to recover the golden days of the early post-war period. That fling of record breaking was to prove NSU's swan-song and the pinnacle of its motorcycle achievements. Truly, it was the end of a golden era.

At dawn, against the dramatic light of the rising sun, NSU team members ready themselves for another record-breaking blitz over the Bonneville salt.

13

Simson model 425 Sport, this roadster engine formed the basis of the factory's quarter-litre racing programme in the immediate post-war period. It featured pushrod operated valves, hairpin valve-springs and helical cut timing gears.

The beginnings of the Simson marque can be traced back to 1856, when its predecessor, the Ernst Thalmann Hunting Weapon Works, began manufacturing armaments in the East German town of Suhl, in the Thuringian Forest.

Like several other manufacturers of arms, the Suhl company needed to diversify during the times when armaments were not in demand. Together with Puch in Austria, FN in Belgium, Husqvarna in Sweden and, of course, BSA in Britain, the German concern needed to put its manufacturing machinery to work in peacetime. So like the rest they turned to building that basic form of transport, the pedal cycle.

The Suhl factory began to turn out bicycles in 1896, and even these were innovative for their day. They were fitted with pneumatic tyres when much of Europe was still having its bones shaken.

However, whereas many bicycle manufacturers made the transition into motorcycle production, the East German concern moved into cars. It was in this new field that the name Simson-Supra first appeared, under which various forms of touring and light sporting vehicles were offered until the mid 1930s.

The company then reverted to making two-wheelers, at first with pedal power. Later, in 1938, it began production, under the name Mofa, of 98cc, Sachs-engined, ultra-lightweight motorcycles. With the intervention of World War 2 in the following year, and the partitioning of Germany in the aftermath, it was late 1952 before the former Jadgwaffen Werke resumed powered two-wheeler production.

First of the new models was the SR-1, a very basic moped with a two-speed gearbox. Its 47.6cc engine developed 1.3bhp and provided just enough power for it to reach 30mph. The specification was completed by 26in wheels and rubber suspension at both front and rear.

Sold under the AWO label, the SR-1 was very similar to the West German NSU Quickly both in appearance and design concept. It was followed, soon afterwards, by the improved SR-2, which proved instantly popular and went on to become the biggest seller of all among East German two-wheelers in the 1950s and early 1960s.

Building on the success of these ventures, the company's next model was the AWO 425, with a 250cc ohv engine. This featured a vertically-mounted cylinder, the crankshaft sitting longitudinally in the frame. The configuration naturally led to the adoption of shaft drive, via a four-speed gearbox. Initially, power output was a lowly 12bhp at 5,500rpm. Running on a compression ratio of 6.5:1, the machine could be ordered in either solo or sidecar guise, each with its own set of gear ratios. The AWO 425 closely resembled both the BMW R25 series and the Swiss Universal. It was typically Germanic with its separate, sprung saddle and plunger rear suspension.

A pair of dustbin-faired Simsons await the start of a race in East Germany.

When launched in early 1958 the dohc RS250 Simson twin was state-of-the-art. With full unit construction, dry clutch and six-speed gearbox. A far cry from the earlier BMW-based ohv single.

Dustbin-faired works Simson dohc twin-cylinder racer, circa late 1950s.

In a market ever hungry for an improved means of transport, the AWO 250cc single soon found its way into competition, both on and off-road. For the 1954 racing season, the factory developed a tuned version to contest the East German road-racing championships.

The first racer managed to be reasonably successful, even though it retained the roadster's pushrod operated valves, engine-speed clutch and shaft drive. However, by the time Rudolph Juhrich rode an AWO to 18th position in the German Grand Prix during July 1954, the design sported swinging-arm rear suspension and a duplex frame.

There then followed a considerable amount of experimentation with the works racers, especially in the engine and final-drive departments. Some machines were tried with single and double-overhead camshaft heads. Various methods of valve actuation were tested, including bevel drive, a train of gears, and chain drive to the cams. There was even an experimental twin-cylinder double-knocker.

The results came thick and fast, the Suhl factory taking the national championships three years running in the quarter-litre category: 1954, 1955 and 1956. Moreover, although it only ever contested the German Grand Prix in the World Championship series, several finishes were recorded, including a 15th place in 1955.

The track successes brought a demand for a more sporting version of the road-going 425. This was coded 425S (Sport). The engine was the

BMW Influence

When Germany was partitioned at the end of the Second World War, the East came under the Soviet yoke and this meant Communism. It also meant a somewhat lower standard of technology - certainly in the early days. This in turn led the East Germans and their Soviet masters to literally steal Western design and nowhere was this trend more evident than in motorcyling. A favourite for the copyists was BMW. Not just the big flat twins, but also the 250cc single with its upright cylinder and shaft final drive. Like MZ, which was originally marketed under the IFA label, so too Simson with its AWO label. It was all part of the centralised bureaucracy so beloved of the Soviet-backed regime.

Examine the illustrations in this chapter and the reader will soon realise the origins of Simsons 1950's racing machinery. However, the East Germans were to be congratulated for the fact that they achieved something BMW never did and that was to race the pushrod single in not only the national championships (in the process winning the title on several occasions), but also entering and finishing a Grand Prix event into the bargain. This racing experience meant developments which eventually led Simson to move away from their BMW inspired origins, with an entirely new series of engines. The cycle parts too moved on and there was even a switch from shaft to chain final drive to complete the transformation.

The 250 AWO (Simson) ohv single on which Rudolf Juhrich finished 18th in the 1954 German Grand Prix at Solitude. Its BMW origins are apparent in this view.

familiar pushrod 247cc single, but with the power bumped up to 14bhp at 6,300rpm, providing a maximum speed of over 70mph. Although shaft drive was retained, the frame was totally redesigned. This was quite innovative, being of pressed-steel with some components of tubular construction. For its day, the result was a machine of exceptionally clean lines.

Even so, it was the much cheaper, two-stroke commuter model which provided the factory with the vast majority of its profit. Luckily, this did not halt development of the four-stroke racing programme. The next machine to appear - and, as it happened, the definitive model - was the RS (Renn Sport) 250, which made its debut in early 1958.

By now, AWO had given way to Simson, and with the capable Hans Weinert aboard, it took many honours, including the national titles in both 1958 and 1959. Although rarely seen in the West, the Simson RS250 was state-of-the-art when it appeared. Its specification included chain-driven, double-overhead-camshafts, full unit-construction, dry clutch, six-speed gearbox, alloy tanks (it had a dry sump) and a full, hand-beaten, alloy dolphin fairing. The forks were of the leading-link type, while braking was taken care of by a pair of massive, full-width alloy hubs, there being a two-leading-shoe arrangement at the front.

Hans Weinert, East German 250cc Champion in both 1958 and 1959, with the final dolphin-faired version of Simson's dohc twin-cylinder RS250. A change of policy then saw the Suhl factory quit road-racing for long-distance trials, such as the ISDT.

One RS250 was raced in the 1959 German GP at Hockenheim, where it displayed a fair turn of speed against the very latest Italian machinery, such as the MV twins and the Morini single. However, with the last of the four-stroke roadsters rolling off the Suhl production line in 1960, the Simson road-racing challenge was brought to an end.

This was due to two factors. The first was that two-strokes had taken over well and truly in the communist bloc behind the 'Iron Curtain'. Perhaps the most important of all, however, was that the East German motorcycle industry had been rationalised under the auspices of the IFA (IndustrieverbandFarhzuegebau). MZ (see Chapter 11) was to produce the larger-capacity machines, while Simson was to manufacture bikes with a maximum capacity of 100cc.

For some four decades, Simson and MZ came under the same state 'umbrella' control system. But when Capitalism replaced Communism as the 1990s dawned, the two marques went their separate ways under private management.

Zündapp

14

On 17th September 1917, Zunderund Apparatebau GmbH, better known in the shorter form as Zündapp, was founded in Nurnberg. The new company, which employed 1,800 workers, was a joint venture between three established firms at the height of the Great War. The commercial stimulus was war production. Zunderund manufactured fuses for artillery guns. At the war's end the new company struggled to find a suitable product to replace the no-longer needed war materials.

Zündapp was acquired in full by Dipl. Ing. Fritz Neumeyer in 1919. Born in 1875, Neumeyer had first displayed his entrepreneurial skills in 1901 by starting a highly profitable metal working company in Nurnberg. This later branched out into various other industrial fields and was active in both home and export markets. For example, one of Neumeyer's best customers before 1914 was Serck Radiators of Birmingham, England.

After the Armistice, Dr. Neumeyer not only built Zündapps but established a conglomerate which encompassed such diverse engineering enterprises as cable and radio, farm tractors, and rolling stock repair yards for the German railways. Neumeyer created a financial empire which eventually wielded world-wide economic influence. While its scope and story are outside the bounds of this book, having Neumeyer at the helm undoubtedly provided Zündapp with a strength that few others within the motorcycle industry could match.

Neumeyer's task of discovering a profitable role for Zündapp after the war was difficult. However, in the autumn of 1921, the company found its new identity, and built its first five motorcycles. These were the forerunners of more than three million machines that the company manufactured over the next 63 years.

The first model, built by what was to emerge as one of Germany's premier marques, was the 211cc Z22. It was powered by a British-made Levis engine. This was a deflector-piston type, three-port two-stroke which produced 2.25bhp, transmitted to the rear wheel by belt. By 21st October 1922, 1,000 of these machines had been manufactured by a workforce which now totalled 600.

Zündapp works rider Hubert Abold at Misano, Italy, with the 79cc single, March 1984.

Zündapp's management realised how important motorcycle sport was for a company's prestige. The very first Zündapp built was ridden in the critical North Bavarian reliability trials on 18th September 1921, by the German champion Metsch, who was later to become a legend within the Zündapp organisation for his exploits on the company's products during the 1920s.

By November 1924, other models powered by Zündapp's own engine designs had been added to the range, including one which used a 249cc version of the original Levis. At the beginning of 1924 Zündapp commissioned its first modern assembly line. By year's end, more than 10,000 machines had been assembled on its conveyors.

The German public first bought motorcycles in high volume in 1924. This boom was greatly helped by a national 17 day touring race which aroused the interest of millions, and brought Zündapp some impressive successes. Although Zündapp only briefly took a serious interest in road racing, and at that only at the very end of the company's life, it found a special niche in endurance trials which followed the early touring events.

From 1926 onwards Zündapp established branches in all the major commercial centres of Germany. The first was in Berlin, followed by Munich, Cologne and Hamburg. This was the beginning of the establishment of a nationwide dealer and service network.

In that year a total of 4,226 machines were purchased. By 1928 this figure was up to 16,877 - and rising rapidly. Several hazardous journeys were undertaken by Zündapp machines. In 1928, for example, two students rode the 7,350 kilometres from Berlin to the Black Sea and back on their small Zündapp two-stroke without a single breakdown, despite often dreadful roads.

The original Zündapp two-stroke single-0cylinder engine of the 1920s, used British technology in the shape of the three-port Levis design, with special piston and transfer-port.

The earliest Zündapp machines were powered by British-made Levis two-stroke engines. This photograph dates from 18th September 1921 and shows the German champion Metsch at the start of the North Bavarian reliability trials. It is believed to be the first showing the marque taking part in a sporting event.

This was followed by more adventures, including a record-breaking demonstration in 1930 when a Zündapp S300 (again a single-cylinder two-stroke) covered the Berlin-Paris route in 17hrs 40 mins - faster than either an express train or the Mercedes car against which it was competing.

By 1928, the four separate Zündapp plants in Nurnberg were cluttered and congested, so a new plant at Nurnberg-Schweinau was constructed. This opened the following year and was hailed as the most modern in the world. In seven short years, Zündapp had risen from nothing to take its place amongst the market leaders. In April 1929, a new monthly output record of nearly 4,200 units was set.

In July Hans-Friedrich Neumeyer, the son of the founder, joined the company. Things may have appeared buoyant, but within a few months he was to witness a real crisis for the company when by December, the sales figures had fallen drastically. A miserable 300 machines came off the production lines in the last month of the year.

Zündapp survived, even though for the next three years less than 30,000 machines were produced. Fritz Neumeyer's role in the company's survival cannot be underestimated. The Great Depression struck, and over 5,500,000 Germans were unemployed. However, it says much for the commercial drive of the founder of Zündapp, that just when the company was passing through its most difficult period, Neumeyer prepared to realise a dream he had long cherished, that of a Volkswagen - the people's car.

As long ago as 1924 he had considered making a small car under licence from Britain's Rover, but nothing came of his offer. Neumeyer never abandoned the idea. In September 1931 a contract was concluded with Ferdinand Porsche. Porsche designed the Type 32 for Zündapp.

Although three prototypes were built, the worsening situation in 1932 brought an abrupt halt to this interesting project. Both Zündapp and Porsche had to wait until 1934 to resume work on the Volkswagen project. Porsche's Type 32 was the father of the legendary 'Beetle'.

By 1933 Zündapp and the German economy were making a massive recovery. Not only did the company produce the first of its four-stroke flat-twins, with capacities of 398 and 498cc, but it also brought out a flat-four of 598cc. These models were designed by Richard Kuchen, and introduced an unconventional, but very successful, chain and sprocket gearbox.

The following year saw Zündapp continuing to make progress. But then its founder Dipl. Ing. Fritz Neumeyer became ill and died on 10th September 1935 - his 60th birthday.

The Nurnberg-Schweinau plant was enlarged in 1937 with a second complex, but the era of private enterprise and free competition in Germany was fast coming to an end. Rationing, raw material quotas and limitations on model ranges were the first unmistakable signs of state control encroaching seriously on the national economy.

A supercharged 600 Zündapp flat-twin, prepared for competition during 1947.

Then came the war and from March 1940, all supplies to civilian customers were discontinued, but unlike many of its rivals, Zündapp retained a majority of its wartime production facilities for the manufacture of motorcycles. Two decades after its first motorcycle, Zündapp's 250,000th machine, a KS750, left the assembly line on 13th March 1942.

The KS750 was a special 750cc model developed by Zündapp for military purposes. It had an integral sidecar with its wheel driven via a lockable differential. The power unit was an air-cooled, flat-twin four-stroke and the KS750 had two sets of four forward and reverse gears. Together with the similar BMW outfit, the KS750 was the definitive Second World War German motorcycle. In reality both had been replaced on the wartime production lines by the simpler, and far less expensive, 350 DKW two-stroke from 1944.

By the end of the war, one third of all Zündapp's production machinery and installations had been destroyed, together with 40 per cent of other buildings. Like rivals such as BMW, it was now a case of producing anything to survive.

So, for the first few months of peacetime, Zündapp made potato mashers, iron axles and various small fittings. Then, using remaining stocks, it built generating sets powered by the flat-twin engine. These were quickly snapped up by the building trade. But the real commercial breakthrough came in the autumn of 1945 when a substantial section of the Zündapp works was committed to the production of urgently-needed equipment for grain mills, principally rollers, extractors and grain cleaning machines. A year later, in November 1946, the two owners of the Zündapp company, Hans-Friedrich Neumeyer and Elizabeth Mann, appointed Eitel-Friedrich Mann, Elizabeth's husband, as managing director. But there was no favouritism in his selection. Born in 1910, Dipl. Ing. Mann was a diploma engineer and doctor of political science who had studied in Munich and Braunschweig, then worked from 1935 to 1939 in various sections of the Siemens-Schuckert organisation in

Nurnberg. Here he was assistant managing director. His appointment proved commercially sound. Under Mann's guidance Zündapp soon regained strength. First with improved mill equipment, then domestic sewing machines, finally in August 1947, came the re-introduction of motorcycle production under the auspices of chief engineer Ernst Schmidt.

At first, Zündapp concentrated its two-wheel production efforts on a new range of two-stroke commuter lightweights, but memories of pre-war Zündapp flat-twins were rekindled by the appearance of the KS600. With its pressed steel frame, inter-connected hand and foot change and dated appearance, this model was to be short-lived.

Keitel and Seeman winning a gold medal with the KS601 outfit, during the 1951 ISDT staged around Varese, Italy during September that year.

The chief excitement was the appearance of the machine which entered service at the beginning of 1951, and would replace the KS600 within two years. The KS601 was a new sports version of the Zündapp flat-twin which had a 597cc (75 x 67.6mm) ohv engine, with a separate 25mm Bing carburettor for each cylinder, cast iron barrels and light alloy heads. Power output was 28bhp at 4,700rpm, with electrical power being provided by a 6-volt 90 watt system.

The four-speed chain and sprocket gearbox was in-unit with the engine and there was shaft final drive, with plunger rear suspension matched to a new telescopic fork. A maximum road speed of 87.5mph was available in virtually all conditions, thanks to the engine's vast amount of torque. The KS601 was the fastest German roadster when introduced.

Besides their solo performance, both flat-twins made ideal sidecar machines, and were greatly in demand. They were also soon to prove themselves as sporting machines in long-distance trials. A KS601 outfit could top 75mph. Development had been proceeding behind the scenes since 1947, but even though Zündapp might have wished to re-introduce its big twins earlier, it could not, if for no other reason than until late 1949, German marques were restricted to motorcycles with a capacity of 250cc or less.

With the 600cc limit for sidecar road racing, a supercharged version of the KS601 engine was built, testing of which was undertaken by factory staff during 1947 and 1948.

Although ultimately Zündapp did not mount an official challenge on the circuits to the likes of BMW and NSU, it proved it was capable if required. Additionally the effort was to pay dividends in the factory's return to the competition front in long distance trials during the next few years.

A unique feature of the Zündapp flat-twin, compared to the similar BMW, was its chain driven gearbox.

ZÜNDAPP

Under Mann's leadership, as well as the original Nurnberg plant there was now one in Munich, then steadily becoming one of the most active industrial centres of the new Federal Republic. Here, a brand-new complex was constructed, which was opened in September 1950 and later substantially expanded. When the move to Munich was first mooted, no one at Zündapp could have visualised that this would soon become the mainstay of the company. By 1951 output was up to 3,000 units a month. And from the beginning of 1952 the plant at Nurnberg came under the direct management of Hans-Friedrich Neumeyer, while the further enlarged Munich complex was under the control of Dr. Eitel-Friedrich Mann.

Besides its well-known flat-twins, Zündapp's most famous production models during the 1950s were the Bella scooter, which debuted in May 1953, selling in hundreds of thousands; various mopeds and the Elastic two-stroke motorcycle, the latter taking over the factory's efforts in the annual ISDT.

During the late 1950s Zündapp was able to survive, not through vast advertising or fielding world beating Grand Prix racing teams, or even dynamic state-of-the-art models, but simply by making the correct commercial decisions as each problem was faced. This included seeing the value and importance of developing export markets for their products before most of its rivals.

Amongst all German motorcycle manufacturers, Zündapp was best able to weather the storm through a combination of having just the right product line, and a strict production policy of making only enough machines to meet orders. This meant none of the stockpiling which led to some of the competitors building up a year's supply, which eventually no one wanted. And unlike the opposition, Zündapp's experience of 1957 was relatively free from trauma.

It was this understated success compared to the turmoil all around which led the German selectors to pick Zündapp, together with another relatively unaffected company, Maico, to form the country's Trophy team for the 1957 ISDT at Spindleruv Mlyn, in North Bohemia from 15th-20th September. The team consisted of Zündapp riders Specht (175), Hessler (250) and Leistner (262) plus three Maico riders; it was an inspired choice of men and machines. By the end of the week it had won six of only 25 medals awarded that year. The performance was good enough to win the coveted Trophy for West Germany for only the second time since the Second World War.

But even these figures conceal just what a great victory it really was. The 32nd ISDT was the first to be held in the Krkonose Mountains (the Giant Mountains) in Czechoslovakia. The little resort of Spindleruv Mlyn welcomed the 246 starters with the foulest possible weather. Apart from fog, the only interruptions to the rain were sleet and snowfalls. Inevitably, there was a toll in riders, 81 of whom gave up on the very first day. This event was one of the most arduous ISDTs of all time. The Germans lasted the whole six days without losing a single penalty point, a performance which absolutely eclipsed the previous year's winners, Czechoslovakia, who were second with 700 points adrift, while Italy came third with 1,613 marks lost.

Zündapp KS601 taking part in the speed trials section of the 1951 ISDT held in Italy.

At the end of 1957 it was announced that the KS601 (nicknamed the 'Green Elephant') was finally to be taken out of production. This was the end of the road for Zündapp's four-stroke flat-twin family and a lineage which many consider today as the classic of the marque. The Sport turned out 34bhp at 6,000rpm and was good for 97mph. Over its final two years, when it was produced as the KS601 Elastic Sport and KS601 EL, it had finally been available with a full swinging arm frame. But with demand for large capacity motorcycles in Germany at an all-time low, only 700 of the swinging arm models were produced, all at the Nurnberg plant, and mostly for export.

At the beginning of 1958, Hans-Friedrich Neumeyer fell ill and was hospitalised. But under his direction, on 1st July that year, the Nurnberg plant was sold to Bosch, the electrical machine conglomerate. This permitted an expansion programme to begin at the remaining Munich complex. 1960 was the year of the great comeback for Zündapp with two wheeler production showing a large increase over the past few years. In the same period many of the previous competitors had disappeared.

But the driving force behind the company's survival and revival, Dr Eitel-Friedrich Mann, unhappily did not live to see the fruits of his work. He died suddenly on 11th August 1960, shortly before his 50th birthday, while in the thick of the reorganisation and construction work that the transfer to Munich, and development of radically revised model range had entailed. Still, Zündapp itself was to benefit from Dr. Mann's foresight and emerged into the new decade much improved by his 'slimming down for better health' campaign.

Zündapp produced 75,000 machines - mopeds, motorcycles and scooters - in 1961 and was at the head of the German two-wheel industry.

The company also made a return to endurance trials in 1961. It not only won four classes of the German national championships, but again provided part of the German Trophy squad and one machine for the Vase 'A' team for the 1961 ISDT in Wales. The 1,200 mile ISDT was staged at the beginning of October and Zündapp was the backbone of the winning team. Germany took the Trophy for the third time post-war, with no marks lost. Zündapp's total medal haul was five golds, including those of the two Trophy men Specht (175) and Hessler (250), plus a bronze. All six entries won medals. An impressive debut was made by a pair of 75cc models and a lone 50cc midget trials iron. Together with similar machines from Kreidler, these flyweights amazed observers with their speed and lasting power.

In January 1962, Ernst Leverkus, professional motorcycle journalist, arch-enthusiast for the marque and Green Elephant-and-Steib owner, organised a rally for fellow Zündapp KS601 owners. It was the depths of winter and hardly a time to drive an outfit to a site chosen near the Solitude race track, but the rally caught the imagination of the enthusiasts to the extent that it became an institution. Taking its name from the machine that inspired Leverkus, the Elephant Rally continues as an annual event.

By 1965, sales of mopeds, lightweight motorcycles and scooters were at near record levels for the Munich-based company. And in reaction to this Zündapp made a big effort in motorcycle sport. This included not only one day trials and endurance trials, but also two new ventures with the appearance of a streamlined record breaker and a road racer. The record-breaking machines were largely the initiative of Dieter Neumeyer, grandson of the company's founder. Their appearance followed the successes of a year before, when a specially prepared standard KS50 Super clocked up 12,247.5 kilometres in 144 hours, representing an average speed of 85.05kph (just over 53.125mph). Zündapp was determined to be even more successful.

The first outing was in April 1965 at Monza in Italy, where the team made an attack on world records then held by rivals Kreidler. But the attempt was abandoned when the bike proved to be down on power. However, after additional work and tuning, the team returned to Italy the following month. Between 13-15th May, the air around Monza Autodrome was filled with the high pitched note of the 49cc two-stroke whose horizontal single-cylinder engine, like the rest of the machine, was wholly enveloped in an aerodynamic glassfibre shell.

In those three days, the revised streamliner broke six world records on the high speed Monza bowl. Volker Kramer took the 10km at 95.355mph, and the 100km at 100.668mph, plus the hour record at 101.045mph. Zündapp's team riders took the 1,000km at 91.121mph, six-hours at 91.841mph and twelve-hours at 85.156mph. All the records were ratified for both the 50 and 75cc classes, and the last record also counted in the 100 and 125cc categories.

The successful Zündapp record breaking team, Monza, May 1965.

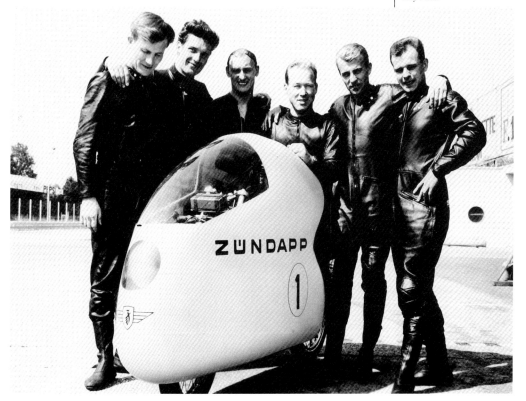

For decades, the name Zündapp had stood for reliability rather than speed, but the Monza record spree changed all this. With the company concentrating on small capacity machines, it was felt important to display that the marque meant both reliability and speed. However, this was not a new policy. As far back as 1937/38, the Nurnberg plant was secretly working on a machine which would challenge existing world records. But this was something totally different to the diminutive Monza record breaker. It was a supercharged, four-cylinder 1,000cc monster with a Rootes blower, designed for speeds in excess of 188mph. Unfortunately, this brave attempt was snuffed out not by lack of technical expertise, but the political situation and the pressure which the Nazis put on Zündapp.

Developed in line with the Monza record breaker was a 50cc class road racer. This was constructed by the Kramer brothers, Volker and Dieter, both of whom were employed at Zündapp. This semi-factory sponsored effort had a 49cc horizontal air-cooled, single-cylinder unit of a similar type to the record breaker with a single rotary valve, coil ignition and ten speeds. Claimed power output was 10bhp at 11,500rpm and a twin gearbox link-up provided ten gear ratios. A five-speed foot-change box was linked to a second gearbox with two ratios, which could be swapped by hand lever, doubling up the ratios in the main 'box'.

Zündapp won the European 80cc road racing championship in 1983, with their new RSM 80 GP machine.

Although it was not raced in the world championships, the 50cc Zündapp racer showed up well against the leading privately-entered Kreidlers in German national events that year. The main reason the racer was not developed further, was due to the level of success Zündapp achieved in off-road sport, where in the world of One Day Trials, the combination of Gustav Franke and Zündapp was to prove hard to beat in 1965. In fact Franke and his 246cc single-cylinder, two-stroke went on to become the first ever European Trials champions, in the process beating such well-known 'feet-up' men as Sammy Miller and Don Smith.

The third Neumeyer generation was at the helm when Zündapp celebrated its first 50 years in 1967. Dieter Neumeyer, born in 1931, had graduated in economics and like the late Dr. Mann had practical experience of both the technical and commercial side of business from Siemens-Schukert. On 8th May 1963, the Zündapp management appointed him joint General Manager with director Schulz, and by 1966 he was running the company himself. As a former endurance trials rider of the early 1950s, Dieter Neumeyer's enthusiasm for motorcycle sport was unabated in the years following his appointment.

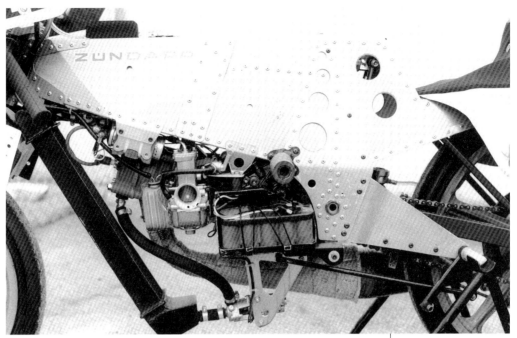

Zündapp's 1984 RSM 80 GP could reach an outstanding 137.5mph, with its 79cc (46 x 47mm) engine developing 30bhp at 14,800rpm.

The Jubilee year saw 1,800 workers employed at the Munich complex who assembled 55,000 machines, of which half were exported to 138 countries. And despite the large workforce, a considerable amount of capital was spent on cost-saving automation.

In 1969 Zündapp 'dabbled' at road racing again. This had been spurred on by some members of the sport's international governing body, the FIM, wanting to limit 50cc racers to a maximum of six gear ratios in order to eliminate factory freaks. With this in mind, in the summer of 1967, Zündapp was testing an air-cooled 50cc six-speeder with development rider Dieter Kramer. The machine had basically a tuned ISDT-type motor mounted in a one-off racing chassis.

But the biggest sporting achievement of the 1960s for Zündapp was to come the following year, when East Germany's five year supremacy in the ISDT came to an end in the Alps of northern Italy, in early October 1968. It was shattered by six Germans from west of the Iron Curtain, mounted on six lightweight Zündapp two-strokes, ranging from only 50cc to a maximum of 125cc.

Other manufacturers benefited from Zündapp technology, such as the Spanish Sanglas company who used Zündapp power for the 72mph, 100cc Sport in the mid-1960s. Rickman of Britain sold large numbers of 125cc Zündapp-engined motocross and enduro bikes mainly to the USA, and in the early to mid-1970s also supplied a number of Zündapp-powered models to the British police. Laverda in Italy used the later, water-cooled 125/175cc engines for its smaller roadsters. Another Italian company, TM, chose water-cooled Zündapp power during the early 1980s.

Stefan Dörflinger in Misano 1984.

Swiss rider Dörflinger piloting his Zündapp to victory in the 1984 Austrian Grand Prix at the Salzburgring. He became the first 80cc World Champion that year.

From a high point of 115,000 units in 1977, Zündapp declined badly in the 1980s with 1980 production down to 70,000. In 1981 it fell to below 60,000 and by the 1982 Cologne Show, Zündapp were struggling, having lost some 41 per cent of the previous year's figure.

Then came the startling news that Zündapp would be fielding a new machine in the 80cc road racing championship, which for 1983 was to be a European championship.

Power output of the racer was claimed to be 28bhp at 14,000rpm but at the time, Zündapp refused to give away any details. The team was to be headed by 24 year old Hubert Abold and sponsored by Krauser, Metzeler and Shell.

The 1983 European rounds were held on 13th March at Jarama, Spain; 27th March, San Marino, Italy; 29th May, Donington Park, Britain; 28th August, Brno, Czechoslovakia; 11th September, Assen, Holland and the final round was 25th September at Hockenheim, West Germany.

Even though Zündapp was struggling with its production models, the RSM 80 racer was unbeatable and ended the season as Champion of Europe. For 1984, the 80cc racer was refined further and at long last its technical detail was revealed. The heart was a 79cc (46 x 47mm) single with disc-valve induction, 16:1 compression ratio, 32mm Bing carb and Bosch transistorised ignition, giving 30bhp at 14,800rpm through a six-speed box. The power unit was finished in white and housed in a sheet aluminium monocoque frame, with adjustable air-sprung, oil-damped Marzocchi forks, taper roller head bearings, box-section chrome moly swinging arm using plain bearings and cantilever rear suspension. There was a ten-litre fuel tank and five-spoke Campagnolo cast magnesium, 18inch wheels fitted front and rear with Michelin 80/70 and 80/80 tyres. Brakes were Zanzani aluminium discs (220mm front and 180mm rear) with Mozzi Motor aluminium calipers. The 1983 machines had smaller triple discs and calipers of a different design, made by Brembo. Altogether, this added up to 123lb dry weight. Maximum speed was claimed as 137.5mph.

Riders were Abold and 35 year old Stefan Dörflinger. As *Motor Cycle News* reported on the 29th August 1984, Dörflinger needed only a seventh place at the final round, the San Marino Grand Prix the following weekend, to take his third world title. The previous two had been on 50cc Krauser-backed Kreidlers.

Dörflinger's team-mate, Hubert Abold, had been instructed that he could only beat his fellow Zündapp rider if engine trouble struck and Dörflinger was not going to make the points he needed to win his crown. But in fact the result was never really in doubt, with Dörflinger scorching home to give Zündapp its first-ever world road racing title. However, this was of little use in stemming Zündapp's financial haemorrhage. A few days after the triumph, Zündapp went into liquidation.

This was just as the Cologne Show was starting, and the show's official catalogue inside front cover displayed one of the company's full colour advertisements, as there was no time to re-print. In the following months, the liquidator searched for a buyer. Unexpectedly, one was found in the People's Republic of China. The factory's name, tooling and stock were shipped east to start a new life on a new continent, under new ownership.

Stefan Dörflinger, 80cc World Champion for Zündapp in 1984 and 1985 - the latter after the factory had finally closed its doors.

When the sale of Zündapp had been completed, special trains travelled overland from China to the Zündapp works in Munich. Each covered rail wagon carried large packing cases to house the remnants of the plant for the journey to their new home. Around 1,500 Chinese made the trip, and to save on cost, the personnel slept inside the packing cases while the loading operation took place. This took several weeks during the summer of 1985. It is worth noting that even with the demise, Dörflinger retained the 80cc Championship in 1985 - with Krauser backing.

Another twist to the Zündapp saga came in 1986 when it was announced that the Enfield India company was producing the K80 ultra lightweight, commuter motorcycle, complete with 'Zündapp§ name, on both the engine castings and petrol tank! Did Enfield India conclude a licensing deal with Zündapp before it went into liquidation or with the Chinese after the sale? At any event, the name, if not the original company, survives.

Zündapp was in many ways the greatest of all the German marques, certainly it was at the forefront of the domestic industry for a longer period than all its competitors, save BMW. It deserves to rank with the true pioneers of the industry, Triumph, Norton, BSA, Harley-Davidson and Gilera.

Stefan Dörflinger winning on the '80' Zündapp during the Italian GP at Misano in 1984.

Index *Figures in italics refer to picture captions.*